THE GODDESS IN
EVERY GIRL

THE GODDESS IN EVERY GIRL

Develop Your Feminine Power

M. J. Abadie

SIMON PULSE
New York London Toronto Sydney New Delhi

BEYOND WORDS
Hillsboro, Oregon

An imprint of Simon & Schuster
Children's Publishing Division
1230 Avenue of the Americas
New York, NY 10020

BEYOND WORDS
20827 N.W. Cornell Road, Suite 500
Hillsboro, Oregon 97124-9808
503-531-8700 / 503-531-8773 fax
www.beyondword.com

This Beyond Words/Simon Pulse edition August 2013
Copyright © 2002, 2013 by M. J. Abadie
This work was originally published in 2002 by Bindu Books, a division of
  Inner Traditions International, Ltd.

SIMON PULSE is a trademark of Simon & Schuster, Inc., and related logo is a
registered trademark of Simon & Schuster, Inc.
Beyond Words Publishing is an imprint of Simon & Schuster, Inc. and the Beyond
Words logo is a registered trademark of Beyond Words Publishing, Inc.

For information about special discounts for bulk purchases, please contact Simon &
Schuster Special Sales at 1-866-506-1949 or business@simonandschuster.com.

The Simon & Schuster Speakers Bureau can bring authors to your live event.
For more information or to book an event contact the Simon & Schuster Speakers
Bureau at 1-866-248-3049 or visit our website at www.simonspeakers.com.

Design: Sara E. Blum
The text of this book was set in ITC Veljovic.

Manufactured in the United States of America

10 9 8 7 6 5 4 3 2 1

Library of Congress Cataloging-in-Publication Data

Abadie, M. J. (Marie-Jeanne), 1933-2006
    The goddess in every girl : develop your feminine power / M. J. Abadie.
        p. cm.
    Includes bibliographical references.
    1. Goddess religion—Miscellanea. 2. Teenagers—Religious life—
        Miscellanea. I. Title.
BL473.5.A23 2013
204'.408352—dc23

                                                            2012031545

ISBN 978-1-58270-427-2 (pbk)
ISBN 978-1-58270-431-9 (hc)
ISBN 978-1-4424-8469-6 (eBook)

To all the teenage Goddess Girls
who want to follow Her way.

And to Laura Schlivek,
my Goddess-loving editor.

CONTENTS

The Goddess Lives!

*Despite persistent attempts to stamp Her into
nonexistence, the Goddess lives in every girl and
woman. Just look around you. The ancient Goddess
is everywhere, within and without. She is Earth
and the Heavens. We experience Her presence
through dreams and creative experiences. She lives
in painting and art, literature and drama, poetry
and song. Yes, men have tried to banish Her, but
they have not succeeded. She has endured. She will
always endure. She gives us the power to challenge
our society's stereotypical images of girls and
women. Her images reveal our true essence—who
we are and who we can become. Just look within
your heart—look closely—and you will
find Her there.*

THE GODDESS LIVES WITHIN YOU

To be a girl today is awesome. For the first time in recorded history, you, as a teenage girl, have the difficult task—and the glorious opportunity—of defining for *yourself* the woman you will one day become.

For thousands of years women in our culture have been defined according to their roles in relationship to men—not by who they themselves were as individuals. For example, here's a popular little poem from the 1950s:

> *Mother, daughter, sister, wife;*
> *You'll always be known*
> *By the men in your life.*

The name for this system of basing a woman's identity on the men in her life is *patriarchy.* In a patriarchal system the balance of power between men and women is skewed; men—and in our dominant religions, a single male deity—hold virtually all the power. As a teen girl you've no doubt already experienced many aspects of our male-dominated, patriarchal culture—in school, on the sports field, even at home. Since the feminist movement began in the 1970s, women have gained some ground—some have become senators and corporate heads, and more careers have opened up to women. But the underlying assumption that men have a right

Goddess Terminology

The Great Goddess: This term is used to indicate the One Goddess who, at the dawn of civilization, was the supreme deity in an essentially feminine Universe that She created. Essentially nameless, She was the single progenitor of "All There Is." She bestowed gifts such as agriculture, knowledge of herbs for healing, the arts and architecture, fire and its use and preservation, the making of pottery, tools, and jewelry, among many other blessings to humankind.

The Goddess: This is a short form of The Great Goddess.

The Great Mother: This is the Goddess in her aspect as Mother of all things, as bringer of life and receiver of the dead. She is the maternal aspect of the Great Goddess and is especially known as Mother Earth, or the Earth Mother, and as such She has been given many different names by different cultures.

to more of the power hasn't really gone away. If a woman ran for president right now, she'd only stand an outside chance of winning, simply because she wasn't a man. See what I mean?

The world hasn't always been this way, though. Some thirty thousand years ago the Goddess reigned supreme over all of Earth's peoples. In that "once-upon-a-time" era, people who were genetically similar to those of us living today celebrated the Great Goddess as their all-encompassing deity. There was nothing supernatural about Her. She was simply Nature and All There Is—giver of life, protector, wisdom teacher, and renewer of life through death.

The Goddess-worshiping cultures had a female-centered way of life—women held prominent positions in these societies, owned property in their own right, and were in charge of social relationships. Because of their power to give birth, women were associated with the Goddess—giver of all life—and were accorded the utmost respect. At the same time, there was a good balance of power between men and women. Though these early societies were mother-*centered,* they were not mother-*ruled.* Men were considered equally important and given their due. Unlike the patriarchal cultures that have dominated recent history, the Goddess cultures were egalitarian.

Now, as teen girls, you stand on the brink of an uncertain tomorrow. Even though we are making mind-boggling technological progress, our world is in trouble. A lack of respect for the balance of nature, and for an equal balance of power between men and women, has brought us to the brink of disaster. The good news is that you have the power to make changes in this unbalanced system that cheats women and hurts our Earth.

Today's girls are approaching a new Golden Age, which they alone can create. And how is this to be achieved? By a return to the Goddess in every girl. One by one, as each of you understands and acknowledges your uniquely feminine Self as your rightful heritage, a great power shift will occur all over the world.

The Goddess is ready to return. She is waiting for you to open the door that was locked against her centuries ago. The time is *now*. It is *your* time. And it won't come again. You must act as if your life depended on it—for in truth, all our lives depend on each and every girl recognizing the Goddess in herself.

It doesn't matter who you are, where you live, what you look like, how much you weigh, what your parents do, whether you are rich or poor, popular or not—you have the power of the Goddess within you. You only have to let it free!

We learn to live consciously through becoming aware of inner and outer events as they are happening. Building a conscious self means becoming increasingly aware of inner events, bodily events, and interpersonal events. A conscious self is able to experience in full awareness all the distinctly different components of the self, including feelings, needs, drives, and values. A conscious self lives consciously.

Gershen Kaufman
and Lev Raphael,
The Dynamics of Power

THE
GODDESS IN EVERY GIRL

*This world is basically feminine, you know. It's
what allows survival. Not "survival of the fittest"—
that's just a male concept. Survival is all about
nurturing, loving, sustaining—the feminine aspects.
Without them, where would we be? Our early
history was predominantly one that honored these
qualities; like your Iroquois, women decided all the
important issues. My culture here worshiped the
goddess, as did people all over the world—all over
Mother Earth—until recent history, a few thousand
years ago, perhaps a couple of thousand years
before Christ.*

Conversation with Viejo Ita,
Mayan Wise Man,
as reported by John Perkins
in *Shapeshifting*

RECLAIMING THE GREAT GODDESS

t can be argued that when the Great Goddess ruled the world it was, especially for girls and women, a better place in which to live than today's world. Some archaeologists think that the reign of the Goddess dates back as far as fifty thousand years—all agree that by thirty thousand years ago She reigned supreme. Our knowledge of such long-ago times is naturally limited. By the time writing had become common and history began to be recorded, patriarchy was already in place and gaining ground. However, archaeological, mythological, and historical evidence shows that when the Goddess reigned, people led a female-centered way of life. Worship of the Goddess was not a religion in the sense that we think of religion today, but a way of living that honored both females and Earth, which was considered to be a living being—our Mother Earth, who gave birth to all things and provided for all. This Great Mother not only birthed everything in the Universe, she also arranged to have all returned to her bosom in death, only to be reborn in an eternal Great Round of Being.

Images of the Goddess have been found all over the world. Many symbolic representations of Her include animals, especially serpents, cats, and horned creatures, such as cattle. Archaeologists have found evidence in these images that the ancient cultures' regard for the Great Goddess went beyond viewing Her as Nature and the Earth Mother. They revered her as the primary Source of

The Earth Mother is a cosmogenic figure, the eternally fruitful source of everything. She is simply the Mother. All things came from her, return to her, and are her. The totality of the cosmos is her body, she gives birth to everything from her womb, and she nourishes all from her breasts. There is no essential change or individuation. Each separate being is a manifestation of her; all things share in her life through an eternal cycle of birth and rebirth.

Encyclopedia Britannica

One of the ways the feminine power is used in [the Shuar] community is to control the men. . . . By control I mean the way they fulfill their role as the nurturers, the ones who are taught by and who honor Nunqui, the Earth, and all that exists, the balance of creation over destruction. In Shuar culture it is the women who are turned to for wisdom. The women are the ones who say, "We don't need a larger house; don't clear any more trees" or "We have enough to eat; don't kill more animals." It is known that if the women fall short of their responsibility to Nunqui and don't let the men know when enough destruction has occurred, Nunqui and the Earth and humanity will suffer in return.

In our culture, who says when enough is enough? What happened when the culture shifted from the fertility and goddess cultures to cultures of male domination, of dominion over the earth? Where is the nurturing? Where is the control? Where is the wisdom? When is enough enough? Who suffers from the dominion and destruction?

Eve Bruce,
Shaman, M.D.

Life and also as the Great Mystery that life is, always has been, and probably always will be, despite science's best efforts to unlock Nature's secrets.

However, to the Goddess people, there was nothing supernatural about Her. As Nature and All There Is, She was not an impossible ideal of some far-removed, judging deity who decided everything and who was to be worshiped by "sinners." It is improbable that She was actually called Goddess, which is a feminine rendition of the relatively modern word *God*, but whatever they named Her, She was supreme.

LIFE AMONG THE GODDESS PEOPLE

The first of these Goddess peoples were what are called "hunter-gatherers," which means that the men hunted for large game and were sometimes gone from a settlement for weeks at a time, while the women and children gathered wild foods and small animals for daily sustenance. These people lived in fairly small groups and moved frequently as they exhausted the food resources of each temporary settlement.

Before long, however, the women who did the gathering realized that they could reproduce food plants and thus have a steady supply at hand without having to constantly move to a new territory. They credited their Goddess for giving them this invaluable knowledge, which by today has developed into not only agriculture, but into agribusiness, run by big profit-hungry companies that favor short-term gain over long-term sustainability. Such "progress" threatens our Earth's delicate ecosystems.

It is difficult for us—with our TVs, radios, cell phones, automobiles, jet planes, internet, supermarkets, modern medicine, and the host of other conveniences and comforts we enjoy—to even begin to imagine what life might have been like when the Goddess was the model for life. For one thing, war was unknown. The people of the Goddess lived in unwalled, unprotected villages where cooperation was the norm. It had to be. And women were the originators of cooperative living. The idea of the "rugged individual" is recent, speaking historically.

We cannot deny that our modern patriarchal civilization has given us many benefits, if comfort and convenience are the preferred standards by which to measure life's value. These modern conveniences, collectively known as "progress," are the result of *linear thinking*.

Women understand that life is not linear but cyclical. Anyone can see that just by looking up at the night sky and seeing the Moon go through her phases from dark to shining sliver of crescent to full and back down again. Although the Goddess in some of her aspects is identified with the Sun and the starry heavens, She is mostly connected with the Moon, which is a common Goddess symbol. The tradition of lunar calendars goes back as early as 32,000 BCE.

Of course, you as a teen girl experience the cyclical nature of life every time you get your menstrual period. For the Goddess people, in their perception of life as basically feminine, the fact of the natural cycles of birth, youth, maturity, old age, and death were seen as sacred manifestations of the Great Goddess and the eternal Great Round, which was Her Being. We can assume that early peoples felt great awe and reverence for the life process. Some have speculated that they did not know the part men played in impregnating women and that therefore birth was considered totally the woman's doing. Others have disputed that notion. We can't know for sure either what the ancient people knew or how they felt, but we can make educated guesses from the evidence they left behind in the thousands of Goddess images that span centuries of time.

The early Goddess people were *matrilineal,* which means that identity and property were passed down through the mother-line.

The Goddess in the Moon

Interestingly, both the Chinese calendar and the Jewish calendar are lunar calendars! Neither of these patriarchal societies was able to eliminate the Goddess entirely, just as the bright Moon continues to remind us of Her.

Another element of the Jewish religion is that in order to be considered a real Jew a person has to be born from a Jewish *mother.* Think about that for a moment. If a Jewish man marries a non-Jewish woman, his children are not officially considered to be Jewish. But if a Jewish woman marries a non-Jew, her children are Jews. Perhaps She still lurks behind the patriarchy's best attempts to deny Her existence.

Old Saying

"It's a wise child that knows its own father."

Among the Iroquois, a council of women chose the tribal chiefs. These women were known as the Clan Mothers, and they had the power to replace the chief if they did not approve of his actions and decisions for the tribe. The Clan Mothers did not dictate to the chief they selected, but it was assumed he would act in the tribe's best interests, and these interests were determined by the Clan Mothers.

Because the biological father of children may have been unknown, children were identified through their mothers. If it is true that men's role in fathering children wasn't understood, the identity of the father may not have been known.

Marriage as we know it today may not have existed. The men may have mated with many of the women of their community, and the women were likely in control of the food—a very powerful position. The identity of a child's mother was self-evident, so it made sense to reckon kinship and inheritance of property through the mother and the mother's family, both for individuals and for entire groups or clans. This form of reckoning is sometimes called *mother right*.

Archaeological evidence suggests that the Goddess people included ancestor worship in their sacred rituals. Ancestor-worship idols are female because they represent the human origins of tribal members. Thousands of sculptures of women have been found in ancient gravesites from as far back as 25,000 BCE. These Venus figures point to the importance of women in early clan society.

It's possible that the mother's brothers may have served the role of father, but it is fairly certain that she had no "husband," and she answered to no man who was lord and master of the household. Thus it was that women owned property in their own names, and the central Goddess temples served as places where governing took place. Justice is always pictured as a woman! These early women formulated laws and created the architecture of the settlements, which grew to be cities in the course of time.

In addition, women were in possession of the knowledge that was vital to life. As food-gatherers, they were also herb specialists, and it was they who invented medicine.

In short, among the Goddess cultures women enjoyed full respect from and equal status with men. They made vital contributions to their societies and received appropriate recognition for their knowledge, wisdom, and creative abilities. So what happened? How did women become second-class citizens defined by the men in our lives, lacking equal rights, and expected to serve men's needs before even considering our own?

What happened was the rise of patriarchy.

THE MYTH OF THE MIND/BODY SPLIT

Ever since René Descartes equated thinking with being with his famous 1637 statement, "I think, therefore I am," the Western world has been hung up on the idea that the mind and body are *separate* realities. The result of this dogma has been to cut off the links of communication between the conscious and the unconscious spheres of the human psyche.

What happened—and is in place to this day—is that the non-rational right brain—considered "feminine" with all the negative connotations patriarchy brings to that word— has had to play second fiddle to the rational, linear-thinking left brain, considered "masculine," with positive connotations. In the dispute, the poor human body—so long considered by patriarchal religions to be the evil repository of sin—comes in a miserable last.

Thus, analytical, logical, rational thinking has dominated our culture for centuries and continues to do so to this very day. However, there is good news: we are standing at the beginning of the twenty-first century and are now in a position to discard this outworn and destructive splitting of the human psyche into bits and pieces. We can declare ourselves to be the whole persons we in fact are— ones whose as yet undiscovered abilities are worthy of our awe and wonder and worthy of development.

THE RISE OF PATRIARCHY

Today, we live under a patriarchal system that, though it has been moderated by recent social and political advances for women, has been in existence for more than two thousand years. The ancient Greeks were the first Western people with a large, settled civilization to develop a patriarchal system of religion and government. They had many gods under a head god, Zeus, and many goddesses split off from the original One Goddess. Though the Greeks were *pantheistic* (worshiping multiple deities) and many aspects of the Goddess still found representation in their recognized goddesses, they embraced patriarchy by giving Zeus the ultimate power over all. The Greeks had learned about the patriarchal system from nomad hordes of barbarian invaders. Waves of Indo-European warriors descended on the communities of vast numbers of people who had followed the ways of the Great Goddess for thousands and thousands of years.

Following the Golden Age of Greek civilization, circa 500 BCE, the rise of Judaism amplified the patriarchal system and added to it another element: *monotheism*. Monotheism means that there is only one God—and in the Jewish religion, that single God was male. The Jewish god, called Yahweh or Jehovah, was stuck firmly in place by the patriarchs who wrote the Old Testament of the Bible.

WHAT IS PATRIARCHY?

Patriarchy: A *socioreligious system* that declares the Supreme Being, the Creator of the World and all in it, to be *male*. Under patriarchy, women are considered inferior to men. In the past, patriarchal systems actually relegated women (and their children) to the status of *property* belonging to men, just as donkeys, horses, houses, and household goods were deemed exclusively male property.

What is not generally known is that it took a long time for patriarchal religions to finally eliminate the way of the Goddess. In fact, for centuries the female-centered populations and the invading patriarchal populations lived side by side. But the invaders were extremely warlike. In their quest to rule the world their way, with their male God in charge, they persecuted and suppressed their Goddess-loving neighbors for centuries. The Bible is full of tales of war and the conquering of nonpatriarchal peoples by the Jewish invaders.

Jewish priests, called Levites, created the story of Adam and Eve to firmly establish the inferior status of women and gain control over them. Their ultimate aim was to conquer the lands and the people who followed the old Goddess ways.

In the wake of the Jews came the Christians—who were, of course, Jews themselves when they started Christianity. In fact, the orthodox Jews considered the Christian cult to be a heresy and tried to stamp it out.

Christians found the story of Adam and Eve much to their advantage and incorporated it and its concept of "original sin" into their developing doctrines. How convenient that man was created in God's image and that woman was an afterthought, fashioned out of an insignificant part of Adam, his rib. She was not created as an equal or even as a mate, but to be man's servant. And just as God had authority over the man, the man was to have total control of the woman. As the great mythologist Joseph Campbell has remarked, "The story of Adam and Eve was a political document."

The later Christians were equally fierce in their determination to rid the world of the Goddess and all who followed her ancient ways. They embarked on a calculated destruction of Her shrines and temples. Many of today's ancient ruins were not destroyed by the natural processes of time but were deliberately knocked down.

Then the prophet Mohammed created what is now known as Islam, claiming to take dictation direct from a God called Allah.

**The Jewish War
on the Goddess**

"You must completely destroy all the places where the nations you dispossess have served their gods, on high mountains, on hills, under any spreading tree; you must tear down their altars, smash their pillars, cut down their sacred poles, set fire to the carved images of their gods and wipe out their name from that place." (Deut. 12:2, 3)

"This anti-sexual attitude was not the result of a more inherent purity or lesser sex drive among the adherents of the Judeo-Christian belief . . . it was probably developed and propagated for purely political motives, aiming at goals that would allow the invading patrilineal Hebrews greater access to land and governmental control by destroying the ancient matrilineal system."

Merlin Stone,
When God Was a Woman

Mohammed and the Bible

Though Western society isn't usually aware of the fact, Mohammed incorporated many of the legends and attitudes of both Old and New Testaments into the Muslim Koran, which is the bible of Islam. For example, Sura 4:31 states that "Men have authority over women because God has made the one superior to the other and because they spend their wealth to maintain them. So good women are obedient, guarding the unseen parts as God has guarded them." An obvious reference to Islam's male ownership of female sexuality!

According to legend, the prophet Mohammed could not read, but where did Mohammed obtain that information if he didn't have access to the Bible? In his *Occidental Mythology*, Joseph Campbell proposes a logical explanation. "One need only suppose a boyhood and youth of alert interest in the oral lore and religious life round about: a little pitcher with big ears; and then a youth of high intelligence, ardent religious sensibilities, and an extraordinary capacity for extended periods of auditory trance."

This religion spread like wildfire in the Middle East, where it still dominates today. Under Islamic law, the subjugation of women was even more complete than under the religions of Judaism and Christianity. Women were—and in fundamental Muslim countries still are—hidden under heavy veils from the age of eleven on, at which time they were considered to have reached adult womanhood. This age coincides, more or less, with puberty and the beginning of menstrual periods.

All of the patriarchal, monotheistic religions have one thing in common: The followers of each consider their own religion to be the only true religion. The Jews declare themselves to be "God's chosen people." The Catholics claim to be the "one true religion," and fundamental Muslims consider non-Muslims to be the work of the devil. And each has a holy book that sets down truth and law. The Jews have their Torah, both the Jews and the Christians have the Old Testament of the Bible, and the Christians have the New Testament as well, while Islam has the Koran. All of these holy books are claimed to have arrived by direct revelation from God. However, "God" does not seem to be a single entity, as there is one god for the Jews, another for the Christians, and a third, Allah, for the followers of Islam. So, monotheism isn't really about a *single* God after all. It's just that each religious system recognizes a single God of its own. And each regards other people's God as a false God.

Followers of these monotheistic religions are often called "people of the Book," and the book is all that matters. This causes confusion and dispute, and countless scholars spend their lifetimes trying to interpret the various religious writings. Disagreement is inevitable.

Is it any wonder the world breaks out in religiously based wars that spread over the face of our beautiful, abundant, irreplaceable Mother Earth? Because humans no longer follow the Goddess, whose Way requires no book but only reverence for life and Her peaceful Earth-honoring ways, we could bring our species to the brink of extinction. Our contentious ways have polluted the planet, its air, and its waters, endangering not only human health but contributing daily to the extinction of nonhuman species.

GODDESS POWER NOW!

Perhaps, until now, nobody ever told you about the Goddess and the Goddess-loving people who once populated our planet. If so, it's not surprising. As you can see, there has been a vast conspiracy to wrest power from the Goddess and drive Her from Earth. The good news is that, outward appearances to the contrary, the conspiracy has failed. The Goddess has been driven underground, but she has not been driven *away*. And today's teenage girls have the unique and marvelous opportunity to bring Her back into the light of day. You can use your inner Goddess power to cut through the many oppressive and falsely founded patriarchal images of females as second-class citizens. You can see to it, one girl at a time—burgeoning into millions of girls all over this lovely Mother Earth—that a contemporary awareness of the once worldwide veneration of the female deity as the wise and all-giving Creatress of the Universe becomes the new reality for us all.

You can bring about the changes necessary to erase the oppressive laws and customs that have been developed by the patriarchal, monotheistic religio-political systems in their attempt to destroy the Goddess. Your hope for the future—and that of all girls and women—lies not in some return to a mythical golden past where the Goddess ruled. It lies in the here and now, and in your future.

Claim your Goddess power and use it well. Be a Goddess Girl!

Just the Facts, Ma'am

It is time to bring the facts about the early female religions to light. They have been hidden away too long. With these facts we will be able to understand the earliest development of Judaism, Christianity, and Islam and their reactions to the female religions and customs that preceeded them . . . we will understand how these reactions led to the political attitudes and historical events that occurred as these male-oriented religions were forming. . . . We will be able to clear away the centuries of confusion, misunderstanding, and suppression, [and examine] the image, staus, and roles still assigned to women today . . . to refute the ideas of 'natural or divinely ordained roles,' finally opening the way for a more realistic recognition of . . . individual human beings . . . and regard the world and its riches as a place that belongs to every living being on it.

Merlin Stone,
When God Was a Woman

What Is a Virgin?

What the word *virgin* originally meant was a woman who was "unto herself," that is, not dependent on a man for her identity or livelihood. It was a title of honor.

An Historical Observation

When a belief cannot be definitely expunged, it is rehabilitated by modifying it [to] conform to the new ideology. That is exactly what happened in the fifth century AD when the Virgin Mary finally supplanted . . . the ancient mother goddess. . . .

[It took] twenty centuries of debate . . . to make one small Galilean who lived at the beginning of the first century AD into the "vast Mother," not a mother goddess, but the Mother of God, which, on the level of the unconscious, returns her to exactly the same place.

Jean Markale,
The Great Goddess

THE GREAT GODDESS AND THE VIRGIN MARY

The Great Goddess, often called "Lady of the Beasts," wore many titles including "Mother of All" and "Mother of the Gods," which clearly show Her to be the direct ancestress of the Catholic Virgin Mary—Mother of God.

So important was Mary to the Catholic Church that an enterprise called Maryology sprang up within the Church itself. Many of the great cathedrals of Europe, built in the Gothic period and in the Middle Ages, are named after Our Lady. Although Mary supposedly kept her maidenhead (the colloquial term for the intact hymen, which is thought to be evidence of "virginity," or lack of sexual intercourse), she lost her rightful status as Goddess.

The early Catholics' attempts to extinguish the Goddess resulted in the watered-down Virgin Mary, a human being instead of a deity. In accordance with their hatred (and quite probably fear) of the Goddess and anything having to do with sex, the priests of the new religion made Mary totally asexual. However, the Christian God, being born of a woman and therefore part human, had to have a Mother. He couldn't just pop up out of nowhere.

Mary did not become an important figure until 431 AD, when she was proclaimed *Theotokos,* Mother of God, at Ephesus. The cult of the Virgin Mary blossomed during the eleventh and twelfth centuries in Europe when the romantic troubadours idealized love in their songs, reawakening ancient images of the pre-Christian divine female. These images were dangerous to the patriarchy, so the Church quickly locked "proper" femininity into the shape of the Virgin Mary. Much later, in 1854, the pope created the dogma of the Immaculate Conception. Now, as well as being a virgin who had given birth without mating with a man (a well-known ability of the ancient Great Goddess), Mary was totally "pure," the only human born without "original sin."

When Protestantism took root, it would have nothing to do with the Divine Feminine. So out Mary went and in came even more severe restrictions for women.

AN INTERESTING QUESTION

"Why do so many people educated in this century think of classical Greece as the first major culture when written language was in use and great cities built at least twenty-five centuries before that time?" asks Merlin Stone in *When God Was a Woman*.

"And perhaps most important, why is it continually inferred that the age of the 'pagan' religions, the time of the worship of female deities . . . was dark and chaotic, mysterious and evil, without the light of order and reason that supposedly accompanied the later male religions, when it has been archaeologically confirmed that the earliest law, government, medicine, agriculture, architecture, metallurgy, wheeled vehicles, ceramics, textiles, and written language were initially developed in societies that worshipped the Goddess?"

The answer to Merlin Stone's most interesting questions is that until very recently *all* scholars who investigated these matters were men, and the great majority of them were either Jewish or Christian. Could their interpretation of the artifacts and data have been biased? There can be no doubt about it, as mentions of the Goddess were always tucked away in obscure references, hidden as much as possible from view.

The Goddess Web of Life

Mother consciousness makes women aware that their bodies and lives are the thread and web that connects all of humanity. And the web is boundless. Because she is in the image of the Cosmic Mother Goddess, a woman's sexuality and creative powers also reflect the divine, life-giving, nourishing energies and powers of the universe.

Donna Wilshire,
Virgin, Mother, Crone

Fingerprints in Clay

In addition to providing food, women created weaving [which] led to the making of pottery and its decoration. We know this was done by women from the fingerprints left in the clay. These female contributions to the civilizing process led directly to art and culture.

Buffie Johnson,
Lady of the Beasts

A GODDESS EXERCISE

THINKING ABOUT WOMEN AND SOCIETY

Keep your Goddess journal close while you read this book. In it, write a short essay, story, or poem on how you feel about the patriarchal system that suppresses women and makes girls feel inferior.

Write a short essay, story, or poem about what you imagine life would be like for women who lived in a society that revered and respected women and believed in a female Creator.

2

ENVISIONING THE GODDESS

THE ARCHETYPE OF THE GREAT GODDESS

When referring to the archetype of the Great Goddess, or the Great Mother, we are speaking not of any concrete image existing in time and space but of psychic images existing in the universal human psyche. Psychologists have demonstrated the workings of archetypal ideas through the whole of history—they can be seen in rituals, myths, and symbols of the earliest people, who left behind vast numbers of artifacts that clearly show how they lived and what they basically thought. It is the archetype of the Goddess that supports Her being. Symbolic expressions of Her have been found everywhere—in artistic creations dating back thousands of years, in the myths that have arisen throughout time, and in our own dreams and aspirations.

Consciousness is a funny thing—sometimes thoughts and ideas just pop into conscious focus and we wonder, *Now where did that come from?* That's your intuition at work, functioning through the archetypal level of your mind.

The Archetypal Feminine

[She] is far from containing only positive features . . . she is the goddess of life and death at once . . . not only a giver and protector of life, the Feminine contains opposites, and the world actually lives because it combines earth and heaven, night and day, life and death.

Erich Neumann,
The Great Mother

The reason humans share these archetypal images is that there is a psychic substratum in which we all participate. It has been called by different names. The psychologist Carl G. Jung invented the term *collective unconscious*. Others have used terms such as *race memory*.

Think of this shared undercurrent in all humans as being like the waters beneath Earth's surface. We see lakes and streams, rivers and oceans, on the surface. But if we could look deeply enough into Earth's depths, we would see one continuous flow of water, all connected. That's how the collective unconscious works. As the poet Robert Moss expressed it, "All the waters of the Earth are one."

WHAT IS AN ARCHETYPE?

An *archetype* is an inward image that functions in the human psyche. Research has shown that archetypes are common to all humanity. An archetype is the product of our own *intuitive* self. It's something we know about deep inside, even if we aren't conscious of knowing it. Sometimes we operate from the heart of an archetype—we all, for example, have a mother figure inside ourselves, even if our real mother was missing.

Your own dreams, fantasies, and creative ideas come from that deep level of your intuition. Like everything else, an archetype is energy. It is psychic energy, and it represents processes that take place both in your unconscious (where you are not aware of what's going on) and in your consciousness.

MOODS—MESSENGERS FROM THE UNCONSCIOUS

Where do moods come from? We all have them and sometimes they arise as a surprise. We wonder, *Why am I feeling this way?* Let's say you get a sudden mood of elation, or despair. Maybe you have no outside reason to feel extra happy or to feel sad and depressed. But there it is: a mood. You didn't ask for it, but it arrived.

Moods are messages from the unconscious. They ask you to pay attention to something inside that's going on even though from an outside point of view your mood may make no sense at all. Moods affect you this way because of the dynamic effect of the archetype working within. A mood can take hold of your entire personality. It can send you off on a tangent, against all logical reasoning. You might want to dance all night, or sleep all day. So it is that an archetype can influence behavior unconsciously. The way to deal with this phenomenon is to make an effort to bring the matter into your conscious mind and understand it.

The Goddess as Lotus

Rising from the depths of water and expanding its petals on the surface, the lotus . . . is the most beautiful evidence offered to the eye of the self-engendering fertility of the bottom. Through its appearance, it gives proof of the life-supporting of the all-nourishing abyss . . . the infinite ocean of that liquid life-substance out of which all the differentiated elements of the universe arise.

Heinrich Zimmer,
The Art of Indian Asia

THE DIVINE FEMININE

This term is used to represent *female*, not the standardized characteristics we today consider to be properly "feminine." The Goddess isn't interested in manufactured or stereotyped ideas of what is or isn't "feminine." So please don't confuse the words with any attitude about what you think is feminine, or what you have been told is feminine. Every female is feminine, and it doesn't matter a bit what she looks like or what she does, or how she does it. If you like ruffles and cosmetics, fine. If you prefer overalls and a bare face, great. It's **who you are** that counts.

If you simply ignore the signals you get from your unconscious, or shove them aside, on the grounds that they don't matter, trouble results. But when you learn to look inward and listen for messages from your Goddess archetype, you can exert a decisive influence on your own moods, inclinations, and personality tendencies. In time, as you get used to working with your unconscious messengers, you will become aware of receiving direction from your own mind—you will get in touch with concepts, intentions, interests, and ideas to explore.

One of the best ways to contact your inner Goddess archetype is through images, as our unconscious archetypes are usually nonverbal. It's on the pictorial plane that the archetype becomes visible to the conscious mind most easily. (For more on learning to connect with your Goddess archetype, see chapter 4: Opening to the Goddess Within.)

A GODDESS GAME

IMAGINING YOUR GODDESS ARCHETYPE

To play this game, you will need some writing implements—markers or pens in various colors, colored pencils—whatever appeals to you.

First prepare yourself by sitting quietly for a few minutes and paying attention to your breathing—just concentrate on the inflow and the outflow until you feel calm and centered.

Then, allow your imagination to drift until you *feel* an image of the Goddess as She exists in your personal archetype. Don't strain. Take whatever comes. If nothing comes, doodle, or try another time.

Draw a picture of your own inner Goddess archetype in your journal or on scratch paper. You don't have to be an artist—stick figures are okay. In fact, you don't even need to make a human image. The Goddess has many symbols. Some are animals, especially the bull, dolphin, dove, and Her favorite companion, the serpent. She is also represented by abstract symbols such as spirals, circles, wavy lines, and mazes (labyrinths). Just be spontaneous and take whatever image comes to you from your unconscious depths.

Use lots of color—or none at all. It's all up to you. She is your Goddess, alive and well inside you! Have fun making an image of Her as *you* see Her from inside yourself.

THE POWER OF MYTH

Myths present us with ideas that serve to guide our perception of reality. They are stories that have the power to hold us in thrall and dictate or determine our behavior and our beliefs. As such, they have great power. Joseph Campbell commented that myths "are not toys for children."

Culturally, myths serve as a way of conditioning us to think and perceive life in a particular way. This is especially true when we are young and impressionable. Myths present specific points of view that reinforce cultural mores but are frequently taught to children as though they were absolute fact. In truth they are only

WHAT IS MYTH?

Essentially, *myths* are stories that people (or an entire population) tell in an attempt to explain the unexplainable. Myths seek to answer the big—and ultimately unanswerable—questions: Where did we come from, and why are we here?

The world abounds with many different creation myths. Every culture on Earth has some version of how humans, and the visible universe, came into being. Science can neither prove nor disprove myths for the simple reason that they are projections of the human psyche.

Be a Goddess Girl

Throughout this book you will find a specially designed graphic motto that asks you to "Be a Goddess Girl." As I worked on the design I kept thinking "Bee a Goddess Girl" because the bee is one of the animals most sacred to Her and one of Her favorite companions. And I thought about the words *be* and *bee*, which sound alike but have totally different meanings. *Or do they?* The bee, literally, has a lot to do with our *being*. In fact, without bees we would all die of starvation as there would be no pollination in the plant world. The animals we depend on for food would die too because they eat the plants before we eat them.

Informed by Her of this food-chain connection, I set out to do a bit of research on the "lowly" bee. Honey, in which animal and vegetable interaction are intimately intertwined, is made from the bee's bodily secretions and is the purest product of organic nature.

ways of expressing differing worldviews. Although they cannot be relied upon as accurate history, they do tell us a great deal about the peoples who lived according to them.

Campbell said, "Myths are other people's religion." He also called myths "public dreams." Apparently, our species is "hard-wired for religion," as the Swiss psychologist Carl G. Jung put it. Thus, the Christian myth is Christian religion; the Jewish myth is Judaism; the Islamic myth is the Muslim faith, and so on. Myths of civilizations that have become extinct—such as the Aztecs and Mayans—were at one time the religions of those people. Native Americans have their own creation myths, as well as other stories, rites, and rituals. These constitute their religious practices.

Because of their power to affect the minds and psychology of young people, especially teens searching for individuality, myths are used by those who would control young, developing minds for their own purposes. Especially when codified into religious "law," they often portray a system of rewards and punishments based on what is considered desirable behavior. Unfortunately, so many of the stories we hear from childhood affect us deeply, even if we later abandon the religious attitude with which we were raised.

These stories become ingrained in our deepest selves—often without our even knowing the process is taking place. The examples we are exhorted to copy or to avoid become internalized into "Thou shalt" and "Thou shalt not." Or, as a friend of mind once commentated, "The shoulda, woulda, coulda." These myths we learn as children affect our attitudes about the world around us—and they make a deep imprint on how we view *ourselves*.

From myths we learn what is "moral" (allowed), how to conduct ourselves (females are to be submissive), what to value both in life and in ourselves (currently, money and consumerism and the copying of celebrity looks and lifestyles if possible), where our "duty" lies, and a general sense of what life is all about and, most important, who's in charge!

The Judeo-Christian-Islam mythology tells us that a male god is in charge and that if we don't obey this figure then terrible things will happen to us. The further command is to submit to male authority, which gives itself the power to decide exactly what is permitted and what is denied. The fact that this makes no sense does not enter into the equation. (I once asked Joseph Campbell why the Aztecs couldn't see that human sacrifice didn't make the crops grow. His answer, which I will never forget, was, "Empirical evidence has no effect on organized religion.") Even if we can rationally understand this system of mythological thought, by the time we are able to think for ourselves, so much damage has been done that it is often a lifetime task to do the repair work and heal our bruised souls.

THE EVOLUTION OF MYTHOLOGY

Where do myths come from, and how do they get written down?

Our earliest information about the Goddess comes not from writing but from images. Before people invented writing, myths were part of an oral tradition; they were stories that were told out loud. Later, as writing developed, the various mythological stories were recorded. Just as the Bible was written over several hundred years, and went through many revisions (some parts of it not being allowed into the official version, the canon), more ancient myths were recorded over time, too, and enlarged by later authors, who made changes along the way.

For example, the first stories we have of the Goddess whom the Greeks named Hera and who became Zeus's wife are very different from later stories about her. Originally, she was a Great Goddess figure, unattached to any man. As such, she was a genuine descendent of the Great Goddess of prehistoric times.

Then, along came the patriarchal Greeks. During what is known as the classical era, around 500 BCE, they wrote many mythological stories about their gods and goddesses, with Zeus holding the

A famous German scholar, Johann Jacob Bachofen, who wrote a book called *Myth, Religion, and Mother Right*, describes the bond between the beehive and the one Queen Mother as being in opposition to the "father" religions. And indeed, the female worker bees who cooperate so smoothly and efficiently to produce honey, raise the young, and protect their mother, the queen, can be seen as a model of the cooperative Goddess cultures who once peopled Earth.

Bachofen notes that in ancient Greece the bee was associated with all the Mother and Earth Goddesses—Demeter, Artemis, and Persephone. It symbolized the earth, its motherliness, and its "never-resting, artfully formative busy-ness," and was representative of the purity of Nature.

So, think twice before you swat a honey bee, and remember to . . .

position of head god. Though Hera was still a powerful goddess, it wouldn't do to give her ultimate power, so they married her off to Zeus. Later, the Greek myths were taken up by the Romans, who conquered the Greeks. They changed the names of the Greek deities, but essentially the stories remained the same.

Prior to the height of the Greek and Roman civilizations, the Egyptian civilization flourished over a very long period of several thousand years. Egypt was a Goddess country in the beginning, and there are many Egyptian goddesses, who can all be viewed as variations of the One Goddess.

However, about midpoint in Egyptian history there came a pharaoh who decided that Egypt had too many gods and goddesses. His name was Akhenaton, aka Amenhotep IV, whose wife was the famous beauty Nefertiti. He decided there should be only *one* deity for all of Egypt. Because he had the power to do so, he declared that henceforth the people would worship a single deity, Ra, the Sun. So, Akhenaton was actually the inventor of monotheism.

Because the old, ingrained ways of people die out very slowly, and because Egypt had such a long history of multiple deities, Akhenaton took the precaution of erasing from the monuments the names of the other deities. No fool, he realized his people weren't going to be happy with this radical change from their centuries-old beliefs, so, to appease his uneasy subjects, he allowed all the former gods and goddesses to remain on the general roster of deities. He simply declared that they were of lesser stature than Ra.

The monotheistic religion Akhenaton forced upon his people died with him.

Zoroastrianism—the Root of "Good" and "Evil"

Monotheism remained dead for centuries until a man named Zoroaster came along in Persia sometime around 1000 BCE. This self-proclaimed prophet, who was extremely influential with the people of his time, announced to the Persians that from now on there would be one and only one god. He gave this supreme being the name of Ahura Mazda.

Though Zoroaster was unfamiliar with Akhenaton, he unknowingly followed the ancient pharaoh's lead in declaring the previous multiplicity of deities lesser beings; in his system they became either "good spirits" or "evil demons." This time the idea of a monotheistic male god took root and along with it developed—for the first time—the idea of a division between "good" and "evil."

Before Zoroaster, there had been no division of the Supreme Being into separate parts. The Ultimate Source—namely the Great Goddess—was presumed to contain *both* "good" and "bad," without any attempt to assign to her various aspects value judgments of "right" or "wrong." In essence, it was simply assumed that although people felt their life experiences to either be happy or unhappy, fortunate or unfortunate, their supreme deity contained elements of both. How these should be distributed on an individual basis was not in question.

But with the coming of Zoroastrianism, the world was split in two. One part good, one part evil, and the two were destined to be forever at war in the battle for human souls. This duality has been a plague on humanity ever since. The kinder, gentler Goddess religion, which saw the cosmic order as an ever-cycling, unchanging, majestic process that could never be altered by human action was dealt a deathblow. As Joseph Campbell stated, the religion of Zoroaster can "be heard echoed and re-echoed, in Greek, Latin, Hebrew and Aramaean, Arabic, and every tongue of the West."

Although the Greeks were soon to come along—in 330 BCE Alexander the Great marched triumphantly across Persia—wiping out the religion of Zoroaster and replacing it with their own pantheon of gods and goddesses, Zoroaster's basic ideas impacted whole nations and affect us still today. Zoroaster's splitting up of what was once a seamless whole under the Goddess left a legacy that has been passed down through the Greeks, Romans, Jews, and Christians—to us.

CHOOSE YOUR MYTH AND CHOOSE IT WELL

The myths and legends that grew from people who followed the way of the Goddess—in which women were revered as wise, valiant, cooperative, loving, and just—were in direct contrast to the later male-oriented religions of the past two to four thousand years. Remember that all myths are simply attempts to explain the unexplainable. As such, despite the persistent attempts of organized religion to convince us otherwise, myths never represent fact or law. You are free to explore the mystery of life in any way you choose—your entire sense of Self will depend on the choices you make.

WHAT IS A SYMBOL?

A symbol is something that points beyond itself to a meaning that cannot be expressed directly. Symbols are usually pictorial, but sometimes they are actual things.

As an example, early Christians, when being persecuted by the Romans, would draw a picture of a fish in the dirt to identify themselves to others as Christians. Non-Christians would not see anything but a drawing of a fish, but because the fish had secretly become a symbol for Christ, anyone who was a Christian knew immediately what the symbol of the fish—originally a Goddess symbol—meant.

The Goddess is represented by many symbols—the first and foremost of these are the serpent and the Moon. The serpent and the Moon are related because each one goes through the same process regularly. In order to grow, the serpent sheds its skin. In symbolic language it sloughs off death to be reborn. This idea is restated in the visible phases of the Moon. The Moon, from our point of view on Earth, "sheds" its own self and is reborn as the new Moon.

The Goddess has many other symbols besides the serpent and the Moon, including:

- Animals such as pigs, hawks, and other birds
- Wild and domestic cats (lions, lionesses, elegant cats, often with a Siamese slenderness)
- Cattle with horns, deer, and sheep
- Double axes (these were most often found in Crete)
- Butterflies (the butterfly is a universal Goddess symbol of transformation: it emerges from its form as an ugly caterpillar into a winged beauty)
- Pomegranates (the seeds are connected with the transformation process of the underworld) and trees
- Pots and vessels of all kinds, used for carrying food or storing oil, also for mixing potions (the typical witch's cauldron is akin to this)
- Water in all its forms, because water flows and is ever changing, reflecting the Goddess's nature, and fish
- Caves and other enclosures, representing the womb
- Items that are shaped like the female vulva, especially cowrie shells, which were once used as currency
- Netlike shapes, spiderwebs, representing the Goddess as Weaver of Life
- X-shaped patterns, representing the four quarters and the four elements

- Circles and spirals, associated with magical rites of women connected to the everlasting cycle of birth-death-rebirth
- Bees (Bees live on the boundary between the plant and animal worlds—both, of course, ruled by the Great Mother. In the oldest times, honey was sacrificed to the Earth Goddess.)

A Goddess Game

Making Your Own Goddess Symbols

In your Goddess journal, practice drawing your own version of Goddess symbols. Look around you in the natural world for inspiration—and look inside yourself to see what best represents Her for you personally. Don't forget about eggs and breasts!

THE GODDESS AND HER SACRED SERPENT

We have seen that the serpent, as a most potent symbol for the way of the Goddess, represents the life cycle of birth-death-rebirth. Because it sheds its skin in order to grow and renew itself, the serpent is, in non-Christian cultures, the symbol of rebirth into the spirit. This motif is deeply embedded in our collective unconscious and arises spontaneously when appropriate to each person's development. Serpent images, whether they come to us through dreams or through spontaneous art production, speak to the deepest mystery of being, to the unfathomable nature of ourselves and the universe. Now, let's look at some specific examples of serpent symbolism.

THE SERPENT AS A SYMBOL OF THE GODDESS AS HEALER

We know women were the first healers and that they invented medicine, usually from their knowledge of herbs and healing plants, but also from their knowledge of the cyclical nature of life. Later, the patriarchal Greeks appropriated the serpent symbol for their own use. But the serpent never died as a symbol of the Goddess as giver of knowledge and wisdom. And this knowledge was always considered to be sacred, from the Divine Goddess Source.

For example, the Greeks saw sickness as the effect of a divine action, which could be cured only by another divine action: The divine sickness was to be cast out by a divine remedy. When sickness is vested with such dignity, it has the inestimable advantage of being the agent of its own cure. Thus, what might be termed *spiritual homeopathy* was practiced in the clinics of antiquity, through the medium of dreams and what today we call altered states of consciousness.

At the classical sanctuaries of healing in ancient Greece, a distinctly spiritual atmosphere was created. Dedicated to the god of healing, these ancient "hospitals" had as their primary aim the connecting of the patient with his or her innermost depths, from where the healing would come. Removed from the distractions and disturbances of the outside world, patients were presented with the

Modern Medicine?

As the emblem of their profession, doctors today still use the caduceus (the symbol of two serpents entwined together on a staff), which they inherited from the Goddess by way of the Greeks. With its exclusive focus on the physical body and chemical processes, modern medicine has turned dramatically away from the Goddess and the idea of healing as a spiritual process. But today's doctors can't get away from Her and Her great serpent symbol. They wear it on their license plates! And She's right at their elbows whether they know it or not!

The *divina afflictio* then contains its own diagnosis, therapy, and prognosis, provided of course that the right attitude toward it is adopted.

C. A. Meier
*Incubation and Modern
Psychotherapy*

opportunity to themselves effect their cure, the elements of which already resided within them.

Asklepios, the patron god of physicians in ancient Greece, carried a plain staff with a single snake coiled around it, and snakes freely roamed his temples. At the Asklepieion, or temple of healing, both patient and doctor made ritual sacrifices, after which the patient retired into seclusion within the temple to await a dream message from the god about the illness and its cure. The mystery of recovery was a private matter between the individual and the god responsible for it. In principle, the mortal physician was excluded from the process.

THE SERPENT AS HEALER AROUND THE WORLD

Many cultures acknowledge the serpent as representative of the divine power of healing into wholeness, and of rebirth into the spirit, or eternal life. Joseph Cambell described a "typical Indian serpent king" at the entrance to a Buddhist temple, in his right hand a burgeoning stalk of the Tree of Life and in his left a jar of the liquor of immortality:

> [These are] the very gifts that the serpent of Eden had in store for our first parents as the treasure of his second tree. . . . The usual mythological association of the serpent is not, as in the Bible, with corruption, but with physical and spiritual health, as in the Greek caduceus.

Many positive serpent images are found from ancient Asia and pre-Christian Europe to pre-Columbian Middle America. For example, a Mesopotamian cylinder seal (circa 2500 BCE) shows the serpent goddess presiding over the Tree of Life. A fifth century BCE stone plaque represents the goddess of the Eleusinian mysteries with her symbolic serpents in attendance (the famous priestess oracle of Delphi received illumination from serpents). Other serpent motifs in Sumer and the Indus Valley go back as far as

2000 BCE. One famous example is the cup of King Gudea of Lagash. It is formed of two serpents entwined about an axial rod—the very caduceus of the Greeks and our medical doctors! We also find representations of snake-headed goddesses. These have extremely slender figures and are usually holding a child. Often they have strongly accented genital areas.

In the New World, serpent symbols abound. In Mexico, Quetzalcoatl, the Lord of Life and Death (whose symbol is the cross and whose mother was a virgin), is known as the Plumed Serpent. The Mayan god Kukulcan sloughed off death to be resurrected. An early stone carving depicts him as the Feathered Serpent—an ornately elegant snake rising up on its own coils to tower over a worshiper holding an offering. And, in a pre-Columbian Aztec altar design, two snakes are intertwined in a perfect caduceus form, their heads facing in opposite directions.

Among numerous North American designs, one engraved shell depicts a pair of ornamented serpent dancers emerging from a rattlesnake skin, their tails intertwined in a caduceus-like shape. Joseph Campbell said of this image that the serpent dancers "reiterate the universal serpent-theme of renewal of life through the sloughing of death."

Did the Greeks Get It?

We don't actually know if the patriarchal Greeks were aware of the serpent as a symbol for the Goddess as Healer, but probably there was some residual understanding still around because the Greeks had goddesses, who were based on the One Goddess. They split Her into many parts and gave names and characteristics to each one.

THE DREAM OF THE JEWELED SERPENT

Here is a dream I had while I was a patient in a rejuvenation clinic in Germany.

> I am given an enormous, beautiful green serpent, the size of a python. Its intensely colored iridescent body is set with sparkling gems: rubies, emeralds, sapphires, diamonds, amethysts, garnets, peridots. This glorious creature's eyes are strikingly clear and luminous, like a cat's.

Suddenly, it begins to thrash around, spewing excrement. Serpents are an unknown quantity to me, and I haven't the faintest idea how to care for it, nor what is wrong. I phone a friend who is an expert. When I ask what is causing this alarming behavior, she tells me that when serpents are upset, they poop all over the place. She then says my serpent is upset because I do not love it.

The message was clear. Though I had initially come to the clinic to recover from physical debilitation, the real problem was much deeper. For several years, I had devoted myself to serving the needs of others. Though I did not regret it, I realized that—as a result of having totally submerged myself in that endeavor—I had lost the sense of my own Self, not only damaging my health but precipitating an identity crisis. I began to rethink my life to find new direction more in tune with my inner Self. Only two months later, I discovered that I have psychic abilities. This discovery served to redirect my life and work. The dream foretold this development.

Interestingly, during the same period I saw an amazing image of the Virgin Mary. It was in the courtyard of a nineteenth-century Catholic church. Having been raised as a Catholic, I was extremely familiar with the plaster figure of Mary trampling a snake under bare feet. But this Mary was different. A wood carving, she stood on her pedestal in the usual pious pose, hands folded, gazing fondly downward.

She was *not* firmly stamping on the serpent of evil and temptation. Instead, I saw to my astonishment that the serpent was curled cozily around her bare feet, like a pet. It was in the position called *ouroboros,* forming a circle by biting its own tail. The circle is a symbol of wholeness and the regeneration of life. I could not help but wonder if the artist was aware of the symbolism and meant it as a hidden reference, or if this amazing representation stemmed from unconscious depths.

DREAM HEALING

The description below, of a lovely sculpture representing the dream cure of the temple sleep, is taken from *The Mythic Image* by Joseph Campbell.

> In the background is the invalid, dreaming, and at the right his own vision of himself standing, as though having just emerged in spirit from his ailing body At the left this figure has advanced to be cured by the . . . god, who is touching his ailing shoulder, while on the couch, simultaneously, the same shoulder is being licked by a snake, which . . . has emerged from the dreamer himself.

Although the serpent symbol was adopted by the male physicians of ancient Greece, the image described above is a clear symbol of the healing power of the Goddess. It also illustrates the wisdom of paying attention to dreams, which is extremely important to the way of the Goddess. Even today, native cultures—such as the Aborigines of Australia, as well as Native Americans and Hawaiians—insist on the necessity of "reading" dreams for their significance and spiritual value.

This image indicates the healing knowledge of Goddess people, from whom the Greeks learned much of what they knew about many functions necessary to maintaining life.

Her followers believed that She had given them all the many varieties of knowledge, including that of medicine, which enabled the women to care for the people of their communities. All healing was considered spiritual in nature, and there was no division between body and spirit, as there is in our society.

A fourth-century Roman carving of the patron goddess of health and healing, Hygeia, shows her with a serpent emerging from a sacred vessel and coiling itself about her body. Hygeia herself

KUNDALINI—
SERPENT GODDESS OF YOGIS

Although India has long been a patriarchal culture, there are many goddesses in Hindu mythology. Vishnu, the sleeping god who heads the Hindu pantheon, rests upon the coils of the great serpent Ananda, the meaning of whose name is "Unending."

In India, "serpent power" is a leading motif of yogic symbolism. There, the primary task of the yogi embarked on the path of spiritual development is to awaken the goddess Kundalini, who is said to be a serpent sleeping coiled at the base of the spine. Kundalini is a subtle spiritual force that rises up the spinal column from the tailbone to the top of the head, through a system of energy centers called *chakras*. Activation of the chakras through meditation accelerates health and well-being and confers enlightenment. This remarkable spiritual force, which unites the energy of Earth with the energy of the Heavens, consists of two snakelike strands of pure energy spiraling up and down the spinal column. These strands intertwine with each other just like the ones we see in the caduceus.

The divine power,
Kundalini shines
like the stem of a young lotus;
like the snake, coiled round upon herself,
she holds her tail in her mouth
and lies resting half asleep
at the base of the body.

Ajit Mookerjee, Kundalini:
The Arousal of the Inner Energy

(from whom we derive the word *hygiene*) was the original healer goddess, until the Greek god Asklepios took over. She then became a sort of nurse figure, not unlike the recent stereotype of male doctors and female nurses (which I'm happy to say is changing now, as medical school enrollments tend to consist of at least half women these days and more men choose to take up the nursing profession).

THE SERPENT AND THE MOON

The Moon is the serpent's celestial counterpart—the cycles of waxing and waning, or "dying" (the new Moon) and being reborn (the first crescent sliver), relate to the serpent sloughing its skin and being renewed. Mythologically, both the serpent and the Moon are symbols of the progress of human life through time, from the mystery of birth through the mystery of death, to be considered as sacred processes of the same One.

Astrologically, the Moon rules bodily functions. Because each of us carries an archive of all of our experiences through life with us—internalized not only in our minds, memories, and emotions but also in our bodies—it is possible to regard our bodies as the record of the fulfillment and deprivation of inward needs. As a symbol of the Great Mother Goddess, who both gives life and devours the dead, the Moon is also related to old Father Time, who is known in India as the Lord of Karma and astrologically as Saturn, the planet of time. Saturn—whose metal is lead, symbolizes restrictions. He represents the necessary limitations placed on human life, of which our bodies are the visible manifestation.

Symbolic of the necessity to accept the limitations of the physical world, Saturn is said to be exalted in Libra, the zodiacal sign of balance and harmony. In a harmonious arrangement, be it a work of

Serpent and Psyche

The serpent also represents the psychic realm; when the serpent appears, it signals that the deepest level of the intuitive mind is sending an important message to the conscious mind.

One of psychologist Carl G. Jung's patients, who knew nothing about serpent symbolism, made a drawing of an eye with a serpent on each side. Each snake was "biting" one corner of each eye. Jung remarks of this middle-aged woman that she, "without being neurotic, was struggling for spiritual development." He felt that the symbol of the eye being bitten by the serpents indicated her new ability to "see" the truth of her inner self, to encounter "the ultimate and moving power of the universe, transcending and overcoming its pain."

Over the Rainbow

The link between serpent and moisture is found worldwide, and the snake is linked to the rainbow in myth everywhere. The Kulu tribe of northern India terms the rainbow *Buddhi Nagin*, or "old female snake." In this culture, the rainbow is associated with a feminine serpent deity. Snake women are also commonly found in myth. These can be powerful, fierce, energetic, or benevolent helpers. Snake maidens rule the bountiful seas, whose underwater treasures, such as pearls and marine life, are theirs to give or keep.

art or a healthy human, there is an integration of the ideal vision with necessary limits: one without the other results in disharmony. Power flows when the opposites are united in a harmonious pattern, as is seen in the intertwined snakes of the caduceus and kundalini. Wholeness and health result from integrating all aspects of our existence, including sickness and death, which cannot be avoided.

A Goddess Game
Meet Your Personal Serpent

Now that you've learned about the positive symbolism of the serpent of the Goddess, spend some time creating in your Goddess journal your own versions of the serpent as Wisdom, or as a healing power, or just as a friendly and beneficial animal. Let your imagination take wing and see what your inner wisdom produces. (One girl I knew drew a charming snaky figure with long eyelashes and a ruffled skirt! Another made a page of wavy lines that looked like water.)

Do what comes naturally—you don't have to be an artist. If you happen to be afraid of snakes, let that show, and then see if you want to make changes. If you use erasable colored pencils, you can redraw whatever doesn't please you. Or cut out pictures from magazines and paste them in the blank spaces. It's your book. Do whatever pleases *you*.

The idea here is to get acquainted with your inner serpent image—and to relate it to your Goddess power within. And, oh yes—to learn to think of the serpent as a wise counselor, not as a symbol of evil. We'll talk more about that when we discuss the fable of Adam and Eve and the Garden of Eden.

THE HEALING MOON THROUGH THE SIGNS

Here are basic descriptions of each moon sign.

Aries Moon teens are active and vital. You need relaxation and meditation in order to "turn off" the thinking motor.

Taurus Moon teens are serene and like a steady pace. You need physically comfortable surroundings, especially if ill.

Gemini Moon teens hate boredom. You need mental stimulation, diversity, and distraction—and lots of talking.

Cancer Moon teens are supersensitive emotionally. You need nurturing and support, especially from your family members.

Leo Moon teens are warm and affectionate, so receiving plenty of affection makes you feel wanted and important.

Virgo Moon teens are fundamentally neat, even fussy. Cleanliness and orderliness are vital to your health.

Libra Moon teens need peace and quiet in calm, beautiful surroundings, and close relationships of all kinds.

Scorpio Moon teens have profound emotions. You need friends who understand your depths to help you identify them.

Sagittarius Moon teens are naturally upbeat and give off an innate sense of optimism. You expect everything to go well.

Capricorn Moon teens are reserved and cautious. You go slowly into relationships and tend to be materialistic.

The Moon in Your Chart

Astrologically, the Moon is important both in analyzing where illness may arise and how healing may be effected. It symbolizes what is most basic to you, thus pointing the way to healing. You can call upon the healing power of the Moon by becoming acquainted with your Moon Sign. To find your Moon Sign, turn to page 214.

Spiritual Philosophy

Emanuel Swedenborg, the eighteenth-century scientist turned visionary, said, "There is nothing in nature that does not symbolize something in the world of spirit."

The Gaia Principle

The "Gaia principle," proposed by J. Lovelock in 1979, states that Earth is a living, breathing organism. Lovelock's idea of an alive, organic Earth—now gradually taking hold upon our collective consciousness—is based on the same principles as ancient shamanism.

Aquarius Moon teens are innately humanitarian. You need freedom at all costs and are often emotionally detached.

Pisces Moon teens soak up the thoughts and feelings of others. You need to learn to set your boundaries.

THE WAY OF SHAMANISM

Originating in central and northern Asia, shamanism spread outward—into other parts of Asia, Australia, Africa, and the Americas. Shamanism speaks directly to the totality that encompasses all life and the environment, both terrestrial and celestial. There is no separation between spirit and body, between human and animal, between human and plant, or between Earth and cosmos. Shamans believe they can transcend both time and space and, in so doing, avail themselves of the invisible powers, which reside in the animal and vegetable kingdoms and in the elements—fire, earth, air, water.

Traditionally, tribal shamans have nurtured spiritual powers and brought them to a high degree of development, passing their knowledge and techniques along to succeeding generations. This practice was common for many centuries among those who followed the way of the Goddess. What women learned, they taught to their daughters and granddaughters. The traditions of learning were handed down carefully.

Wise in the lore of herbs and plants known to have healing properties, these early women fused the practice of spiritual magic with the practice of healing. Indeed, there was no separation between the two—the practice of shamanism presupposes that we live in a psychospiritual as well as physical ecosystem.

In this view, the entire world and all in it are imbued with Spirit—all life is in communication at a deep level, beneath our awareness.

Animals have their own type of consciousness and can know our thoughts and sense our feelings (as anyone with a pet cat or dog can attest).

Leading-edge scientists such as physicist David Foster and former Cambridge University biologist Rupert Sheldrake postulate that natural, if unseen, forces possess both intelligence and purpose. Sheldrake's concept of "morphic fields," in which there is a consistent if invisible communion between all members of a species, is similar to the shamanistic idea of an archetypal or "master" animal for each species.

WHAT IS SHAMANISM?

Shamanism is a general term for what is thought to be the oldest form of religion in the world. The basic tenet of this worldview is that life exists simultaneously in two realms— the everyday or "natural" one and the transpersonal or spiritual one. In traditional shamanistic societies, the spiritual aspect of life is always a natural part of the physical or bodily realities. What I call "the invisible world" is every bit as important as, and even more potent than, the manifest, or visible, world.

Put simply, shamanism is a point of view and a practice that respects Earth and everything in the Universe. It is more than a religion: it is an entire way of life. Today, many native peoples around the globe (those who have not been converted to Christianity or any other organized male-god religion) practice shamanistic ways, and scholars believe that the ancient people who followed the ways of the Goddess were shamanistic.

RETURNING TO WHOLENESS

It is sad that in our society the correspondences between religion, magic, and medicine have been all but lost. Members of the medical establishment have fallen prey to the negative aspects of Saturn—narrowing and restricting their view to the physical body and the material aspects of illness, health, and life itself. Thus, they are prevented from practicing the healing magic of the serpent god. Though they display the intertwining serpents on their license plates, they have lost the sense of the living symbol of their craft. This is because they do not—will not—see that nonphysical forces animate and support the manifest world, including that of the physical body.

Although the contributions of science to our welfare are undeniable, the mind-set of the male-god–dominated community does not allow for the interplay of all the energies of mind, body, and spirit. Therefore, it is up to each and every one of us—and especially up to teen girls—to take responsibility for recognizing the need for wholeness and integrating it into our lives. The return of a worldview that respects and reveres the way of the Goddess, and that honors the natural world and all in it, is an urgent necessity today. We must heal ourselves *and* our societies *and* our planet.

We cannot wait for those who do not grasp the concept of wholeness, which lies at the root of the way of the Goddess, to give us permission to explore our own natures and use them fully. By so doing, we incorporate the divine serpent power into our daily lives and enable ourselves to make far-reaching changes in both ourselves and our society.

Each day we have the opportunity to re-create ourselves by tuning in to the Goddess within. When we activate our energies in the form of impulses and desires, when we fearlessly seek out both our strengths and our weaknesses, when we test our abilities anew by coping with the challenges life presents, we then develop into the unique individuals we came into this world to be.

But when we hesitate, hold back, and court fear instead of trust, we stultify our essential life energies. Because the psyche persists in realizing what one is born to be, when the quality of our lives becomes less than we basically know it should be, warning bells sound in the form of physical illness and psychological distress. Crisis arises to command our attention to what is wrong, forcing buried issues into the light where we can recognize our deep inner needs and attend to them.

In support of this point, here are some observations made by Edward C. Whitmont in his book *Alchemy of Healing:*

> The unfolding of our life's development ever and again leads us into critical impasses that cry out for resolution and healing. . . . These are bent upon connecting and reconnecting us to [our] essence and its reordering stream of information.

And, as we act to realize our true selves, we help others and the environments in which we live—family, community, the species, the planet.

True, there is much that is negative in our world—as the TV newscast nightly confirms—and in our individual lives, which are often upset by confusion, emotional pain, and physical disorders (though these physical and emotional symptoms often point to spiritual problems seeking recognition).

I am one, however, who firmly believes that it is better to light a candle than to curse the darkness. One lighted candle can serve to light millions of other candles—ultimately creating a blaze of light that will illuminate the entire world.

We do not just receive the fire of life and pass it on unchanged, like an Olympic torch relay runner. In bearing that living flame,

I Asked the Spirit of the Plants

When shamans from South America travel to the United States to do healings, the plants with which they are familiar do not grow here. One time a visiting Otavalan shaman performed a healing at my home and wanted to be able to add herbal remedies to his prescriptions for the patient afterward. The Otavalan market where he would ordinarily send his patients to obtain plants for healing is a very long way from Baltimore. He took a long walk on my property. Coming back to the house armed with bundles of "weeds," he announced that he had learned specific uses and ways to prepare the plants. Not having his familiar helper plants available, alternates were found. Although he had never tried them before, and without any knowledge of herbal uses of temperate plant species, he used them with excellent results.

"How did you find out what these plants could do?" I queried this great shaman.

"I asked the spirit of the plants," he explained.

Eve Bruce, *Shaman, M.D.*

A ZULU HEALING DREAM

In Eve Bruce's book *Shaman, M.D.,* Eve has an illuminating conversation with Credo Mutwa, a Zulu shaman from South Africa. Credo is concerned about the epidemic of AIDS sweeping through South Africa and wants to build a series of clinics throughout the country for AIDS patients. When Eve hears the description of his dream clinics she is struck by their uncanny similarity to the clinics of Hippocrates in ancient Greece. An excerpt of their conversation follows.

"Let me show you the clinics I hope to create. I'll draw out the rough plans for you now, a prototype. The idea is to build something cheaply that can be replicated throughout the townships, throughout the land."

He drew his plan on a piece of scrap paper—a simple building with many windows and a veranda so that light and air flow through the main room. There were aromatic plants and water pools with falls so that the sound of trickling water and healing aromas continually caressed the senses. A few beds for the sick people to sleep in were placed in the room, with hammocks strung for the severely ill so that they needn't die in bed. Some areas of the floor would be hard, while others would be sandy so that people could feel the earth under foot, and someone with seizures would have a soft place to fall. Surrounding this building he drew huts for the staff, and many huts for the families so that they could stay and care for their kin.

"The clinics should not be isolated," he went on, "people who have recovered sufficiently to leave will be asked to return to give hope to those who are more ill."

We went over the drawing and the concepts at length and then I had a sudden realization. "Baba, you know of course of Hippocrates, said to be the father of allopathic medicine?"

"Yes, I do," said Baba Credo, "the Greek."

"I just realized the similarities. His clinics are said to have been very much like what you have described! It's astounding, really; he lived so many years ago, and his words and ideas have been distorted in so many ways. His clinics were places of deep true healing, more like spas where all the senses were brought into the healing process and where lifestyle was emphasized. You have the same dream as the very father of modern medicine."

How wonderful! An old Zulu man going back to the roots of Zulu healing ways, and through this bridging the very roots of allopathic medicine. Perhaps it is time for true healing all over the world.

we add that which is uniquely our own to its power and glory. Life is a vast ecosystem in which we all play our parts—just as does each rock and plant, bird and bee—and every individual contribution is of vital importance. Each of us has the potential to increase the sum total of positive energy in the world.

For myself, I know that the closer I get to expressing the reality of who I am, the more whole I become. It is in this spirit that I bring you the serpent's message. I believe that we owe it both to ourselves and to the totality of life on Earth to heed its wisdom as shown by the way of the Goddess.

We read books to find out who we are. What other people, real or imaginary, do and think and feel is an essential guide to our understanding of what we ourselves are and may become.

Ursula K. LeGuin

ADAM AND EVIL

Having learned about all of the positive readings of the serpent that have come down through the ages from the days of the Goddess, let's take a new look at an old (well, not *that* old) story.

We all know the biblical story of Adam and Eve and how the evil serpent tempted Eve to take a bite out of the forbidden apple of the Tree of Knowledge. In fact, most of us have had this story drummed into our heads and psyches since we were infants, imbibing it with our mother's milk, so to speak. And few of us have ever questioned it.

Why this reversal of the order of nature—that all humans, male and female alike, are born from a woman mother—took such deep root in Western culture is a mystery unless you understand that it was driven in at the point of a sword. To once again draw on the words of Joseph Campbell, from his wonderful, illuminating book *Occidental Mythology*: "This tradition, exemplified by a God who lived in a distant realm separate from Earth and who revealed His will and wisdom through male prophets, is proclaimed superior by the *sword*." Campbell went on to say:

> When the Goddess had been venerated as the giver and supporter of life as well as consumer of the dead, women as Her representatives had been accorded a paramount position in society as well as in cult . . . opposed to such, without quarter, is the order of the Patriarchy, with an ardor of righteous eloquence *and a fury of fire and sword* (my italics).

As we saw earlier, the concept of a male god separated from his own creation did not spring into existence overnight. A close reading of the Hebrew Bible makes it clear that this victory of the male god over the Goddess was achieved only after a long and bitter

"How does one grow up?" I asked a friend. She answered, "By thinking."

May Sarton,
Journal of a Solitude

struggle. The first books of the Bible themselves tell of the religious war waged on the Goddess and Her people.

Interestingly, even the ever-so-wise King Solomon couldn't help himself when it came to female divinity. At the same time he was engaged in constructing his famous temple (to the greater glory of Yahweh), he was seeing to it that sanctuaries to the Goddess, or the various goddesses who bore different names in different places, were also built. One might say he was, religiously speaking, a split personality!

ST. PAUL AND THE DEGRADATION OF WOMEN

I should say a few words about the famous St. Paul, whom the French scholar and historian Jean Markale claimed was "the true founder of Christianity."

Paul was originally named Saul. He was born Jewish and tended to be something of a fanatic. When his astonishing conversion to Christianity came about, he transferred his natural fanaticism over to his new religion. As part of his fanatical nature, Paul was a woman hater. (The technical term for this is *misogynist*.)

Evidence suggests that the Jewish Saul was homosexual. Now, in the way of the Goddess, homosexuality is no problem—all sexuality is accepted as natural. But, as a Jew, Saul would have been taught that homosexuality was "an abomination against nature." The Old Testament is clear and firm on the Jewish ban against homosexuality. We can conclude that Saul felt guilty and ashamed of his sexuality. When he became Christian, his hatred (or perhaps it was jealousy?) of the rather free-wheeling sexual customs of the Goddess people translated into a hatred of women in general.

From a modern psychological point of view, we can assume Saul/Paul had some pretty serious issues around his sexual orientation. And probably some related to his mother as well. He hated women so much that one of his most famous pronouncements was, "Women are good only for childbirth. Let them give birth until they die of it."

One of the instructions to Jews from Yahweh was to "go forth and multiply." So childbirth was ordained, but the women who were responsible for this sacred process were degraded. Why? This one-word question brings us to the crux of the story of Adam and Eve and the famous serpent in the Garden of Eden.

FROM MOTHER GODDESS TO FATHER GOD

Historical research shows that there was a point in time—we cannot date it nor know if it was different in different regions—when a reversal of the natural order took place. The Mother Goddess was turned into the Father God.

The earliest evidence is the story of the world-famous shrine at Delphi, where priestesses gave oracular counsel. Originally, the god of the shrine was a serpent named Python who was served by women.

Then, out of the north, came Greeks who had a god named Apollo, their sun god. Apollo killed Python and took over his shrine. And the people began to worship Apollo. And yet—and yet—it was always a woman priestess who gave the oracular pronouncements at the shrine.

As Joseph Campbell said, these serpent gods just don't die. And the Goddess religion wasn't that easy to stamp out either. As you can see, it was only a partial victory, but this incident (or legend) marks the beginning of the transition from the Goddess to male-god patriarchy.

Even though early societies still followed the way of the Goddess for centuries to come, the stage had been set for the biblical fathers. It was among the elite scholar-priests that the concept of patriarchy was developed—and along with it the story of Adam and Eve. Their goal was to eliminate the ancient Goddess and to strip away the power and status of real women in these societies.

Jean Markale remarked in the introduction to his *Great Goddess* that "without too much risk of error, we can thus conclude that it was the priests who imposed the concept of a father god, creator of all things . . . as the legend of Delphi clearly reveals."

Other scholars have commented that the story of Adam and Eve was concocted in "scholarly priestly circles." And Joseph Campbell stated flatly that the story was intended as a "political document." In other words, propaganda!

Propaganda, unfortunately, can be extremely effective—why else use it? The evidence of the success of this particular bit of propaganda is all around us even today. The challenge—your challenge— is to put things back into their rightful order.

RETHINKING THE STORY OF ADAM AND EVE

How is this reordering to be accomplished? We can't go back to the old ways of the Goddess, but we can rethink what we have been taught to believe. Girls can question the validity of the story of Adam and Eve. They can commit spiritual disobedience, just as those who fought for civil rights in the 1960s and 1970s committed acts of civil disobedience in order to right long-standing wrongs.

Let's take a look at some of the details of our story. First of all, just what is a serpent doing in Yahweh's perfect Garden of Eden? Apparently, this god isn't even in control of his own backyard!

And why did the serpent talk to Eve—who is presumably inferior to Adam? Well, we already know the answer. The serpent represents the Goddess, whom the patriarchs were finding extremely hard to eliminate. It shows up in the garden as Her symbol and speaks to Her daughter. That's only sensible.

Back to Babylon

Another scholar, Professor Edward Chiera, makes the point that the Bible provides *several* creation stories! He comments that the Adam and Eve tale must have been widely circulated, for many copies have been found. But in piecing together fragments of an ancient Sumerian myth he discovered that, although a woman played the dominant role in the Sumer myth, she bore no resemblance to the silly Eve who messed up a good thing (Paradise) by foolishly listening to the evil serpent. Quite the contrary, says Chiera: "Poor Eve has been damned by all subsequent generations for her deed, while the Babylonians thought so much of their woman ancestress that they deified her."

A Catholic Priest's Testimony

Women, dominant up until then because of their fertility, which put them in a natural, biological relationship with the divine, were to be punished precisely by that which was their glory: their pregnancy and maternity. Henceforth, these would be sources of suffering rather than of glory.

André de Smet,
La Grande Déesse n'est pas mort (Paris, 1983)
Quoted by Jean Markale in
The Great Goddess

And why is Yahweh so angry that his first couple eats of the fruit of the Tree of Knowledge (of Good and Evil)? Wouldn't it be a good thing to know about right and wrong?

The truth of the matter—one that is not stressed in Judeo-Christian teachings—is that there were not one but *two* trees in the garden. The second tree was the Tree of Immortality. (We've already seen a Goddess figure with serpents and a crescent Moon offering the liquor of immortality to a worshiper.)

In the story what makes Yahweh furious is the fear that his children would have the nerve to eat the fruit of the second tree and become immortal—divine—themselves. So, he throws them out. Not only them but the serpent as well. And he fiercely condemns the serpent to henceforth *crawl*. Excuse me? Does he think the serpent walked upright before the incident in the garden? We need a reality check here. Then, for good measure, he pits the serpent against Eve, the woman. In other words, women are to be prevented from following the ways of the Goddess.

Still unsatisfied and monumentally pissed off, Yahweh declares that after their expulsion from the Garden of Eden it would be the woman who desired the man instead of the other way around. This reversal was intended to set men above women as "spiritual" (a term reserved for males) and to blame women for men's sexual desires. Oh, come on, Yahweh—get a life! Any teen girl could tell this god a thing or two about *that*. Aren't boys always after the girls? Sure, girls have sexual desires too (thanks be to the Goddess), but according to this upside-down view, they aren't supposed to *enjoy* sex, and its sole purpose is supposed to be making babies.

In calling women "carnal," which is a reference to the patriarchal view of the human body as a nasty bit of business (these people had some real hang-ups on that score), and in blaming Eve for "tempting" Adam, the patriarchal Bible writers revealed not only their political ambitions but also their psychological sexual problems. How handy to have females to blame.

Take a look at this statement written by André de Smet, a Catholic priest, in *La Grande Déesse n'est pas mort* (Paris):

> Since feminine religions have it that men desire women, which gives the latter mastery over the former, in the masculine religion that is now established, it will be woman whose "desires will be directed toward your husband, and he will have mastery over you." The woman becomes the slave of the man. This is a radical change. Another civilization begins when man is given predominance, since up until then, it had been given to woman. As to woman's familiar element, Mother Earth, it is cursed. "Because you have listened to the voice of the woman [that is, because you have turned your back to the cult of the goddess], you must henceforth command her . . . and cursed will be the ground because of you." (This [biblical] passage taken from Genesis 3:17–18.)

The author went on to explain that the cursing of all natural, earthly processes—in other words, the ways of the Goddess and the recognition that life goes in cycles—marks the "historical beginning of masculine society."

Next we get the famous statement of Eve's punishment for following her Goddess and listening to Her representative, the serpent: "You will give birth in pain."

Now, quite possibly, the women who followed the Goddess knew about special herbs and plant preparations to ease the pains of childbirth. (I wrote a book on herbal medicine and found lots of herbs for that purpose going back thousands of years.) We already know women were the first doctors and the inventors of medicine. Cutting off women from their Goddess and their knowledge of the natural world would result in painful childbirth.

The curse against the serpent, and consequently, against the [Goddess], extends to women, suspected—rightly—of being the partisans of this deity. This suspicion gives rise to the Church fathers' constant warnings against women, as well as their banishment from the priesthood and active participation in the church, and, in a more aberrant, vicious, and tragic form, the 'witch hunts' that began in the thirteenth century and continued until the end of the seventeenth century, at least in western Europe.

Jean Markale,
The Great Goddess

A Goddess Exercise

Eve and Adam

It looks really *different* when you put Eve first, doesn't it? Now, using what you have learned about the Goddess, Her ways, and Her sacred serpent, and about patriarchy's forcing women into the position of second-class citizens (or outright slavery), rewrite the story in your Goddess journal. Have fun!

3

ONE GODDESS— MANY NAMES

oddess religions invest nature and the body with spiritual meaning and value. From earliest times, cultures based their values and worldviews on the worship of the Great Goddess, which underlies the beginnings of all civilizations.

Nevertheless, the Goddess—though She never died—has lain hidden and dormant for centuries upon centuries. Now, She is ready to return. And a good thing that is, too!

In his wonderful 1992 book *Return of the Goddess* (I really recommend this book to girls who are serious about becoming what I call "Goddess Girls"), psychologist Edward C. Whitmont, MD, told us:

> At the low point of a cultural development that has led us into the deadlock of scientific materialism, technological destructiveness, religious nihilism, and spiritual impoverishment, a most astounding phenomenon has occurred. A new mythologem is arising in our midst and asks to be integrated into our modern frame of reference. It is the myth of the ancient Goddess who once ruled earth and heaven before the advent of the patriarchy and of the patriarchal religions.

What Does the Future Hold?

Sooner or later a choice will have to be made: to continue on a willful . . . path in which one tries to secure autonomy and self-determination, or to embark on a spiritual path in which one seeks ever-greater willingness to become part of the fundamental processes of life in self-surrender.

Gerald May,
Will and Spirit

Whitmont continued, "The Goddess is now returning. . . . The patriarchy's time is running out." To return, She needs *your* help.

After being denied and suppressed for centuries, while world conditions deteriorated under the male-ego–dominated sociopolitical structures and the status of women sank lower and lower, She is ready to make a comeback. And not a moment too soon. Our society is in dire danger, with wars breaking out all over the place. A new one erupts almost every day and old ones go on and on and on. Many of these conflicts are sparked by the more fanatic members of male-god religions. They are constantly fighting one another. At the same time, our beautiful blue planet is under heavy environmental assault from people with the same power-hungry mind-set, who seem to think natural resources are their personal property! But, as Chief Seattle pointed out to the white European conquerors of the far West, no one can own the land. *It belongs to everyone.*

Thank goodness the Goddess *is* returning. In spite of the spreading violence and environmental degradation, I can see many hopeful and encouraging signs of Her return. For one thing, prior to the time I started writing about the Goddess in 1975, I could find hardly any books about Her, and all that I did find were by men. Since then, dozens of Goddess books have been written by women. Goddess resources on the internet abound! And women writers and scholars who study the Goddess are abundant, some calling themselves thealogians to differentiate themselves from theologians, who study male-god religions.

In the book that started it all, *When God Was a Woman* by Merlin Stone, the author noted that she "found the development of the religion of the female deity [in the Near and Middle East, where Judaism, Christianity, and Islam all were born] was intertwined with the earliest beginnings of religion so far discovered anywhere on earth."

SHE OF THE TEN THOUSAND NAMES

Artifacts and clay figurines representing the Goddess date back to prehistoric times and have been found all over the world. Accounts of a female Creator of all existence—not only the creator of people but of Heaven and Earth and all its creatures—have been found in Sumer, Babylon, Africa, Australia, India, and China. Some five thousand years ago, the Goddess was known in many forms and by many names—in fact, the Goddess has often been referred to as She of the Ten Thousand Names. She was revered everywhere as wise counselor and prophetess, as lawgiver and sage dispenser of righteous justice.

In Egypt, Hathor, the Great Celestial Cow who carries the Sun between the horns of the Moon on her head, was much beloved as the great all-providing, maternal figure who nourished Earth and its peoples with her milky rain. Another Egyptian Goddess was Nut, the Sky Goddess shown with her star-spangled figure arched over Earth, a male named Geb. Nut represented the feminine principle identified with the generational power of the Sun.

Great Isis, an Egyptian goddess to whom the Romans erected dozens of temples as well, was queen of Heaven. She provided the power that gave the pharaoh his authority—he sat in her lap as a child! She was the throne, a sacred symbol of the Great Mother with its origins in Goddess symbolism. There are many sculptures of Isis with the baby Horus on her lap or nursing at her breast.

Clearly, Isis was the prototype for the later Christian Madonna, with the baby Jesus either nursing or sitting in her lap. Because the Jews lived in Egypt for several generations, they derived their symbolism from the sacred figures of that ancient culture. And because the first Christians were Jews, they followed suit—all the while claiming *theirs* was the original religion!

The Eternal Female

British archaeologist Sir E. A. Wallis Budge called Her the "personification of the eternal female principle of life which was self-sustaining and self-existent and was secret and unknown and all-pervading."

Bast, the Egyptian goddess of love and beauty, fertility and harmony, was revered everywhere. Represented as a cat, her temples contained thousands of statuettes of cats brought there by those seeking her blessings. The cat was also sacred to lion-headed Sekmet and to Isis. Is it any wonder that in medieval times cats—thought to be familiars, or servant spirits, of witches—were burned at the stake along with the accused and convicted victims of the Inquisition?

Neith, the lady of the West and twin sister of Isis, is one of the oldest and most widely distributed Egyptian deities, going back to the predynastic era, before Egypt had a central government ruled by a succession of pharaohs. The Roman historian Plutarch wrote this about her: "I am all that has been, and is, and shall be, and my robe no mortal has yet uncovered." Clearly, Neith had her beginnings in representations of the Great Goddess.

A GODDESS GAME

TRYING YOUR HAND AT BEING CATTY

Cats lived in the temples in Egypt and were much loved and honored by the population. They were companions to the priestesses, and they also served as temple guards. In addition, we can assume they were valued as protectors of the food supply, keeping rodents out of the stored grain after the yearly harvest.

To play this game, find some pictures of cats in magazines and paste them in your Goddess journal or on a larger piece of scrap paper to make a collage honoring these mysterious, sacred animals. Or if you prefer, draw your own cat figures. As you do this activity, imagine yourself as an Egyptian priestess of the Goddess.

THE GODDESS SPEAKS

One of the earliest written accounts of the Goddess is from *The Golden Ass of Apuleius*, in which the Goddess Herself speaks:

> I am she that is the natural mother of all things, mistress and governess of all the elements, the initial progeny of worlds, chief of the powers divine, queen of all . . . manifested alone and under one form in all the gods and goddesses . . . my name, my divinity is adored throughout the world, in divers [*sic*] manners, in variable customs, and by many names.*
>
> *Adlington translation—The Modern Library

In Babylonia, the Great Goddess was called Queen Innana. In Mesopotamia, Her name was Ishtar, known as Directress of People and Lady of Vision. To the Greeks (who split the One Goddess into many), the Great Earth Mother was known as Demeter. The Romans called Her Ceres. And, at the time Christianity was getting started, the Romans named their most important goddess Cybele. Cybele's priests wore feminine clothing—long robes—as a statement of identification with their feminine deity. Some even castrated themselves to be less masculine.

Isn't it interesting that Roman Catholic priests and monks today still wear long gowns? They haven't a clue why anymore, but their clothing is a direct descendant of the priests of Cybele! At the time the worship of Cybele was so prevalent it almost kept the new Christian religion from gaining a foothold in Rome. It took a few hundred years and the conversion of the Roman emperor Constantine in about 300 AD for the Christians to finally win out over the Great Goddess.

Celtic tribes, in what is now northern Europe and the British Isles, acknowledged Cerridwen as the goddess of intelligence and knowledge; to the pre-Greeks, as Gaia, she provided the wisdom of divine revelation.

The last known high priestess of the Great Goddess, Ariadne (daughter of the legendary King Minos) lived in Minoan Crete (an island in the Mediterranean that is now part of Greece) around 2500 BC. Her temple was crowned by a pair of horns representing the Moon, and sacred dancers who performed feats of daring bull leaping, vaulting over the backs of live bulls, were consecrated to

Celtic Societies

Technically, only countries where a Celtic language is spoken—by at least a part of the population—can be called Celtic. The countries that fall into this category are Ireland, Wales, the Brittany region of France, Scotland, and the British possession the Isle of Man. However, the Celts migrated into other parts of France, Belgium, Germany, and Switzerland, as well as taking up residence through the whole of the British Isles during many waves of migration. They came originally from the great plains of Central Asia around 1000 BCE.

A GODDESS EXERCISE
WRITING HYMNS TO THE GODDESS

Few of the hymns to the Goddess have come down to us, with the exception of those from India. However, we are free to write our own hymns to Her, praising Her and telling Her what we feel about Her and our feminine connection to Her.

To get you started on your own writing of hymns to the Goddess, here's an example I wrote:

Our Mother, who art the Earth,
Hallowed be Thy Name.
Thy Queendom beneath our feet,
Thy Will, its harmony.
Blessed all Thy spaces,
Sacred all Thy creatures.
Give us this day our food and drink,
And prevent us from Thy despoilation.
Forgive us our trespasses against Thy holy body,
And teach us to reverence Thee always.

> Now in your journal or notebook, try your hand at writing a hymn to the Goddess. Just say what's in your heart, and it will be perfectly acceptable to Her.
>
> Once you've written your hymn—or hymns—try singing them out loud, or just humming as you repeat your words. You don't have to be a musical genius, or even be able to carry a tune. Just let the sounds flow freely from your heart to Her ears. You may surprise yourself and find singing your hymn to Her an enjoyable way to feel deeply connected to your own Goddess center. If you play a musical instrument, you can accompany yourself.

her. Images of bull leaping are preserved in the remains of the palace of Knossos on Crete. In Ariadne's temple, hymns were sung in praise of the Goddess, their composition being one of the functions of the colleges of the holy isles of the Mediterranean.

THE WOMEN BEHIND THE GODDESS

Although the many names of the Goddess let us trace Her around the globe, it's important to remember that behind Her Ten Thousand Names there stood millions of real women, who were once teenage girls like you. The qualities and achievements of our long-ago foremothers were the basis on which the feminine divine was modeled.

One of their most important contributions was the development of medicine, which grew out of women's knowledge of wild plants. Even today, many prescription drugs are based on herbal components! And, according to Evelyn Reed in *Woman's Evolution*, "Very little has been added to this remarkable ancient collection of medicine."

Medicine and the Moon

The root *med* derives from the root word for *moon*. And the Goddess was often identified with the Moon in regions all over the world. Celtic women are said to have developed medical substances from plants that became part of women's mysteries and were kept secret because of their amazing abilities and because of their spiritual Goddess-related context.

Ancient people credited the Goddess with giving humanity writing, agriculture, preservation of fire, domestication of animals, and pottery making. Pottery vessels were all important for storing and transporting foodstuffs.

Her priestesses discovered and researched the healing arts, learning the characteristics and powers of herbs. Their women's arts led them to profound knowledge of nature that enabled them to distinguish between poisonous and edible plants; propagate wild grasses and weeds into our staple grains, fruits, and vegetables; tame wild animals; and make and fire ceramics. Unfortunately, later on in the medieval Christian era, the women who employed some of these wise women's talents were accused of witchcraft.

In ancient times, because of women's connection to pottery making, pots were considered sacred vessels. As hollow forms, they

WOMEN'S WORK

The word *medicine* originally meant "knowledge of the wise woman," and those women who practiced herbal healing were revered for their wisdom. They could perform what then seemed magic. Evidence exists that they were able to revive people from comas, that they performed operations (the complexity of which still baffles our modern doctors), delivered babies while easing or eliminating the pain of giving birth, knew which herbs would bring on menstrual periods (possibly aborting unwanted pregnancies).

All of their healing work was considered sacred, as it came from the Goddess. Whether they were treating wounds or illnesses or psychological problems, they kept their formulas secret and restricted the use of drugs and intoxicating potions to medical, and when appropriate, religious applications.

were symbolic of the hollow womb of the Goddess from which all life flowed. Over the centuries of the development of civilization, even the most abstract matriarchal symbols maintained a relationship to the vessel-body of the sacred Feminine. (Interestingly, it is the pot shards dug from archaeological sites that have given us the most information about extinct cultures! So, we have women to thank for this historical information.)

In these ancient civilizations, the Goddess was revered as the Mother of All. She both gave life and "ate back" the dead. The Goddess as Mother was carved on the walls of Paleolithic caves and painted in the shrines of the earliest known cities, on the Anatolian plateau. The great stone circles—known as *henges* in the British Isles—were raised in her honor, as were the later dolmens and cromlechs of the Celtic peoples. The great centers of Goddess worship—in Anatolia, Malta, Iberia, Brittany, and Sumeria—are ruins now, with only the silent stones left standing to attest to the ancient reverence for the Great Mother as the progenitor of all things. Nonetheless, the tradition of Goddess-centered life lives on in the hearts and psyches of people everywhere, tracing its roots back to the time before the ascendance of patriarchy.

In contrast to this ancient view of life, our society, and by extension our approach to what we consider to be sacred or holy, is conditioned by patriarchal domination, which includes the mechanistic view that Nature has no soul and was designed entirely for the benefit of humans. The God of patriarchy generously gave human beings—male human beings, that is—dominion over all other life-forms. Thanks to this notion, many life-forms are now extinct or seriously endangered. As a by-product of the patriarchal worldview, humans are slowly destroying our home planet.

No wonder governments dream of conquering space! But do they really think they can colonize the Moon or any other celestial body? The TV program *Star Trek* was entertaining, but no sensible person could believe it represented the real future.

The destructive results of this philosophy that denigrates the age-old feminine principle cannot be tolerated. She is Mother, and She is Earth. Upon Her bosom we rest, upon Her soil we trod, from Her fructifying womb come all living things, and within Her sacred body lie all those precious resources that enrich the lives (and the pocketbooks) of humans. But because She has been declared dead and inert by the high priests of patriarchy, we take from Her without thought or consideration for the consequences. Though some of us express concern for "the environment," few of us see that *we* are part of that environment, that humanity itself is an endangered species.

"The sacral relation of the woman to the pot originates . . . in the symbolic significance of the material from which the pot is made, namely, clay, for clay belongs to the earth, which stands in a relation of *participation* with the Feminine."

Erich Neumann,
The Great Mother

A GODDESS GAME

CREATE A GODDESS POT

You are going to choose a pot that will represent the Goddess to you. It doesn't matter whether it's something you already have or something you find, make, or buy. The only requirement is that it be a pot, which is to say something rounded with an opening.

My own preferred Goddess pot is a very special one. About four inches high, it's wonderfully round and fat—like a pregnant belly—and was handmade by a friend. When she took up pottery, it was the first piece she made and fired, so her making it a gift to me means I treasure it all the more. It's light-blue with dark-blue dripped markings that remind me of the color of the sky at day's end. The French call this time of day *l'heure bleu*, or "the blue hour." It marks the time of transition from day to night.

Choose your Goddess pot with care—hold different objects and see how you respond to their vibrations. You'll know when you have got the one that's "just right."

When you have selected your Goddess pot, you can use it to receive Goddess guidance. Here's how it works. Write any of your wishes, dreams, aspirations, questions, problems, ideas, or desires on little pieces of paper and put them in the pot. Perhaps you've had an argument with a friend and can't figure out how to make things right. Maybe you're trying to think of an inspired way to earn some money. Or you're attracted to someone and you'd like to come up with a good plan for letting that person know it, without being too obvious, of course.

The purpose of the Goddess pot is to have a container for all your thoughts. Remember, the Goddess contains the whole Universe. You might want to consider your Goddess Pot as Her mailbox!

Inside your Goddess pot, magic will take place. Once you've put a slip of paper inside, don't obsess over getting an answer. Let it be. Trust that She will guide you. As with seeds planted deep in the dark earth, a growth process will begin. Sprouts of ideas and answers will gradually form within you.

YOU ARE THE KEY TO THE RETURN OF THE GODDESS

No legislation can solve or eradicate our environmental problems. Only we, within ourselves as individuals and in our schools and our communities, can do that. And *you,* as a teenage girl who has the potential to grow into a powerful Goddess-oriented woman, are going to be the most important factor in the return of the Goddess. If we honor her properly and allow Her out of the depths where she has been buried and from which She is now arising, there is still hope.

We must honor the Goddess within ourselves and then in our world at large. If we refuse to acknowledge Her, She may just get

Goddess Magic

The most difficult part about working magic, and sustaining one's belief in it, is dealing with that apparent time lapse which sometimes occurs when nothing seems to be happening, but that is precisely the time when everything is actually happening—in the Invisible World.

Marion Weinstein,
Positive Magic

Expect the Unexpected

As angel-book author Sophy Burnham has commented, "Many people pray and receive the answer to their prayers, but ignore them—or deny them, because the answers didn't come in the expected form." Be alert for answers, ideas, and dream images and learn to accept the Goddess in whatever form She expresses Herself.

The New Science

Developments in psychology and science—including the new explorations into the realms of intuition, ESP, global harmony, and the relationship of mind to matter—have shown that our currently impaired concept of the feminine is wreaking havoc in our world.

"We are creating dysfunctional societies that are breeding pathological behavior—violence, extreme competitiveness, suicide, drug abuse, greed, and environmental degradation. . . . Such behavior is an inevitable consequence when a society fails to meet the needs of its members for social bonding, trust, affection, and a shared sacred meaning."

David Korten,
When Corporations Rule the World

rid of us altogether. But if we grant Her the reverence She deserves, she will become a compassionate guide. She has the power to effect the transformation without which we are doomed.

The patriarchal concept of the feminine—the result of centuries of mythological representation (and misrepresentation)—reaches deep into the fabric of our society, and into the fiber of our beings. But no matter how deeply ingrained, patriarchy is neither ordained by divine revelation nor proclaimed by biology—though it claims to be both. It is merely a system of thought that can be rejected or revised to suit ourselves and our needs. However, in order for it to be changed, it must first be challenged. Feminist theologians are doing this, but all of us who wish to live lives authenticated by the Self need to join them in this work.

In *The Changing of the Gods,* Naomi R. Goldenberg asked, "If a woman comes to the conclusion that the patriarchal religions of Western culture do not help her in her life and, in fact, may very well hinder her sense of well-being, what can she do?" In her answer she presented two options: One is to withdraw all energy from spiritual concerns; the other is to give energy to the formulating of spiritual concepts that allow a religious view apart from the forms prescribed by traditional religions. She encouraged women to discover "the spiritual processes at work in their own psyches independent of religious processes endorsed by contemporary religion."

These feminist theologians are concerned about the need for holistic vision and for getting in touch with our bodies and nature, realizing that, as Mary Daly said, "this becoming of *whole* human beings will affect the values of our society, for it will involve a change in the fabric of human consciousness." For thousands of years, the era of the Great Goddess provided support and comfort to all humanity. My hope is that through honoring the Goddess we can reconnect to the inner wholeness She provides.

Will we be able to succeed at this daunting task? The answer ultimately will depend not on who the prevailing culture says we

A GODDESS EXERCISE

HOW DO YOU SEE YOUR FEMININE SELF?

In your Goddess journal, write about your own view of yourself as a female in this patriarchal society. Review your words and think about what changes you could make now. Then write out those changes in as much detail as you can.

Embodying Spirit

The Goddess is manifest in the world; she brings life into being, *is* nature, *is* flesh. Union is not sought outside the world in some heavenly sphere or through dissolution of the self into the void beyond the senses. Spiritual union is found in life, within nature, passion, sensuality—through being fully human, fully one's self. . . . There is no [separation] between spirit and flesh, no split between Godhead and the world.

Starhawk,
"Witchcraft and Women's Culture,"
in *Nourishing the Soul*

are but on who we determine ourselves to be, and why. Though the attitudes emanating from the male mythologies have worked their way deep into the minds and hearts of our entire society, a new tide is rising, an inner shift that will not be denied. This shift is issuing out of the deep mythological wells that feed the psyche: all pressures are not social; some come from within. The good news is that the Great Goddess, though banished and seemingly lost through the past millennia, is once again making Her presence felt in modern consciousness. She is whispering in your ear right now!

DISCOVERING YOUR INNER GODDESS

To attain true psychic health and achieve his or her full potential, everyone—especially today's teen girl—needs to escape the patriarchy's powerful enmeshment. To lead successful, fulfilling lives, girls today must examine the prevailing point of view toward the feminine and understand that it needs changing, which will demand a shift of emphasis within. Girls need to embark on a

WHAT IS PAGANISM?

In ancient times, when Christianity was just getting started, non-Christians were called pagans, a derogatory term for country people. The use of the term arose because city people were the earliest converts to Christianity, while the old nature-based religion hung on longer in rural areas. In Latin, the word *pagan* means simply "country," and *pagaini* are "country people," as opposed to city dwellers. So, for early Christians, pagans were country bumpkins who did not practice the "correct" religion but clung to their old ways.

Today, there is a resurgence of interest in paganism. This form of nature worship is being taken up by those concerned with the environment who see that nature is to be revered, not exploited. However, there is no actual pagan tradition—paganism was never a religion, as such. Christians called *all* non-Christians pagans, including the ancient Egyptians who had a sophisticated religion of their own.

Currently, a new religion, called Wicca, is very popular with those interested in a return to reverence for nature. People who practice Wicca are involved in following the cycles of nature and celebrating the festivals that revolve around the solstices and equinoxes, as well as the cross-quarter holidays such as Halloween, that fall halfway between the solstices and equinoxes on the calendar. They call these holidays sabbats and esbats.

The Wiccan/pagan movement can be seen as an attempt to reconnect with the Great Mother Goddess and the ways of nature. However, though its practitioners base their rituals and celebrations on nature's cycles, Wicca is a modern religion, not an ancient one. Wicca is just one of many new religions arising today—some arise as offshoots of traditional religions, while others make attempts to re-create pre-Christian ceremonies and beliefs. Wiccan religious traditions have been created by those who practice Wicca today and do not derive directly from any ancient traditional source.

journey—not the outward journey of the traditional male hero, but a feminine-oriented inward quest. The goal of such an inner journey is not primarily to change the world—it is to change yourself, to enable you to become the fully free and feminine person you inherently are right now.

Knowledge of who we are within cannot exist without conscious knowledge of the options available from which to choose. Traditional religion, abetted by science, has sold us a cheap bill of goods—a shoddy half-life around the masculine power structure. By consciously reclaiming the power of the Goddess, we can take back responsibility for our lives and reweave the torn fabric of our self-image and self-esteem. (Remember that the Goddess is the weaver.)

To integrate the divine Feminine is to be in harmony with the inner person, not merely fulfilling the socially accepted and politically ordained roles assigned to both women and men. To accomplish this shift in consciousness, we need to examine the cultural

A Psychologist's Prediction

The investigation of . . . the feminine psyche is one of the most necessary and important tasks [for] the creative health and development of the individual. [It] has equal importance for the psychologist of culture, who recognizes that the peril of present-day mankind springs in large part from the one-sidedly patriarchal development of the male intellectual consciousness, which is no longer kept in balance by the matriarchal world of the psyche. In this sense, the exposition of the Feminine is also a contribution to a future therapy of culture.

Erich Neumann,
The Great Mother

A GODDESS EXERCISE

HOW MANY GODDESSES CAN YOU NAME?

Though the Great Goddess is really one being encompassing all there is, it might be easier to relate to Her and invite Her back into your life if you focus on some of the individual aspects assigned to Her throughout history.

Now that you've learned quite a bit about the ten thousand names of the Goddess, list in your Goddess journal all the Goddess names you can remember from this book, from other books, or from school. After you write down a name, write whatever you know about that particular aspect of the Goddess.

symbols that shape our view of the world. By reorienting ourselves to the symbols of the divine Feminine, we heal the inner split that came about when the Great Mother Goddess was replaced entirely by the Father God.

Although this task must fall squarely on the shoulders of each individual, it is only through collective effort that we can transform our dominant belief systems and values, thereby making the institutions of our societies responsive and responsible to ourselves, our planet, and everything on it. Ours is a time of transition. The old patriarchal structure affects the entire planetary society. This is no longer a viable way for conducting life on planet Earth.

OPENING TO THE GODDESS WITHIN

4

A spiritual quest is a deeply personal intimate journey. No two are alike. There is a Way of the Goddess, but each girl sets her footprints on that path in her own individual way and finds her own spiritual framework. Yet, as all roads up a mountain lead to the summit, the end result of each journey is the same. The journey to your Goddess center will be a process of transformation leading to renewal and rebirth into spiritual wholeness. It will give you freedom in the most complete and powerful sense of that word.

There are four basic modes of preparation that will enable you to reach the Goddess inside yourself and get acquainted with Her.

- Silence
- Solitude
- Conscious breathing
- Relaxation

Cultivating these states will help you get to know Her, hear Her, and receive guidance from Her. By practicing them, you will put yourself in a state of readiness to explore your inner spiritual land-scape. In other words, you will build your temple to Her on solid sacred ground.

COMING INTO SILENCE

Practicing Silence

"Daily silence experienced in humility and fervour as an indispensable exercise in spiritual nourishment gradually creates within us a permanent state of silence. The soul discovers in such a silence unsuspected possibilities. It realizes that life can be lived at different levels."

Pierre Lacout,
God Is Silence

"Silence is golden," says the proverb. Yet today it seems as if we experience silence as terrifying. An increasing cacophony of noise produced by humans assaults our ears daily. The Goddess people were awakened by the cock's crow or birdsong. Today, most of us awaken to the buzz of our cell phone or the random offerings of a digital clock, so that even the first few minutes of our day are filled with mechanically delivered sound. Often the TV accompanies us while we dress and eat breakfast. Those of you who drive to school usually have music playing, often with the volume turned up high. (Many American kids have impaired hearing from listening to music at full blast.) And school buses are just plain noisy.

In school, artificial sound is everywhere. Bells jangle to announce class changes. Announcements are piped into every classroom over the public address system. And our leisure hours, too, are wired for sound. When exercising, we strap on headphones. The music and movie collection becomes as much a part of our vacation luggage as our suitcases. We go online every chance we get. Many people turn on the TV or computer the minute they enter the house—not because they really want to watch or look at anything but because they feel more comfortable in the presence of background sound.

Constantly plugged in, we tune out. We can't hear the still, small voice deep inside that's desperately trying to get our attention. Enjoyment of natural sounds—a rushing brook, birds singing, insects croaking—have all but disappeared from many lives. Teens especially are rushed and stressed by overexposure to excess noise. We have ratcheted the decibel level up so high that noise pollution has become a civil and political issue.

The irony is that we've gotten so used to the constant presence of sound that silence actually causes anxiety. Consider, for example, the usual reaction to a lull in conversation. No one knows why, but when conversing, people pause naturally about every twenty minutes, creating an unexpected pool of silence in a previously animated atmosphere. This lack of talk often causes embarrassment. Anxious and inclined to nervous laughter, people feel as if they've done something wrong and immediately try to get the conversation going again. They fail to realize that silence comes of itself, for its own reasons—a natural pause that punctuates conversation. Faced with unexpected silence—whether a few moments or a few hours—most of us apprehensively reach out for the nearest sound with which to distract ourselves. To find the Goddess within, you will need to make a regular practice of allowing silence into your life.

A GODDESS EXERCISE

BALANCING SOUND AND SILENCE

To tap into your inner Goddess Self, you may have to make some changes in how you regard the use of sound. To gauge the balance of sound and silence in your life, ask yourself these questions:

- How much silence do I experience in an average day?
- Am I addicted to constant sound—music, TV, videos, internet?
- How can I eliminate excess noise in my life?
- Do I find silence uncomfortable?
- Do I use various forms of noise to reduce anxiety?
- Would I like to experience more silence in my life?
- How can I make room for some daily silent time?
- How can I achieve a balance between necessary (or unavoidable) noise and the amount of silence I desire?

A Goddess Exercise

Creating Silence

To do this exercise, you will need a pen and your Goddess journal and at least twenty minutes of quiet, undisturbed time. When you are feeling clear and relaxed, make three columns on a page and give each one of the following headings:

1. Silence I want to manifest in my life
2. Noise I want to get rid of in my life
3. Balancing sound and silence in my life

Now, list everything you can think of in the first two columns, including how you feel about each category. Let your imagination roam freely—don't worry right now about how you are going to achieve results. Just list what your true wishes are. Staying focused on what you want to achieve is the key to success. Knowing what you don't want allows you to focus more clearly on what you do want. Focusing on your true desires will activate inner direction.

Once you have gotten all your thoughts down on paper, go over the first column carefully and ask yourself if you truly want to be rid of all the things on your list. Perhaps there will be items that feel beyond your control. Look for modifications. For example, you may want to stop hearing your brother's blasting heavy metal, but you don't have the say-so to forbid him to play his music. You can, however, let him know that it's bothering you and ask him to use headphones at certain agreed-upon times.

Next, ask yourself if you are willing to do what is necessary to obtain the silence you say you want, whether it is a mere half hour, a whole day or a half day, twice a week. You have to be sure that you truly want to achieve the level of silence you have listed for yourself.

After reviewing what you have listed in the first two columns, write down in the third column whatever comes to mind about how you can balance the two. Then, put the list away for a week and don't think about it. Let your deep inner mind provide you with the answers you need. Review your list the following week to see if you want to make any changes, or if new ideas have occurred to you. Repeat this procedure for an entire month without discussing it with anyone. This process must be a reflection of you and your needs. It shouldn't be based on anyone else's idea of how much silence you should need or want.

After a week, take your list and work with it by arranging the items in columns one and two according to the following priorities. Give each an A, B, C, or Z code.

A is for Absolutely Must Have.
B is for Better With than Without.
C is for Can Do Without if Need Be.
Z is for Zilch—You Know This Isn't Important.

If you have more than three entries in A, B, and C, reconsider until you have only two or three A items in both the "get rid of" and the "want to achieve" lists. This is your focus list. It tells you what your rock-bottom demand for silent time is, where you feel you can be flexible, and where you will have to compromise.

Demanding silence for one's self in this society isn't easy. Our busy lives shout at us constantly, but to make contact with the Goddess you will absolutely need to build some quiet time into your schedule. In order to experience the sacred in yourself, you must dare to turn off the sound.

You could view this action as a personal declaration of spiritual independence. A major component of the spiritual journey is time for reflection, but without silence, one cannot reflect. Because the popular culture does not value silence, it effectively denies us reflection. Reflection is a threat to the established order. It leads to questioning—and questioning leads to independent thought. This in turn leads to weakening of social, political, and religious authority. When *those* barriers begin to come down, you might just be able to hear the Goddess.

She is there within you, but She speaks in that still, small voice that is drowned out by the level of noise we permit, and even encourage, in our lives. Contact with the sacred occurs in stillness, when mind and heart are at rest. Your internal point of silence is comparable to the still center of the turning wheel, and this unmoving center is your gateway to the realm of the Goddess within.

Silence is not merely the absence of sound. It is a restful space that we inhabit when we are at our most free and uninhibited. It allows us to intuit the next step we need to make in order to continue our growth and development. Try turning off all the electronic sound conveyors and listen instead to the simpler sounds around you—you might hear a baby bird peeping, a child babbling, a cat's footfall, rain dripping, or your own breathing. You might also become aware of the silences that occur naturally in the flow of ordinary life.

Remember too that not all noisy invasions come from outside ourselves. When they sabotage our efforts to be silent, we must quiet our internal voices as well. Often, just slowing down enough to observe the mind at work is an illuminating experience. It allows us to peel away the layers of inner chatter that prevent us from contact with the Goddess.

Silence is the royal road to the center of the Self. It is in our silences that we understand unity and recognize ourselves as being part of the All. This is the essence of the spiritual search for the Goddess within.

Almost everyone has had the experience of feeling at One with the Universe—perhaps when sitting by a lake in solitude, gazing up at a star-filled summer sky, or being caught alone and awestruck by a magnificent sunset on a country road. These mystical moments connect us to the realm of the Goddess. They transfix and transform us. We do not have adequate words for that sense of stepping outside our normal boundaries into something grand and inspiring. But everyone knows what the experience feels like. And it always happens in silence.

Ordinarily, we slip into such experiences accidentally. They are fleeting, and vague. But we can find them regularly if we can learn to be silent and wait for them to appear before our inner eye. These hints of another reality—this momentary lifting of the veil between the worlds—come to us when we are aware and listening for their soft tread in our inner landscape. They are gifts from the Goddess.

In her book *Everyday Sacred*, Sue Bender told the story of a trip she made to see the renovated warehouse that had become the downtown Guggenheim Museum in New York City. She described the room as "uncluttered long white space [that] floated—a limitless expanse of calm and stillness, with white walls covered with white paintings. . . . This was what a temple should feel like: a 'temple of the soul.' . . . The space was silent. . . . The word *purity* came to mind. . . . This was the 'immensity within ourselves' . . . infinite possibilities."

Invite silence into your life frequently and you will tap into your Goddess Self and hear Her divine voice.

SEEKING SOLITUDE

If silence is golden, solitude is a precious jewel. The historian Edward Gibbon called solitude "the school of genius."

Solitude for the Soul

Abraham Maslow, the psychologist who identified "peak experiences" as those moments of unity, or a recognition of the Self in the All, said that the ability to have peak experiences is dependent upon being free of other people. In his words, "[This means] we become much more . . . our authentic selves, our real identity."

Maslow's approach differs considerably from those who propose that the entire meaning of life is derived from interpersonal relationships.

Solitude, however, is as difficult to attain as is silence. For many teens, it is especially hard to come by. You have constant demands on your time and energy. What with school, homework, sports, social activities, and the maintenance of family relationships and friendships—not to mention boyfriends or girlfriends—it's amazing you ever find a free moment to just be by yourself.

Most of us haven't even learned to seek solitude. If we fear silence, we see solitude as the ultimate negative state. Instead of being recognized as a treasure house of sublime gifts, being alone is viewed as a noxious condition to be remedied at once. If we cannot have the company of living people, the flickering images on the television screen will do as well. Yet, like silence, solitude is the necessary thing. Without it we will be lonely despite the presence of others—lonely because we are not in touch with our own deepest Self. Neglecting or abandoning this innermost Self reaps a bitter harvest. We feel that we don't know who we truly are—because indeed we do not, never having bothered to find out by finding the Goddess within.

Many of us feel that to be alone makes us somehow inferior. Without the presence of others, or lacking friends, we think there's something wrong with us. This is a big mistake and one that torments many teenage girls, who tend to look to others for validation and approval. The truth is that solitude (some of the time) is necessary lest we lose ourselves. Many of the world's most creative artists and writers have, by and large, preferred solitude to company.

Complete happiness, that oceanic feeling of perfect harmony between the inner and outer worlds, is at best an infrequent experience. When we do enjoy this most profound psychological and spiritual state, we almost invariably experience it internally, witnessed only by the indwelling Self. Rarely is this sense of well-being related to interaction with other human beings.

Our adaptation to the world is largely a product of the imagination and the development of an inner world in which to shield the Self from the uncertainties of the outer world. Without a strong and

THE USES OF SOLITUDE

In the winter of 1934, Admiral Byrd insisted on manning an advanced weather base in the Antarctic *alone*, because of, as he wrote in his diary, " . . . one man's desire to know that kind of experience to the full, to be by himself for a while and to taste peace and quiet and solitude long enough to find out how good they really are." On April 14, 1934 he recorded this experience:

> I paused [on a walk] to listen to the silence, and went on to add that what came out of the silence was a gentle rhythm, the strain of a perfect chord, the music of the spheres, perhaps.
>
> It was enough to catch that rhythm, momentarily to be myself a part of it. In that instant I could feel no doubt of man's oneness with the universe. . . .The universe was a cosmos, not a chaos. . . .

From Richard E. Byrd, *Alone*

The necessary thing is, after all, but this: solitude, great inner solitude. Going into oneself and for hours meeting no one—this one must be able to attain.

Rainer Maria Rilke,
Letters to a Young Poet

well-built structure within, the outer world seems threatening and dangerous.

It seems that the human psyche is so constructed that the discovery or creation of unity in the internal world produces a sense of wholeness or unity in the outer world, like a mirror image. This is what is meant by the New Age saying, "You create your own reality." Outer happenings and inner experience interact with one another. Mind and matter are not only inseparable; they affect each other. Thus, when the inner plane is in harmony with itself, harmony with the outer world seems to follow suit almost magically.

We are not sure *how* or *why* this works, but the evidence suggests that communion with the inner Self aligns us with the cosmos, with the right and natural order of all things.

A GODDESS EXERCISE

CREATING INNER SOLITUDE

While you are working out a way to find more solitude in your life, you can use a place of solitude within. Once you have connected with this inner space and it has become real for you, a sense of calm and ease will suffuse you. Think of this as your inner sanctuary, a place where you can recharge your batteries and make contact with the Goddess within. Creating a place of inner solitude is not difficult. Here's how it is done:

Find a time when you can be alone and undisturbed for half an hour. Spend a few minutes breathing slowly and rhythmically and allowing your body to relax completely.

Now, create in your mind a picture of a lovely place—it might be a secluded spot in a woods or a private ocean cove. It can be outdoors or indoors. Letting yourself feel relaxed and free, think leisurely about what a sanctuary would mean to you. As this picture emerges (you don't actually have to *see* it, you only have to *know* it), let yourself be absorbed into its beauty, silence, and sense of comforting solitude.

When you have an image in your mind or a feeling about what your sanctuary is like, continue to fill in all the details. Imagine what a "room of your own" would be and feel like. What would you put there? A comfortable chair, a bowl of fresh flowers, pictures on the wall? Make this image as complete as you possibly can, with colors, smells, textures. Walk about the environment you are creating and claim it as your own personal place of inner solitude.

When you feel that you have taken complete possession of your special place, perform a symbolic gesture—such as writing your name on something in the space or placing a favorite object there—that will enable you to return to your sanctuary at will. The purpose is to make it easy for you to recall this experience. After you have done this, breathe slowly and quietly for a few minutes before returning yourself to normal waking consciousness.

You have now created a place of inner solitude. It is yours to command. You can return anytime you want, whenever you need a space in which to practice being alone and quiet.

BREATH AS SPIRIT

Breath is life. When breath stops, life stops. The vital force of life comes into our bodies as we breathe. Yet, we take breathing for granted and often neglect to breathe fully and deeply. We could hardly function if we had to consciously remember to breathe, but until we find ourselves winded from running or our breathing is impaired by a cold, we are rarely aware of the quality of our breath.

We would do well to pay attention, though, because conscious breathing has the power to connect us to the Goddess within. Awareness and control of the breath allow us to open ourselves to Her sacred realm. In many traditions around the world, working with the breath is a form of spiritual practice. Most Eastern philosophies teach that we live in a sea of vital energy—and that we absorb and activate this energy within ourselves with our breath. The Hindu yogi tradition calls this energy *prana*. Eastern mind-body balancing techniques, such as acupuncture and shiatsu, refer to this vital force as *qi* (or *chi*). The Hawaiian Huna tradition calls it *mana* (*mana loa* in its highest form). In the Hawaiian language, the word for "to think" is *mana-o*.

Controlled breathing permits us to extract new energy from the air. Our physical bodies can store this energy in the same way food

A Goddess Exercise

Breathing with Color

Breathing consciously develops a communications link between consciousness and the unconscious, between body and mind, between spirit and body. Adding your imagination increases the benefit. This is a yoga exercise often referred to as polarization. In preparation, lie faceup in a comfortable position, either on your bed or on a mat on the floor. Align your body to Earth's magnetic field, with feet pointing south and head north. Stretch your arms out alongside your body, palms up.

Begin breathing slowly and rhythmically and, as you breathe, imagine that you inhale one color and exhale another. If you breathe in a warm color, breathe out a cool one, and vice versa. If you want to energize yourself, breathe in a warm color such as red, the strongest; orange, which enlivens; or yellow, which promotes optimism. Breathe out a cool color, such a blue or green. For a calming or relaxing effect, do the opposite.

Think of the incoming breath as a positive current, the outgoing breath as a negative current. Imagine these polarized currents circulating through your body one after the other, cleansing and purifying, healing and reviving. By breathing in these two polar opposites, you move your energy toward balance and health.

is stored as fat. When this subtle energy is in short supply, we feel "down." Listless and tired, we are more vulnerable to physical ailments. When it is in abundant supply, we feel "up." We're energized, optimistic, and full of pizazz. Though this energy is subtle, it is very real.

You can prove its existence to yourself by paying attention to the ion content of the air you breathe. Air is charged with positive and negative ions. Think of how you feel when a storm is brewing and the sky lowers darkly. A surplus of positive ions in the air causes an oppressively heavy atmosphere that saps our energy. Negative ions release uplifting energy into the air. After the storm has broken, negative ions predominate and the air feels clear and refreshing. Your spirits lift and your mood brightens—you're energized and ready to go. By practicing controlled breathing, you have the power to calm and energize yourself at will. Proper deep breathing has the effect of saturating your system with negative ions, releasing tension and contributing to mental calmness.

Yogis claim that proper breathing revitalizes the body and also nourishes the spiritual self. A high content of energizing prana in the system stimulates our natural abilities—mental, physical, emotional, and spiritual. The breath is a powerful tool. Prana is there whether we are aware of it or not, like the oxygen in our lungs, but when we make a deliberate effort to increase it through conscious breathing, blocked channels of information open. Breathing techniques are easy to learn, and if practiced daily they will release their power to you. You can think of practicing conscious breathing as breathing in Goddess energy.

A Goddess Exercise

Rhythmic Breathing

Breath, like food, nourishes our every cell, and cleanses our blood. But we insist on starving ourselves of this vital nutrient. The good news is that changing breathing patterns is easy. Anyone can do it. Changing your breathing starts with becoming aware of it.

This is a simple exercise, a form of relaxing meditation, a way to harmonize body, mind, and spirit. It can be used anytime and anywhere—sitting quietly at home, in study hall at school, in your car, or on a train. In the middle of a bustling city, I sometimes slip into a church, sit in a back pew, and breathe in spiritual energy.

Relax and bring your attention to your breath. Observe your breathing pattern, but do not make any attempt to alter it. Merely pay attention to the breath going in and coming out. Now, begin to breathe slowly and deeply. Feel the coolness of the breath of fresh air coming in; feel the warmth of used air leaving your body. Imagine yourself being cleansed and energized by each breath.

Next, listen to any sounds you make while breathing. Do not judge; just listen. Also notice whether you breathe in shallow or deep breaths and where the air goes, into the diaphragm or into the belly. Does your chest rise and fall, or does your abdomen rise and fall?

As you breathe, be aware of the flow of air coming into and leaving your body. Follow the inhalation/exhalation cycle, and see if you can find the point where they intersect. Actually, breath is one continuous movement, but we tend to separate the in-breath from the out-breath when we think about breathing. Continue doing this for several minutes. The object is to become aware of your own breath, to monitor its natural cycle of movement, nothing more. Don't worry if distracting thoughts arise. Let them float off like soap bubbles in the air (you can tell them you will consider their needs later) and return to attending to your breathing. Imagine your breath filling up all the cells of your body just as you would fill a balloon by blowing air into it. Let the sense of being filled with prana spread throughout your body. Breathe easily—do not force or strain.

THE POWER OF RELAXATION

You lead a busy and often stressful life—there's so much to do and not enough time in which to do it all. Considering all you have to cope with on a daily basis, it's no wonder relaxation is hard to achieve. When tension isn't released, it is stored—and it causes trouble. Tension makes concentration difficult and can bring on emotional upsets. It can also cause physical symptoms, from head-aches and eating disorders to unnecessarily painful menstrual periods. As a teen girl, you are especially vulnerable to storing tension because of your more sensitive nature.

There are two basic techniques for achieving physical relaxation—the sequential method and the tense-and-release method. Though they don't focus specifically on the muscles, breathing exercises are also good for relaxing the whole body. They reach deep inside the psyche and produce a feeling of inner peace and calm.

Below are two relaxation techniques for you to try. Experiment to see which works best for you. Once you have mastered either of them, or have found that you could achieve a relaxed state by using one of the breathing exercises included earlier, you'll be ready to try the mini-relaxation shortcut on page 79. But you need to try out the longer techniques first to be sure you know what complete relaxation feels like.

Relaxing Affirmations

- ❋ I now let go of all tension, worry, and anxiety.
- ❋ I now allow myself to relax totally into peace.
- ❋ I now release all negative thoughts and ideas.
- ❋ My body and mind are now fully relaxed into my inner Goddess self.

A GODDESS EXERCISE

SEQUENTIAL RELAXATION TECHNIQUE

Lie in a comfortable position and breathe deeply several times, consciously inhaling fresh energy and consciously exhaling all negative tension. Then, starting with your toes, focus on each part of your body in turn: feet, ankles, calves, knees, thighs, hips, lower back, upper back, abdomen, chest, arms, hands, neck, head. As you focus on each part, instruct it to relax completely, and linger there until you feel the muscles loosen. Tell each set of muscles to go limp and feel yourself gradually sinking into an inert state of being. When you have finished with this sequence, do it again, beginning with your head and moving to your toes.

The Relaxation Response

In the late 1960s, Harvard cardiologist Herbert Benson, MD, was involved in physiologic tests on people who meditated. He discovered that relaxation methods, of which there are many, caused both psychological and physiological changes that served to counterbalance the body's fight-or-flight response to stress. He called this the "relaxation response."

Not a technique itself, but a coordinated series of internal changes that occur when the mind and body become calm and tranquil, the relaxation response can be achieved by numerous means, such as deep breathing, muscle relaxation, meditation, visualizations, and prayer. The simplest of these methods is focused meditation. Benson's tests showed that people who simply sat quietly with their minds focused on a single word, idea, or thought could markedly change their physiology, decreasing metabolism, slowing heart and respiratory rates, and exhibiting brain waves comparable to those associated with the dream state.

A Goddess Exercise

Tense-and-Relax Technique

To do this exercise, choose a time and place where you can be alone and quiet for at least thirty minutes. Prepare your environment by lighting a candle, playing soft music, scenting the air, or doing anything else that appeals to you for creating an atmosphere in which to relax completely.

Sit comfortably in a chair or lie down on the floor or a bed. You are going to progressively tense and relax each of the major muscle groups of your whole body, beginning with the feet. Take a deep breath, let it out slowly, and gradually tense the muscles in your feet. Do this cautiously as feet and legs tend to cramp. Hold the tension for a count of three. Relax, tighten again, and relax once more. Repeat this entire sequence a third time. Leaving the foot relaxed, move up to the calf muscles and repeat the three-time procedure. Continue up to the thighs, the abdominal muscles, the buttocks, each time in sets of three. Proceed to your chest, arms, and hands—tighten, relax, tighten, relax, tighten, relax. Next, work on your neck and shoulders. Move up to your face and make a monster face with your mouth wide open and your tongue stuck out as far as it will go. This is known in yoga as the lion face and is used to prevent wrinkles and sagging face muscles. Finally, squinch your entire face up tight, with your lips pursed and your eyes squeezed shut; then relax your face completely. Do this three times. Remain still for a few minutes, enjoying this state of being.

A GODDESS EXERCISE

INSTANT MINI-RELAXATION

Once you have fully experienced relaxation and have fixed the sensation of complete relaxation firmly in your memory, you can achieve instant relaxation simply by calling up the feeling you have memorized of your totally relaxed self. To do this, take a comfortable position and remember what it felt like to be completely relaxed. This kind of body-awareness memory is called kinesthetic memory. Your subconscious mind can remember everything. Tell it that you are going to take ten deep breaths and that when you have finished you will be as completely relaxed as when you went through the entire relaxation process before. Then, slowly and gently begin to breathe, counting to ten breaths. Let your subconscious do the rest.

OPENING TO THE GODDESS WITHIN

Being open enough to contact the Goddess within, to receive Her wisdom and guidance and to fully identify with Her as you, and you as Her, is a major step to becoming a Goddess Girl. The following Lotus Meditation is a wonderful way to reach this open state.

Remember the earlier quotation from Heinrich Zimmer about the lotus being the visible form of that which lies deep in the waters of Earth? This lovely image inspired the following meditation, which I hope you will enjoy and use frequently.

A GODDESS EXERCISE

LOTUS MEDITATION

Prepare for this meditation by choosing a quiet place where you can be alone and comfortable for half an hour. You might want to read the meditation out loud and record it before beginning so that you can allow the spoken directions to guide you through the meditation while you relax. If you don't choose to record the meditation, read it over several times before you begin so that you can remember the directions. Don't worry about speaking the words exactly as they are written here. The Goddess will respond to any heartfelt attempt to reach Her. If possible, relax first in a warm bath scented and softened with salts or oil. This meditation is best done naked or only lightly clothed, preferably in white. Light a white candle and lie down or recline in a comfortable position. If the air is cool, cover yourself; if warm, remain nude.

Now, breathe slowly and deeply several times and allow your body to relax completely.

Say to yourself:

I open to the possibilities within my Goddess Self.
Goddess spirit flows through me as I open to Her.
All obstacles to the experience of my Goddess Self are
    now permanently removed.

Now imagine yourself a seed at the bottom of a deep pool where all is dark and tranquil. Feel yourself begin to put out roots into the nourishing bottom and anchor yourself there.

Next, feel a stem begin to grow up and out of you, reaching upward for the light above. Feel it move through the dark water of the abyss until it breaks the surface.

Then, feel yourself putting out little new leaves on the surface of the water, stretching in all directions.

As your leaves grow larger and stronger, feel the bud of a beautiful lotus begin to form. Let this bud rest on the surface, in the light, for a few minutes and then—slowly—begin to open up your petals. Release them one by one, until you have unfurled a glorious blossom—fully opened and gently floating on its undulant stem, yet still firmly rooted in the earth at the bottom of the pond.

Feel the light on your petals, soak up the warmth of the sun, breathe in the cool of the air.

Say:

I am open. I am open.
I now open fully to all my Goddess-given possibilities.
I open to my inner healing powers.
I release and let go all constraints, restrictions, limits.
My openness brings happiness, pleasure, reward, and health.
I remain open to the Goddess within.
My roots are strong so I have no fear of being open.
My state of openness brings me all good things.

The spirit of the fountain
    never dies.
It is called the mysterious
    feminine.
The entrance to the
    mysterious feminine
Is the root of all heaven and
    earth.
Frail, frail it is, hardly existing.
But touch it; it will never run
    dry.

Lao-tzu,
Tao Te Ching

Remain with this feeling of being totally, safely, and completely open for as long as the feeling lasts. When it begins to fade, slowly return to waking consciousness by breathing gently and easily, while you continue to feel open to your inner possibilities. Rest quietly until you feel yourself retracting into the bud state.

Now that your lotus self has blossomed fully, you know you will always be able to open when you wish. But you do not need to be fully open all of the time—you can rest in the bud state, or even return to the seed state to gather new force.

In your Goddess journal or notebook write what you felt and thought during the meditation so that you can recall it.

5

GODDESS MYTHS

In the beginning—as far back as any available archaeological and written records go—the Goddess was nameless. There were no individual myths about Her because She was the Great Goddess, the Supreme Power, the All.

VIRGIN, MOTHER, AND CRONE

In very early times, She began to be viewed as the Triple Goddess, in recognition of the three phases of womanhood—Virgin, Mother, and Crone. The Triple Goddess also represented the three phases of all of nature's cycles: blossoming, fruiting, and dying and decaying from which new forms emerge. To the Goddess people, the word *virgin* did not mean what it means today. To be a virgin simply meant to be independent and aloof from involvement with males. The maternal role of the Goddess is obvious. Her Crone stage is that of old age, the stage of the Wise Woman.

Originally, there were no divisions among the three aspects of Her divinity. But over time people began to identify each of her personas with a different stage of conscious development. First,

Goddesses Worldwide

In addition to the Egyptian, Greek, and Roman myths, there are stories told about differently named goddesses all over the world—Pele, the Hawaiian volcano goddess, is still considered alive and well by the islanders. African goddess forms are worshiped in the new world by followers of African-based religions, such as Santeria, an Afro-Cuban religion that came to this hemisphere by way of imported African slaves. Other African-based religious practices also refer to goddesses. All have different names. Many have different functions. Still, all derive from the original One.

of course, is the young female, full of possibility: you, a teenage girl, personify this virgin side of Her. Next comes the mature woman. Whether she actually gives birth and raises children or not, a girl changes both physically and psychologically as she matures into a woman. Her consciousness expands as she gains experience both of herself and the world around her. Finally, there is the stage of the elder female. In ancient times, older women were sought out for their Goddess wisdom and accorded great reverence.

Today, because they are no longer sexy or able to conceive babies, older women are virtually invisible. We badly need to get back to the ancient point of view. Though we ignore and neglect the elderly of both sexes, men often have a better time of it. Many older women live in poverty and many more are warehoused in nursing homes under deplorable conditions.

INDIVIDUAL GODDESS MYTHS

By studying the myths of the Goddess from around the world we can enlarge our understanding of this great and powerful feminine figure that is the sustainer of life. As the world progressed beyond the earliest times, people of many cultures began to tell stories about various individual aspects of the Goddess, which they personified with individual names. The Egyptians, as we have seen, had many goddesses, but they understood that these separate goddesses were merely aspects of the One Goddess.

Although the Greeks had a patriarchal society, they did not try to eliminate the Goddess as the Jews and Christians did later. They just put Her to use for their own purposes! Their method was simple. They had their head god, Zeus, impregnate whatever local goddess was around, thus assimilating the resident divinity into their developing system. They developed the tales we know as myths to support their political and social aims. Yet, they too under-stood that these "personalities" were but facets of the One Goddess.

Even though we must bear in mind that the Greeks tampered with the original myths, we can learn from them. They are the historical myths with which we are most familiar, in particular the myths of Artemis, known as the Lady of the Beasts (called Diana by the Romans); Aphrodite, the goddess of love (named Venus by the Romans); and Athena, goddess of wisdom (Minerva was her Roman name).

The Greeks also gave us Demeter (called Ceres by the Romans), a grain goddess who was Mother Earth, along with her daughter, Persephone (also known as Kore). These two cannot be separated as they are two sides of the same goddess coin, and their stories intertwine. And the Greeks created—or reinvented—Hera, who was once the Great Triple Goddess all by Herself, but became the wife of Zeus, the Greek head god.

We can relate the Egyptian goddesses to Greek versions. Hathor is a Great Mother. Bast is responsible for love and fertility. Isis is the giver of knowledge as well as the one who presided over rebirth. The correspondences are not exact, but the Greeks, and the Romans after them, had a lot of contact with Egyptian civiliza-tion and no doubt borrowed many concepts from that ancient religion.

During the long patriarchal period of Greece, dozens of different myths about the different goddesses and gods were invented and circulated. There is no *one* myth for any of these divine figures.

As we consider the Goddess it is necessary to realize that—no matter which of Her aspects is told about in the myths—we are really talking about the One Goddess. And, because all of this took place so long ago and because the original Goddess was split up to serve the various purposes of the Greeks and other patri-archal societies, we can feel free to interpret Her today as we choose.

The Named Goddesses

You might want to explore Her many aspects under the different names she has been given and read the stories that have come down to us. These are interesting and can be useful to identify *which* particular aspect of Her you are expressing at any one time.

For example, you might be expressing Aphrodite when you are in a love relationship. You might be using Athena's energy when you are studying for a test. An outdoor event, such as exploring the wilderness, might bring forth Artemis, who was known as the Lady of the Beasts.

LET THE GODDESS BE YOUR ROLE MODEL

Many of the difficulties that girls (and women) face today come from our changing social structure. A lot of the changes are good; women have reclaimed some of their original power by moving into fields of action that have traditionally been reserved for the male of the species.

The women's liberation movement of the sixties and seventies made it possible for women to enter the traditionally male workplace. But as your grandmothers and mothers have moved into the workplace, they have increasingly had to take on the competitive male model of action. Though they've been released from the bondage of the household and are pursuing distinct careers, women are functioning without female archetypal models. It's vital for girls to realize that fitting yourself into the male model may make you lose some of your own feminine nature—your innate Goddess Self. The problem is that there are no female mythological models for today's fast-changing world.

Remember that for some four million years the social relationships modeled by the Goddess women were cooperative—not competitive. It is to that cooperative model that all of us must return as we share the increasingly difficult challenges to maintaining and supporting life on our beautiful Earth. But in order to change the social order back to the cooperative model of the Goddess people, you as girls are still in the position of having to create your own Goddess myths—from within. The traditional biological roles of females, to give birth and rear children, and of males, to support and protect, are both falling apart. As girls today, you have more choices open for your future than ever before in history. Choose wisely. Learn now to anchor yourself in your Goddess being in order to build yourself a fulfilling life. As a feminine person, *you* are someone in your own right, apart from any relationship with a male.

This is a challenging task, but you have the ability to meet it fully. Today, you have the opportunity to accept the challenge and respond as the distinctly female personality you are—not as a mere biological archetype, and not as an imitation male, either. As you delve into the Goddess's ways and practice them, Her awareness will be your guide.

It's no use pretending this is going to be an easy job. There are no models in our mythology to represent the individual girl's quest to be herself. And this is what makes being a teen girl today so tough.

We are in a time of transition of greater magnitude than the world has ever seen. Never before has the development of teen girls been of such importance. Without models to follow, each of you must make your own way. But you will receive much assistance from the Goddess, who lives within. As you move into your future, you have the power to shape your own life and to create new mythic models for your children and their children.

The Great Goddess is like a finely cut and polished diamond with many facets. Each one is a bit different. Each will shine brightly in its own way. Whichever facet of Her oneness you look at, you will see Her face in another of Her countless forms.

As Walt Whitman said, "I contain multitudes." And so do you. You too are a complex being. No single named goddess will represent the totality of who you are. This is why I repeatedly stress that She is *One.* Yes, She has many names and many faces and She has been interpreted in many different cultures. But underneath— and at your own deepest feminine level—She is *all* of the named aspects of Herself.

Find, if you like, one or more of Her aspects (names) and stories that fit how you see yourself. Use them to express your own many different facets. As Her daughter, how could you not be just as multifaceted as the Great Goddess, Mother of All?

THE MOON—SYMBOL OF THE TRIPLE GODDESS

The most universal symbol for the Goddess is the Moon, whose three aspects represent the three faces of the Great Triple Goddess: As the newborn crescent, the Moon is maiden, the virgin—not chaste, but belonging to herself alone, not bound to any man. She is associated with Artemis, or the Lady of the Beasts, and all in nature that is wild, free, and untamed. At the full Moon, She is the mature woman, sexual and maternal, giver of life. In this phase,

A GODDESS EXERCISE

THE PHASES OF THE MOON

From the nights in which we observe the newborn Moon's slim shining crescent to those when her full and glowing face illuminates all, and back again to the opposite-facing sliver, she is passing through what are known as lunar phases.

The waxing, or increasing, Moon brings with it an energy of expansion. This is a positive influence, no matter which sign of the Zodiac the Moon occupies at the time of waxing. It is the best time to concentrate on issues of growth or a new beginning of any kind. Whatever is seeded now will grow into fruition.

When the Moon is full, the energy moves toward the completion of what was previously set in motion. The lunar energy is at its strongest and most powerful. You can focus this energy by using the appropriate meditation and affirmations. As the light of the full Moon eliminates shadows, this is an especially good time to clarify your understanding of conditions that have vague symptoms and are difficult to diagnose. Ask for identification of the source of the problem in order to determine appropriate treatment.

During the period of the waning Moon, the lunar energy works toward decreasing and, finally, at the dark of the Moon, eliminating any unwanted problems. This phase is ideal for dealing with negative issues you want to eliminate from your life, including ill health. Now is the time to practice releasing and letting go. Use the waning phase of the Moon to help you discharge all negativity from your life.

The energies of the Moon change slowly, segueing from one phase into the next. After the night of the dark Moon, for example, the energy of the new Moon slowly increases into the expansive growth phase that will culminate in the full Moon. The energy of the full Moon begins to build two days before the total fullness is achieved, and it continues in effect for another two days afterward, only somewhat diminished in power as the waning phase takes over. The energy of the waning Moon fades slowly as its visible area decreases.

You can increase your sensitivity to the Moon and your lunar self by making direct contact with her. To do this, sit facing the direction of the visible Moon. If you cannot see her, acknowledge her by closing your eyes and imagining the beautiful silver crescent or disk in the dark sky. If possible, position yourself in front of a window or go outside where the rays of the Moon can shine on you. Sit quietly for several minutes until you can feel the Moon's energy contacting you. Imagine her luminosity entering your body, connecting your soul to her, the soul of our planetary system. Feel the magnetic pull of the Moon on your sensitivities and allow yourself to be touched within by her softly glowing light. Let it illuminate your "dark night of the soul," inspiring and uplifting you.

Symbol and Myth

Symbol is myth's vehicle, the chariot by which legend and story, and myth's higher form, religion, are drawn through the heart and mind, and through time, the pages of history. Symbols express underlying patterns of thought and feeling stemming from the mythological roots that still affect us in a very real way.

She is associated with the great grain goddesses—Demeter, Ceres, Isis—and also with Aphrodite, the goddess of love and beauty. At the end of her cycle, the waning Moon about to turn dark is representative of the wise old woman whose years have ripened into wisdom. Here, as prophetess, diviner, and inspirer, She is associated with the powerful goddesses Hecate, Ceridwen, and Kali.

Symbolically, the Moon serves to illuminate the unconscious side of human life, and in her diffuse light we often can see more clearly than in the glare of the noonday sun. The light of the Sun enables us to see the world around us—what is outside ourselves. But the Moon allows us to shine light into our inner spiritual world, to illuminate what springs naturally from inside ourselves. In moonlight we are more aware of the shadings and nuances of our feelings and inner perceptions; we more accurately tune in to the spiritual vibrations of others, and our Self is more in tune with information from the Universe.

THE MOON AND THE SOUL

During the hours of night, our subtle senses are more open and receptive to our inner spiritual harmony. The Moon has been called the "soul of life." Without it, we would have only the mechanical, an endless solar efficiency, which, in the end, is soulless. Without the Moon we would have no poetry, literature, art, music, dance, or dreams. Artists are notorious for being "dreamy," and it is at night, when the Moon reigns, that we dream.

Astrologically, the Moon represents the soul, which is the link between Spirit (Sun) and Matter (Earth). Your lunar self is the channel for the flow of the universal, or divine, energy. One of the legacies of the patriarchal era is that in our society we give far more weight to the Sun (or logical-rational) functions of ourselves than we do to the Moon (or intuitive-nonrational) functions. What our culture values most are the traditional masculine traits of action and linear thinking. Although the feminine lunar traits are vital to our well-being—encompassing crucial domains such as dependency and nurture, security and safety, and the ability to relate emotionally—they are not highly valued by our masculine solar culture. It's the hustling salesman, the profit-driven executive, the hard-nosed lawyer, the tough politician, the professional athlete who get the attention, the money, and the applause.

Adopting the Sun as masculine, our society has both neglected and denied the Goddess, as She expresses Herself through the Moon. Thus, we find ourselves out of balance.

The Moon passes through all twelve of the zodiacal signs every twenty-eight days, which coincides with the female menstrual cycle. Thus, each person is said to have the Moon in a particular sign. Knowledge of your Moon and how it operates will give you clues to the Goddess within. Although there are Sun goddess myths told in many different cultures, the Goddess has so long been associated with the Moon that we have all but forgotten Her solar aspect. Your Sun sign will show how you put the Goddess into action, but your Moon sign will reveal how She operates in you on an inner, intuitive level.

A GODDESS EXERCISE

GODDESSES IN THE ZODIAC

To tell all the myths of all the named goddesses would take a huge volume. Therefore, because of my long involvement in astrology, I have identified—out of the hundreds and hundreds of named goddesses all around the world—twelve who I believe express the essence of each of the twelve signs of the zodiac.

Your astrological chart expresses the essence of *you*. Most people know their Sun sign, but the Sun only represents a part of your unique personality. The zodiacal placements of the Moon,

The advent of a new phase of spirituality is upon us in the shape of the Goddess. Many people are discovering her for the first time, yet for humanity in general this is not something new but the resurgence of a once familiar deity.

Caitlin Matthews

Mercury, Venus, and Mars have profound influences on your being as well. In the appendix at the back of this book, you can look up your astrological signs for four of these planets—Sun, Moon, Venus, and Mars. Armed with that information, you'll be able to relate each planet to the goddess aspect that expresses it. These goddesses will become your personal pantheon—bestowing the wisdom of the ages upon your everyday life.

Locating Your Personal Goddess Aspects

Go to the appendix and look up your planetary placements for the Sun, Moon, Venus, and Mars. These will give you hints as to how the Goddess works in different areas of your life.

- The Sun relates to your life purpose.
- The Moon represents your body, emotions, and instinctual nature, all that is interior.
- Venus (called Aphrodite by the Greeks) tells of your love nature.
- Mars, although the name of a male god, represents your physical vitality and your sexual desires.

Once you have found all four of your planetary placements, you can identify each of your planets with one of the twelve Goddess aspects. The twelve goddess myths follow, arranged in order by astrological sign.

If, for example, you have the Sun in Aries, the Moon in Pisces, Venus in Taurus, and Mars in Sagittarius, your personal pantheon would look like this: Energetic Artemis, patroness of freedom, would rule your outer life. You would resonate emotionally with watery Oshun, a goddess who has the power to heal with love. The Egyptian cow goddess, Hathor, would give you an earthy sensuous love nature. And Athena, the goddess of wisdom, would impart a passion for learning and exploration.

Have fun assembling your own goddess pantheon. Some of you will discover connections to four different Goddess aspects. Others will find that you have two or more planets in the same sign. Your connection to the goddess who rules that sign will be all the more profound.

ARIES

I seek the Goddess through seeking myself.

Any planet in the independent sign of Aries means that you likely express the Goddess in Her aspect of Artemis. In the realm of Artemis, patroness of all that is wild and free, you want to set your own course and not be restricted by the rules and regulations of others. Typically, you are a natural competitor, with energy to spare.

You are independent of spirit and you love to explore. You want to be the first at whatever you do. Courage is a quality you have in abundance. You always want to see what's going to happen next.

ARTEMIS GODDESS GAME

As the Lady of the Beasts, Artemis hates any cruelty to either her animals or her wild spaces. Think of how you can help to heal the environmental damage to our planet and make a list of ideas in your Goddess journal or notebook.

Using crayons, colored markers, or whatever pleases you, draw your own personal image of Artemis. Just let the image emerge from inside yourself and don't worry about "art." The idea is to make a symbolic representation of this goddess as you experience her within yourself.

Because of your free spirit, you are a nonconformist, not so motivated to please your elders as are many other girls. You know what you want and go after it. Physically, you are graceful. Mentally, you are alert.

Artemis's main symbol is the Moon, so if your Moon is in Aries your spiritual path most likely is one you choose yourself without regard to tradition.

Artemis was a virgin goddess who had little to do with men, and she never produced children. Nonetheless, she protected women and guarded not only the wild places but the nymphs who inhabited them as well.

When expressing Artemis, you are likely to see both girls and boys as friends rather than as romantic connections. Artemis was always accompanied by her bands of nymphs, so it's likely you'll have many friends to keep you company.

TAURUS

I seek the Goddess through my senses.

Planets in the sign of Taurus—especially the Moon, which is astrologically considered to be exalted or in honor, in Taurus—put you in the realm of the great cow goddess, Hathor, who wears the horns of the Moon. She is the representative of nurturance. Your spiritual path will involve nurturing others and Earth itself.

Most beloved of the Egyptian goddesses, Hathor is one of the oldest goddesses known. There is some evidence that she was originally a Sun goddess, and the Sun held between the horns of the Moon on her head confirms this possibility.

Hathor likes music and dance and all that is sensual. Her Egyptian followers liked to play musical instruments, often of the percussion type, and to sway rhythmically to their songs. Because

HATHOR GODDESS GAME

As mistress of joy and queen of dance and music, Hathor loves to help her followers enjoy themselves through their senses. Think of ways you can enjoy your sensuality and make a list in your Goddess journal or notebook.

Using crayons, colored markers, or whatever pleases you, draw your own personal image of Hathor. Just let the image emerge from inside yourself and don't worry about "art." The idea is to make a symbolic representation of this goddess as you experience her within yourself.

of her relationship to sensuality, Hathor is called a love goddess and her ancient festivals were joyous ones of song and dance. At her temple in Dendera, Hathor was honored annually by a ritual of merrymaking, during which she was worshiped with dances of an orgiastic nature. Quite possibly the dances to Hathor were something like the raves that teens enjoy today.

The famous Golden Calf that Moses so wanted to destroy was actually a representation of Hathor in all her golden glory!

GEMINI

I seek the Goddess through what I learn.

Planets in the sign of Gemini exhibit dual natures. I have chosen the lovely Iris, goddess of the rainbow, to link to Gemini because she too exhibits a dual nature—combining light with water. Her multicolored bow that we see so beautifully displayed in the sky (if

"It's terribly amusing how many different climates of feeling one can go through in a day."

Anne Morrow Lindbergh

we are lucky that day and the sun shines through the rain) can be seen as symbolic of Gemini's dual nature.

Gemini's chief trait is the gathering and passing on of information. Iris, known as the messenger of the gods, is often seen as winged, flying about as she takes messages here and delivers them there. Carrying messages among the gods and goddesses, Iris represents the idea of assimilating divine ideas. She is also known as an angel, which is another term for a being who carries divine messages. As such, she is a goddess of inspiration and learning, and her energies mesh with the energy of Gemini because those born under the sign of Gemini are always mentally on the go.

Represented by twins, Gemini is both male and female, and as the Sun is considered male and water female, this combination represents the eternal feminine principle that is self-sustaining and all-pervading.

The spiritual path of the Gemini girl is to reunite both of your selves, to reconcile your natural tendency to be everywhere at once with your need to be whole and undivided.

IRIS GODDESS GAME

As goddess of the rainbow and messenger of the gods, Iris loves to help her followers gather information from many sources. Think of the multiple ways you collect information and make a list in your Goddess journal or notebook.

Using crayons, colored markers, or whatever pleases you, draw your own personal image of Iris. Just let the image emerge from inside yourself and don't worry about "art." The idea is to make a symbolic representation of this goddess as you experience her within yourself.

CANCER

I seek the Goddess through what I nurture.

With planets in Cancer—especially the Moon, which rules the sign—you are in the realm of the Great Mother Goddess Herself. She has many named representatives, but perhaps the most well known of these is Demeter, the Greek goddess of grain, who presided over Earth's bountiful harvest.

Demeter is shown as a beautiful and mature woman usually holding a sheaf of wheat or grain. (The Romans knew her as Ceres, from which we get the word *cereal*.)

Planets in Cancer indicate not only the desire to nurture—be it plants, animals, babies, or children—but also the *need* to nurture. As a teen with Cancer planets and a strong relationship to this maternal goddess, you may marry young and want to have children early. If you plan to attend college or pursue some form of higher education beyond high school, you probably lean toward

DEMETER GODDESS GAME

Part of Demeter's name, *meter*, seems to suggest "mother." She was always worshiped as a Mother Goddess. Think of ways that you nurture in your life and list them in your Goddess journal or notebook.

Using crayons, colored markers, or whatever pleases you, draw your own personal image of Demeter. Just let the image emerge from inside yourself and don't worry about "art." The idea is to make a symbolic representation of this goddess as you experience her within yourself.

entering one of the helping professions, such as nursing or social work.

Demeter was extremely emotionally connected to her maternal role. Whether you express your nurturing self through having children or through providing nourishment for others, your spiritual path finds its expression through the feminine maternal element personified by the Great Mother Goddess. She was said to have set the constellation of the Crab in the sky.

LEO

I seek the Goddess through what I create.

With planets in Leo, you are in the territory of Bast, the cat goddess who symbolized fire to the Egyptians. One of the oldest of the goddesses, Bast originated in the Nile delta, but her worship quickly spread far and wide. Through her kinship with the Moon, she belongs to the unitary world of the feminine accented by the power of fire. As goddess of the east, she represents birth and what is new, because the Moon, as well as the Sun, is "born" in the east and "dies" in the west.

In Egyptian art, Bast sometimes appears as a cat-headed woman. Cats were sacred to her, and her followers filled her many shrines with cat images. The nocturnal cat—whose eyes are thought to become as round as the full Moon at night—is associated with pregnant women. Thus, Bast is honored as a goddess of fertility and is associated with children's welfare.

A goddess of pleasure and creativity—dancing, music, and art— the center of her worship was Bubastis, where many great celebrations were held. The Greek historian Herodotus reported that her worshipers arrived by the thousands for these festivals.

Life shrinks or expands according to one's courage.

Anaïs Nin

Courage is not the lack of fear, it is acting in spite of it.

Mark Twain

The sign of Leo also relates to children and creativity. If you have one or more planets in Leo, your relationship to Bast indicates that your spiritual path lies in the realms of love and creativity.

BAST GODDESS GAME

As the primary goddess of creativity and one of the oldest of the matriarchal line of goddesses, Bast is powerful and has a close cousin in the lion-headed goddess, Sekmet, who is the eye of the Sun. Think of ways that you use creativity in your life and make a list in your Goddess journal or notebook.

Using crayons, colored markers, or whatever pleases you, draw your own personal image of Bast. Just let the image emerge from inside yourself and don't worry about "art." The idea is to make a symbolic representation of this goddess as you experience her within yourself.

The best and most beautiful things in the world cannot be seen, nor touched . . . but are felt in the heart.

Helen Keller

VIRGO

I seek the Goddess through duty and order.

With planets in Virgo, you are in tune with Hestia, the goddess of the eternal flame that burns in temple and home alike. Hestia represents order and the care of the everyday and ordinary. She makes home a sacred place and attendance to small chores a holy endeavor.

Hestia was called Vesta by the Romans, and her Vestal virgins are well known as the keepers of a flame that must never be allowed to go out. Because of her relationship to a fire burning on a round hearth (round being the essential feminine shape), Hestia was not given human form by artists of the period.

Hestia stayed aloof from the romantic intrigues of her fellow Olympians. With planets in Virgo and a strong relationship to Hestia, you as a teen are mostly immune to the volatile emotions

HESTIA GODDESS GAME

As Hestia is associated with the hearth and home, so Virgo is associated with the keeping of order—both physical and mental. Your private personal space is important to you. Make it into a comfortable sanctuary for yourself and tend it carefully. Think of the ways that you express Hestia in your life and make a list in your Goddess journal or notebook.

Using crayons, colored markers, or whatever pleases you, draw your own personal image of Hestia's round hearth of fire. Just let the image emerge from inside yourself and don't worry about "art." The idea is to make a symbolic representation of this goddess as you experience her within yourself.

and high drama of your peers. You have a capacity for self-sufficiency along with a tendency for self-effacement.

The stronger the influence of Virgo (who is representative of the great virgin goddesses who were "unto themselves alone") the more likely it is that you will pursue your own interests away from the roar of the crowd. You are not likely to waste your time just hanging out with friends. Intellectual pursuits interest you more than social dawdling.

Always mindful of your duties, you finish whatever you start. Your spiritual path is to concentrate on your inner, subjective experience.

LIBRA

I seek the Goddess through what I unite.

With planets in Libra, you relate to Juno, the Roman goddess of marriage. Libra is the sign of relationships, and Juno represents the relationship of marriage. She is the goddess who personifies wife. Even today we honor Juno when we speak of June brides, because June is named after Juno. Those who marry in June are—perhaps without knowing it—hoping to get the blessings of this goddess.

Libra is a complex sign—just as marriage is a complex relationship. Teen girls with Libra planets are inclined toward forming early romantic relationships. Juno is no lightweight, however, merely concerned with love and marriage. Just as marriage takes a female through all the stages of life, Juno rules the reproductive life of women, from marriage through the birth process.

Based loosely on the Greek goddess Hera, Juno herself was considered the ruler of femininity by the Romans. The Roman word *juno* was not only the name of the goddess. It also referred to that which was incarnate in the female as her personal spirit, the enlivening inner force of the feminine principle. The Romans had great

Each relationship you have with another person reflects the relationship you have with yourself.

Alice Deville

JUNO GODDESS GAME

As Juno is associated with marriage, Libra is related to relation-ships of all kinds and aspires to create balance. The more Libra influence you have in your chart, the more you tend to dislike being alone. Think of the ways that you express Juno in your life and make a list in your Goddess journal or notebook.

Using crayons, colored markers, or whatever pleases you, draw your own personal image of Juno, who was also queen. Just let the image emerge from inside yourself and don't worry about "art." The idea is to make a symbolic representation of this goddess as you experience her within yourself.

respect for this goddess who was one of the trinity that ruled Rome, along with Minerva and Jupiter.

A Moon goddess, Juno symbolized the regular cycles of time. A demonstration of her time keeping is your monthly menstrual periods. With Planets in Libra, your spiritual path is expressed in the realms of relationships and balance.

SCORPIO

I seek the Goddess through transformation.

With planets in Scorpio, you are in the realm of great Hecate, the goddess of the underworld. Mistress of magic, she is the spinner of human life and of darkness as well as of light. She rules the West Gate, the entrance to the underworld, and as such represents the ultimate mysteries of life, sex, death, and rebirth.

Like the sign of Scorpio, which represents the unseen depths, Hecate is a mysterious figure. Some say she was not Greek but traveled from her home of Thrace. She is a dark figure, like the night. One of her favorite places is where three roads come together, an indication that she is also a Great Triple Goddess.

Her worship included the sharing of magical knowledge in secret—and her followers kept their secrets close. If you are strongly Scorpio, you are attracted to the mysteries of life and want to learn about your inner soul. You are fearless in this quest.

As queen of night, Hecate is connected with the Moon's dark phase, when many magical rites are conducted under cover of the lightless sky. She is also an Earth goddess who rules the land of the dead. She is often represented with serpents, torches, and swords and can be taken to symbolize the Crone phase. Her transformations are renewals and rebirths. She is said to whisper her secrets to dreamers.

With Hecate as your patron goddess, your spiritual path lies in inner transformation and the journey into your own depths.

> The turning point in the process of growing up is when you discover the core strength within you that survives all hurt.
>
> Max Lerner

HECATE GODDESS GAME

As Hecate is related to magic and mystery, Scorpio is to intensity and inner experiences. It relates both to sex and the complexity of human sexuality. If you have Planets in Scorpio, sex is a preoccupation. Think of the how you express your sexual nature. Make a list in your Goddess journal or notebook.

Using crayons, colored markers, or whatever pleases you, draw your own personal image of Hecate as queen of the night. Just let the image emerge from inside yourself and don't worry about "art." The idea is to make a symbolic representation of this goddess as you experience her within yourself.

SAGITTARIUS

I seek the Goddess by seeking Her constantly.

With planets in Sagittarius, you are in the arms of Athena, the goddess of wisdom, representative of the highest feminine intelligence. As protectress, she carries a spear and spindle, symbol of her as spinner of human destinies.

Athena was originally an aspect of the Great Triple Goddess, until the Greeks rewrote her history in their efforts to establish their Olympic gods with Zeus at the head. According to the later myth, Zeus gave birth to Athena—as a grown woman fully armored with weapons—from his forehead!

Actually, Athena was the daughter of the goddess Metis, whom Zeus swallowed in order to make himself a mother. The Greeks then installed her as the protectress of Athens, where her huge

ATHENA GODDESS GAME

As Athena is related to wisdom and mastery of skills, so Sagittarius seeks knowledge of all kinds. Relationships of the romantic kind are often seen as restrictive to intellectual pursuits. With planets in Sagittarius, travel for learning attracts you. Think of how you express your desire for freedom and knowledge. Make a list in your Goddess journal or notebook.

Using crayons, colored markers, or whatever pleases you, draw your own personal image of Athena as your patron goddess. Just let the image emerge from inside yourself and don't worry about "art." The idea is to make a symbolic representation of this goddess as you experience her within yourself.

statue in their beautiful and imposing Acropolis was covered in pure gold.

The Athena archetype has come down to us and indicates a girl who is self-sufficient and adventurous. Like the freedom-loving sign of Sagittarius, an Athena girl doesn't like to be tied down. An optimist and enthusiast of the outdoors, the girl influenced by Sagittarius doesn't usually have any problems with self-esteem. She trusts her own judgment and relies on the wisdom of her patron goddess.

Your spiritual path lies in the acquisition of wisdom and the practice of valor.

CAPRICORN

I seek the Goddess through usefulness.

With planets in Capricorn, your patron goddess is Isis, the enthroned goddess, upon whose lap the ruler sits. She is the mountain mother, and it is Capricorn's nature to climb mountains. She is the Earth goddess who has her seat on Earth.

One of the most important goddesses of antiquity, Isis was worshiped for thousands of years. She is said to have given humans all of the arts of survival—how to grow and grind grain, spin flax, weave cloth, make papyrus into paper—in other words, how to use what was available to make life more comfortable.

Isis is famous for having restored her murdered husband, Osiris, to life and then giving birth to the little sun god, Horus. She is often depicted with the baby on her lap. This image is representative of her as the power behind the throne.

A complex figure, she was the giver of material boons to her followers. Often seen with wings, she is nonetheless very much the Goddess who has her seat firmly on Earth, as does the girl with Capricorn in her chart.

Life is either a daring adventure or nothing. To keep our faces toward change and behave like free spirits in the presence of fate is strength undefeatable.

Helen Keller

Until we learn whichever life lesson we're meant to at the time—self-acceptance, self-determination, self-discipline, self-esteem, self-forgiveness, self-interest, self-knowledge, self-respect, self-sufficiency, or self-worth—our lessons will keep coming back to us.

Sarah Ban Breathnach

Planets in Capricorn give girls good powers of organization, and your ability to hang in there when the going gets tough is legendary. Isis searched the land until she achieved her goal of finding and reviving her dead husband. With Isis as your goddess guide, your spiritual path lies in the proper use of the material world as you ascend the mountain.

ISIS GODDESS GAME

As Isis is a goddess of great strength and endurance, so Capricorn never gives up until the goal is reached, no matter how long and difficult the road. Your seriousness is profound, and you are capable of planning ahead successfully. Think of how you express your practical nature to the world and make a list in your Goddess journal or notebook.

Using crayons, colored markers, or whatever pleases you, draw your own personal image of Isis as your patron goddess. Just let the image emerge from inside yourself and don't worry about "art." The idea is to make a symbolic representation of this goddess as you experience her within yourself.

AQUARIUS

I seek the Goddess through humanity.

With planets in Aquarius, your patroness is Maat, the Egyptian goddess of justice. Her chief function is to test souls and her symbol is the Feather of Truth, which she uses to weigh against them. Her primary characteristic is impartiality.

Planets in Aquarius, an air sign, are indications of a girl who is primarily interested in the welfare of all of humanity. This is an important sign for the newly born Age of Aquarius, the only one of the signs of the zodiac that is represented by a human being.

The waterbearer is a human figure pouring liquid from a jug, which represents the divine spirit watering Earth. The Egyptian goddess of truth, Maat was responsible for weighing the souls in the underworld to decide if they had lived just lives. This humanitarian symbol relates the Aquarian desire to see justice done for all the souls on Earth.

Because of your concern for humanity at large, people born under the sign of Aquarius have a reputation for emotional coolness and remoteness. Girls heavily influenced by Aquarius may find friendships more rewarding than romantic relationships. There is a warning to be delivered, however: Do not give yourself so totally to the noble cause of seeking justice for humanity that you neglect your personal life.

There were no temples or shrines to Maat. She simply was Truth. Your spiritual path is to seek your Self through impartially serving humanity.

For thousands of years, the feminine in the form of a hearth or fire goddess was central to many cultures. Known by many names, her energy was remarkably consistent around the world. She was the keeper of the hearth and the knower of the spiritual nature of human beings. She was a doorway into the inner world of the soul.

Anne Scott, *Serving Fire*

MAAT GODDESS GAME

The Egyptian goddess Maat represented the essential order, rhythm, and truth of the Universe. Aquarius is the sign of humanity (the only sign represented by a human), so you are concerned with all that is righteous and good: human rights. Think about how you express these concerns and make a list in your Goddess journal or notebook.

Using crayons, colored markers, or whatever pleases you, draw your own personal image of Maat as your patron goddess. Just let the image emerge from inside yourself and don't worry about "art." The idea is to make a symbolic representation of this goddess as you experience her within yourself.

PISCES

I seek the Goddess when I seek love.

With planets in Pisces, you relate to the lovely African goddess Oshun, who came to the Western world with her people when they were captured into slavery. As Pisces is the most watery of the water Signs, it is only natural that a Piscean girl would relate easily to a water goddess.

Oshun was originally the Yoruba goddess of the river named for her, but she is actually the water of the river itself. Africans call their divinities *orishas,* and Oshun (whose name, interestingly enough, sounds like *ocean*) is much beloved by her people.

Followers of the Santeria religion conduct ceremonies called *bembes* in which they invite their divinities to enter the participants. During these rituals, the followers go into altered states of consciousness.

Pisces planets in your chart give you the natural and easy ability to enter into altered states, for it is the nature of Pisces to flow, like Oshun's river. Her connection to the living waters (a symbol for the flow of life itself) suits girls with Pisces in your charts. The danger is in becoming addicted to the lovely flow and the feeling of oceanic love, which transcends mere human love. Nevertheless, Pisces needs water as much as air to breathe.

Pisces is all about self-sacrifice for love, and about healing love. The essence of Oshun's value for her followers is her power to heal through love.

Your spiritual path is to renew yourself and others by inhabiting two different worlds, the seen and the unseen.

One is taught by experience to put a premium on those few people who can appreciate you for what you are.

Gail Godwin

OSHUN GODDESS GAME

As Oshun represents universal love and compassion, the ultra-sensitive, compassionate, kind, loving nature of Pisces finds it difficult to live on the hard earth and longs for the fluidity of water. If not positively expressed, the Pisces nature can produce escapist tendencies and addictions that are self-destructive. Think about how you express your watery self and make a list in your Goddess journal or notebook.

Using crayons, colored markers, or whatever pleases you, draw your own personal image of Oshun with her river and her healing power of universal love. Just let the image emerge from inside yourself and don't worry about "art." The idea is to make a symbolic representation of this goddess as you experience her within yourself.

INTERPRETING YOUR GODDESS PANTHEON

As you read through the descriptions of the signs of the Zodiac and the goddesses I have chosen to relate to them, you learn much about your Goddess within—or about several versions of Her—depending on which signs your planets were in at the time of your birth.

Some of these ideas may seem to conflict with one another. Don't let that bother you. Always remember that there is really only one Goddess. All the many names given to Her by different cultures reflect (or indicate) Her varied functions and multiple facets.

You are a complex person—and you are in the process of learning about your inner Self through your experience of emotions, thoughts, feelings, and ideas. You are a process of continual change. No day is like the one before. No day will be like the one to come.

A GODDESS EXERCISE

SUN/MOON IN-TUNE-MENT

Prepare for this exercise by first walking about and taking a good long stretch to loosen your muscles and ready yourself for an inner experience. Then, sit or recline in a comfortable position that you can hold for ten or fifteen minutes. Loosen or remove any tight clothing and close your eyes. First, pay total attention to your breath, without making any changes; simply observe the breath coming in and going out for several minutes until you feel a sense of relaxation and unwinding as you proceed to your inner Self.

Now, imagine yourself holding your Sun in one hand and your Moon in the other. You may want to do this with your hands outstretched, or in your lap, or whatever feels comfortable. Allow yourself to feel the weight of each of the "lights" you are holding, as if you were trying to discover the differences between them. Choose one and put the other down. Then, with both hands, turn your chosen light about in your hands as you would an object that is new to you. Feel the size, texture, weight of it. See if it has any other characteristics such as smell or sound or color.

Spend a few minutes, or as long as you feel comfortable with the first light, making friends with it as you might with a new puppy or kitten, and then put it down and take up the second light in your hands, repeating the procedure.

After familiarizing yourself with the two lights on an individual basis, feel intuitively how they relate to each other. See if you want to say anything to either or both. You may want to ask questions, find out the best way to use the energies, or see what each needs of you. You can ask both Sun and Moon if it feels fulfilled or if you can bring more of its energy into focus in your life. Ask how to do this. Do this procedure with both lights.

Then, take them both up together, one in each hand, and see what happens—you may feel that they want to dialogue, or that they have something to give each other, or work out together. Give them equal time.

The more often you do this exercise, the more you will be in touch with your inner Sun and Moon and their relationship to each other within you and in your life.

You can do this exercise with any two planets in your chart and let the different goddesses they relate to talk to you. Or, let them talk to each other.

Always be a first-rate version of yourself, instead of a second-rate version of somebody else.

Judy Garland

6

A JOURNEY TO YOUR GODDESS CENTER

Where do myths and the symbols that represent them originate? Myths and mythic symbols arise from the depths of the human mind, what we have identified as the unconscious. A unique characteristic of our minds is their power to make images. The great Greek classical dramatist Euripides has Medea's nurse warn her that "images the mind make work their way into life." Symbolic images arise from the deepest levels of our beings and carry with them great power to affect our emotions and bodies. Thought-images sunk deep into the subconscious work upward into life. While our conscious minds are able to deceive us and create illusions about who and what we are, the images produced by our unconscious are invariably true. The unconscious knows all and does not lie.

You are about to take an important journey into your Self, where the Goddess dwells. This experience will enable you to identify areas of your life where the Goddess is working well, areas where you need Her help, and areas where you haven't yet made contact with Her powers. This inward journey is all about symbol making, the creation of images that gives you important information about yourself.

Our knowledge of the ancient Goddess cultures has mostly come down to us in the form of images left behind by those who revered Her and practiced Her ways. True, we have written texts as well, but these have been "doctored" again and again over the centuries to serve different political aims or to conform to new religious ideas.

Images (if they have not been altered) are different. They are a pure statement direct from the unconscious of the person who created the image.

Unless we are writing something commercial, such as a television drama or advertising copy, our culture discourages us from using our imaginations. Therefore, we no longer associate our powers of image making with the sacred. Yet, it is from this sacred font within that symbolic images arise.

For thousands of years, art was not used for mere decoration or visual pleasure; it was the vehicle by which sacred tradition was transmitted to the populace. Before general literacy, the only way to instruct the illiterate masses in the religious forms of their culture was through images.

Our ability to program (or reprogram) our deep inner minds with images, connects our conscious minds with our unconscious—the gateway to the inner Goddess realm.

As you take this imaginative journey into your own center, you use your inner Goddess power to produce images that clearly reveal your true feelings about important areas of your life. You may get some surprises! So often what we think we feel isn't the reality of what's going on inside.

Once you have identified these inner images, you can judge whether they are ones you are comfortable with, or if you want to make changes. The beauty of this process is that you have the power to change anything you don't like. By tapping into your unconscious to spontaneously generate specific and meaningful symbols, you give yourself the power to change negative images into positive ones that will make your life work better. (This process is not to be confused with ordinary positive thinking, which tries to replace a negative idea with a positive one.) If you feel an image that has been given to you isn't who you really are—or who you want to be—you can go back within and re-create that image to more correctly express your Goddess Self.

Once you are aware of the images you carry within you at an unconscious level—where they operate very powerfully—you can change them permanently. When you have replaced a negative image with a positive one, the new image sinks deep into your very being and becomes your sacred truth.

A GODDESS EXERCISE

PREPARATION FOR JOURNEYING TO THE GODDESS WITHIN

There is inside you—right now—an unobstructed Goddess center just waiting to be discovered. This self-guided meditation will help you to identify those areas of your life that can benefit from the use of Her guidance.

Each of the experiences you encounter in this exercise has a specific correspondence to how you truly feel about a particular area of your life. These correspondences will be revealed after you have finished this activity. It is easier to do this meditation with another person present to guide you through the steps. However, if you prefer to do it alone, you can memorize the steps or record them. If at any time during the meditation you feel uncomfortable, *stop*. You are in total control. Wait for another time to complete the exercise.

Read the outline on the following pages carefully before starting.

First: Get into a comfortable position where you can remain for about thirty minutes, sitting, reclining, or lying down. Make sure you are totally comfortable physically and that you will not be interrupted. Eliminate all outside distractions, such as noise, before you start. Do not do this if you are tired or hungry.

Second: Relax your body and mind using a relaxation technique or a breathing exercise. Gradually, let your breathing become slow and deep. If you are working with a partner, arrange a hand signal before you begin the relaxation for letting your partner know when to begin reading. And be sure to arrange another hand signal for indicating that you want to stop. If you make a recording of the sequence, leave sufficient blank time at the beginning for the relaxation.

Third: Know that whatever imagery you produce during this exercise is perfectly all right. However you respond to those images is okay too. Nothing is right or wrong. This is about *you*. Approach the entire episode in a playful manner. You are going to have a fantastic adventure.

Fourth: When you have reached a state of deep relaxation, signal your partner or wait for the recording to begin.

Fifth: When you have completed *all ten parts* of the journey, return slowly to full waking consciousness. Then, in your journal, write your experiences down in as much detail as you can remember. Or make a drawing of what you saw. Remember that much of what we know about the Goddess people comes from images.

Note: Do not interupt the journey to write or draw. Complete the entire sequence first.

Reflect on your descriptions for a while and see what they mean to you before you read about the symbolic interpretations for each step of the journey. Examine your feelings about each experience. Write down any negative feelings and think about how you could change those images.

Sixth: After you have reflected upon each part of your personal adventure, turn to the very end of the activity to compare your experiences with the symbolic interpretation given for each of the journey images. Reflect again upon the images you produced to reach an understanding of their meaning for you and your life. Decide if you want to make any changes. You can repeat the meditation at a later date and change any of the images that you feel need improving.

Important Note: Do not peek at the interpretations in advance. To get the truest and best results from this process, you must experience it with no advance knowledge of what the symbols represent. Cheating will invalidate the journey, preventing you from getting a spontaneous reading of your inner landscape

THE GODDESS ADVENTURE TRIP

One: Your Special Place (Allow three minutes.)

You are going to find a wonderful, special, secret place. It can be any outdoor place you choose—a beach, a meadow, a park, a forest. It is a place you like to be, where you feel comfortable and safe. If at any time during the exercise you feel uncomfortable, you can instantly return to this place. When you have found a locale, spend a few moments experiencing it. Notice how it looks, feels, smells. Are there trees, birds, flowers, water? Sniff the air, pick a flower, listen to a bird singing, hear the roar of the ocean waves or the lapping of a lake's waters. Maybe there isn't any water. Maybe you have chosen the desert, or a hidden garden.

After the relaxation component of this exercise, title a page in your journal or notebook My Special Place Experience and then write or draw what you experienced during relaxation.

Two: Your Personal Path (Allow two minutes.)

Now that you have found your secret place and feel comfortable there, look about you for a path. There will be a path somewhere. It might be right in front of you or you might have to explore a little to find it. Take your time. The path is there and it is the right path.

Once you have found the path, notice everything about it. Is it broad or narrow, smooth or rough, paved or dirt, straight or crooked, open or obstructed? Are there any people or animals on the path? If so, feel free to interact with them and note details of the interaction to help you remember it later. If the path is empty, go on alone. Notice how you feel about the path—is walking on it pleasant, or is it difficult? Do you like being there or would you prefer to be elsewhere? Do not analyze your response; merely notice it.

After coming out of relaxation, title a page in your journal or notebook My Personal Path Experience and then write or draw what you experienced of your path.

Three: Finding Water (Allow two minutes.)

As you proceed along your path, taking note of everything around you, you encounter a body of water. Describe the water to yourself. It might be a placid lake, a burbling stream, a rushing river, the crashing ocean, or a fresh spring. You may or may not be able to see the water. It might be hidden or in the distance. It doesn't matter. If you like, spend some time with the water. Listen to the sounds it makes, gaze into its depths, go wading, splash around, or dive right in and take a swim. Again, if you meet any people or animals—perhaps you'll see fish or a playful otter—take note.

After the relaxation component of this activity, title a page in your journal or notebook My Finding Water Experience and then write or draw what you just "saw."

Four: Finding a Key (Allow two minutes.)

When you are ready, leave the water and continue once more along your path. Find a key. Describe the key to yourself. Is it large or small, plain or ornate? What is it made of? How do you feel about it? Where was it, out in the open or hidden away? Put the key in your pocket and continue along the path.

Title a page in your journal or notebook a Key Experience and then write or draw what you experienced during relaxation.

Five: Finding a Chest (Allow two minutes.)

As you walk along your path, continue to notice the details—sights, sounds, smells, other creatures. Now you find a chest. Notice everything about it. Is it wooden or metal, large or small, open or locked? Does the key fit the chest? Is it full or empty? Examine the contents, if any, and see how you feel about the chest and what it contains. If you like, you can take along something from the chest on the rest of your journey.

Title a page in your journal or notebook My Finding a Chest Experience and then write or draw the chest you "saw" during relaxation.

Six: Finding a Cup (Allow two minutes.)

Continue to proceed along your path, noticing if there are any changes. If the path started broad, has it narrowed now, or vice versa? If it was smooth, is it now rocky? Continue to be aware of your surroundings as you stroll. Now, you find a cup. Examine the cup. What is it made of? Is there anything in it? What? How do you *feel* about the cup? Is it pretty or plain, clean or dirty, used or new, whole or damaged? Is it something you'd like to keep or leave behind?

After completing the relaxation component of this exercise, title a page in your journal or notebook My Finding a Cup Experience and then write or draw your experience.

Seven: Encountering a Bear (Allow two minutes.)

Continue along your path, remaining aware of what is around you and how you feel about it. Now, you encounter a bear. Where is the bear and how does it look? Is it on the path coming toward you, or off in the woods going away from you? Is it a large bear or a small one? What color? Does it notice you or is it intent on its own business? Do you feel threatened by the bear? How do you react to finding a bear on your path? Are you scared? Thrilled? Indifferent? Does the bear have a smell? Does it make any noises? Do you make eye contact with the bear? Remember the details.

Remember the details because after you come out of your relaxation state, you should title a page in your journal or notebook My Encountering a Bear Experience. Write or draw this experience.

Eight: Reaching a House (Allow three minutes.)

Soon you see a house in the distance. What does it look like? What is it made of? How do you feel about it? Is it large or small, wood or brick, old or new, empty or inhabited? What about the grounds? Are they landscaped or overgrown, spacious or cramped, inviting or dismal?

When you reach the house, check to see if the front door is open or shut. If it is locked, see if your key fits the lock. If you are able to, enter the house and look around. How many rooms are there? How are they furnished? Are there any people? Is there an upstairs level, an attic, a basement? Go exploring.

Write or draw your exploration, on a page in your journal or notebook titled My Reaching a House Experience, after you come out of your state of relaxation.

Nine: Finding a Vase (Allow one minute.)

As you explore the house, you find a vase. Describe the vase to yourself. What is it made of? Is it large or small? Beautiful or plain? Ornate or serviceable? How do you feel about the vase? Is there anything in it?

After the relaxation component of this activity, title a page in your journal or notebook My Finding a Vase Experience and then write or draw the experience you had.

Ten: Seeing a Fence (Allow one minute.)

Go to the back of the house and look out the window. You see a fence. What kind of fence is it? What is it made of: wood, rock, chicken wire? Is it high or low? Old or new? Well kept or run down? Nearby or at a distance? Pleasant to look at or ugly? What is your reaction to this fence? How does it make you feel?

Write or draw the fence and your reaction to it in your notebook on a page titled My Seeing a Fence Experience.

INTERPRETING YOUR INNER SYMBOLS

Now that you have taken this inner journey, read through the symbol correspondences for parts one through ten below. Remember, there are no right or wrong interpretations. The purpose of this exercise is to give you information about yourself and your perceptions of various areas of your life where negativity may reside. If there is anything you do not like, remember that you can always change it. Life is not static; it is always in flux. You are in a continuous process of growth and change, even when you are not aware of it.

This exercise serves as a powerful guidance tool to show you where your attitudes stand at any given time. The beauty of the sacred mind is that it exists to help each of us find our true Self.

When we carry images that are not right for us, the power of the sacred mind to create new images allows us to reprogram ourselves toward truth. You can repeat this process as often as you like. Once you have learned the steps, you can activate your symbol-making faculty to tune in to your current inner state, changing anything you want. While you cannot change your past experiences, you can rearrange how you think about them, thereby releasing feelings that may inhibit you from becoming your authentic Self.

One: The Special Starting Place

The starting place represents the environment to which you naturally resonate. This is important information. If you felt uncomfortable in your starting place in any way, you may fear beginning new things. If the experience was unpleasant or something unexpected happened that rattled you, you may feel timid about embarking on a new course of action in your life, such as taking up a spiritual practice.

If your starting place was comfortable and felt good and safe to you, you are already on your way to accepting the great adventure of living through your Self and building a goddess temple within.

Two: The Path

The path represents your life's path as you currently view it. If your path was open, broad, smooth, and free of obstacles, you view your life as proceeding along quite well. However, a path free of obstacles may indicate that you are unwilling to take risks or forge ahead in a new direction. It can indicate a satisfaction with the status quo.

If your path was narrow, overgrown, hilly, rocky, or otherwise hard to traverse, you are generally unhappy about the current state of your life. You see your way as difficult and obstructed. However, a difficult path can indicate that you are a person who is used to overcoming obstacles and does not fear a rocky or uncertain way. Perhaps you enjoy taking on a challenge.

The path of one girl I worked with was a deep rut in which she walked two feet below the surface of the surrounding ground. The message was unmistakable: She felt she was in a rut—and she was. This information, revealed by her sacred mind, enabled her to face a reality that she had been refusing to acknowledge and then to make corrections.

At a time of transition in my own life, I entered this meditation and found my path to be a level bricked walkway, very pleasant and lovely to walk upon. On one side the surroundings were landscaped like an English garden, with neatly clipped hedges and well-tended flower beds. Everything was tame and civilized and totally in order. But the other side (the left-hand side) was bordered by a virgin forest—dense, dark, unknown, wild. The garden side held no charm for me (nor challenge). I found myself drawn to the wild side, wanting to know what lay beyond the safe, neat path I had chosen. I could hear rushing water in the distance, deep within the forest, and I imagined a swift-running, deep, clear river of great power.

The imagery told me that I must choose between two options. I could continue to lead my life in a safe and orderly, but unchallenging, manner, or I could risk the adventure of going off into the unknown, uncharted regions of myself. The second choice promised exhilaration but hinted at possible dangers as well. I chose the uncharted forest, setting off in search of my authentic Self, in spite of what others might think or the dangers I might encounter. I found the wild side to be full of exotic flora and fauna that I would never have experienced in the English garden. It was peopled, too, with magical beings I would never have met except in this mysterious deep dark wood.

The image of the path is an important one. It can reveal a great deal about how you approach the spiritual journey that is your life.

Examine your feelings about your path. Did you enjoy being on it? Would you like to continue on this path or create a different one?

THREE: THE WATER

The water that you encounter on your journey represents sex: how you feel about it and how you experience it in your life. Attitudes and feelings about sexuality are deep and far-reaching. They can cause conflicts and inhibitions. Your sexuality can be the focus of compulsions, obsessions, fear, or lack of interest. Again, nothing you come across on your journey is right or wrong. The information you gather simply enables you to release blocks so that you can move toward your authentic, sacred Self.

Water that is calm and placid, such as a quiet lake, represents a passive (or inhibited) sexual nature, one that is not easily aroused but that causes you little trouble. Or, it might represent a temporary period of quiescence or abstinence when sex is not an issue for you. A rushing river, deep and dark, can mean a turbulent sexual nature, exciting and at the same time frightening. The ceaseless ocean indicates a restless sexual nature that makes it difficult for a person to settle into a monogamous relationship. A country pond bordered by flowers, with ducks swimming on it, suggests a person who is either sexually content or not sexually adventurous, preferring to remain with what is traditional. A fog-shrouded bay indicates someone for whom sex seems mysterious or unobtainable. A stagnant pool, where nothing grows, implies that one is cut off from spontaneous sexual feelings. A cascading waterfall represents abundant sexual energies that need to be appropriately channeled.

You must interpret your own image. What you feel about the image you produce is key. Sexuality is a vital and intimately personal element in our makeup. No two people are alike in their inner sexual beings. As does every other human energy, sexuality ebbs and flows—with the days, with the months, with the seasons, with the years. How we use our sacred sexual energy is up to us, but it is important to realize that this is a power source within, never to be misused or taken lightly. Rising out of the second *chakra* (or spiritual energy field in the Hindu system), sexual energy fuels the sixth chakra, where we contact the Higher Self or the divine within. It is worth pondering what your sacred mind chose to give you for a water image. Ask yourself how you felt about the image, whether you liked it, if you wanted to immerse yourself in it, if you wanted to leave or linger. Were you comfortable with the water you encountered, or did it make you feel uncomfortable, shy, or embarrassed? Did you enjoy the experience? Was there anything about the water you'd like to change?

FOUR: THE KEY

The key represents how each of you value your Self. The image you received tells you how you feel about yourself—your intrinsic worth—way deep down. It is not the description of the key itself that matters but how you react to it—that is, how you react to what you find inside yourself.

For example, one woman I know found a key that was ornate and beautiful, but she didn't like it because it seemed useless. She was a "trophy wife"—young and beautiful and decorative to her rich older husband—but she felt herself to be of no significant use or value.

On the other hand, a man I know found an ordinary-looking house key. It seemed uninteresting—merely utilitarian. But upon careful examination and reflection, it proved to be a master key capable of opening all locks. Because he considered himself to be just a plain and simple guy, this man had low everyday self-esteem. But his sacred mind knew better, and it showed him that he was a master in his own right, possessing many abilities, which he did not value because to him they seemed ordinary. After doing this meditation, he began to appreciate himself more.

An artist I worked with who felt that her talent was limited in comparison to what she wished to achieve, found a very small key. It was, however, made of solid gold and beautifully worked. This image allowed her to acknowledge that her talent was, if not commercial, nonetheless genuine and valuable.

Consider your key carefully. What feelings does it call up in you? Are you happy to be the possessor of such a key or dismayed to own it? Would you be upset if you lost it, or does the key generate negative feelings in you? Do you dislike it? What would you change about it? Would you prefer a substitute? If so, what?

FIVE: THE CHEST

The chest represents the value you ascribe to your mind (or brain) and the knowledge it has gathered to date. An open chest signifies that you feel able to access and use your mind freely. If the chest is locked, you feel locked away from your own inner resources, an indication that you do not believe your mental faculties are readily available. When the key fits the lock of the chest, it is an indication that you are in possession of the key to your own mind. If the key does not fit the chest, you may mistrust your mental abilities.

The contents of the chest give you clues about how you view your mental attributes, such as knowledge and experience, intelligence and intuition. They also offer clues about how you value those attributes.

The size and shape of the chest are indicators of your attitude toward your mind and its abilities. The chest can be old or new, large or small, plain or fancy, open or closed, full or empty. You must interpret the symbol your sacred mind gives you in the light of your own self-knowledge. An empty chest need not be a negative—it might just be waiting to be filled up. A student just beginning college, for example, experienced a shiny new chest, like a footlocker, that stood open and empty. He interpreted it as waiting to be filled with knowledge and experience to see him through his life. An overflowing chest may indicate a cluttered mind or one filled with inappropriate knowledge, or it may indicate an abundance of mental riches. No one but you can say what your chest means to you.

One woman's chest was locked tight and bound with iron. Her sweet little key, the kind a young girl has for her diary, was totally ineffective in the face of the huge rusty lock. As she had never been good at left-brain, rational thinking (the kind of thinking most valued in school), this woman felt her brain was of no use to her at all. Although she had artistic leanings, she had never bothered to discover or develop any talents she might possess, for fear of failing. Her parents had made her feel small and childish (hence the symbolic child's key), even after she reached adulthood. At age forty-two, she did not feel like a grown-up. Once she saw what was blocking her, she was able to access her sacred mind and discover the truth about herself. Her artistic talent flowered as she progressed on her spiritual journey into the Self.

Another person, an accomplished intellectual, not surprisingly encountered a chest both open and well stocked with books. What was surprising was that this man found the book-filled chest a burden and kicked it off his path. I instructed him to dump out all the books to see if there was anything else at the bottom. There was: a music score. He was a frustrated composer who had been forced into an academic career by his professor father—and he had lost his authentic Self along the way. However, though it was buried under the book learning, his Self was still there—and his sacred mind showed him that. He now plays in an amateur string quartet and writes music on weekends.

Six: The Cup

The cup represents your attitude toward the positive/negative polarity of life. Was your cup half full or half empty? Was it a sturdy mug, a piece of fragile china, a throw-away paper cup? Did it contain something lovely to drink, perhaps fragrant tea or steaming hot chocolate? The cup represents how you feel about the hand life has dealt you and the experiences you have sustained. Remember, whether your cup was full or empty, beautiful or ugly, you have the power to change the feeling it represents by changing the image and recovering your authentic Self.

As with all of these symbolic representations, you are your own best interpreter. You are already the world's expert on yourself. Meditation upon the images you receive clarifies their meaning. What is positive for one person may be negative for another, and vice versa.

For example, one woman's cup was a lovely piece of Limoges porcelain, of great monetary value. It was a delicate teacup. A nice image, isn't it? But she hated it because it represented her constricted ladylike life, which required her to give "proper" tea parties and always be the model of decorum. As the wife of a rich man with traditional values, she was restricted to doing charity work and caring for a large, expensively furnished house. She was slowly dying, she said, of things. In a return to the meditation, she smashed the Limoges teacup—symbolically breaking out of her restraints. Now she has a job—and a sturdy earthenware coffee mug.

In another example, a young man, who thought life had given him a raw deal, found a discarded Styrofoam cup that had once held coffee. A cigarette had been crushed out in the bottom, leaving a disgusting mess. He was revolted by what he saw and threw his cup away, which was what he wanted to do with his life. In a return meditation, he decided upon a brand-new cup—white, clean, and shiny—which he could fill with his authentic Self. By using his sacred mind, this man realized that he'd been viewing his life as fit only to be discarded. Faced with this realization, he found the strength to make changes.

Seven: The Bear

The bear represents the outside world and our feelings toward it. It also stands for authority of all kinds imposed upon us from without. The bear gives important clues about the factors that have prevented us from realizing our authentic Selves and how they operate in us. It also shows the way to reconciliation of the inner world with the outer world. Bears come in all guises: cuddly teddy bears, fierce and scary wild beasts, threatening, neutral, or friendly. If your bear was a mean one—well, just remember he is your bear, and you can change him at will. Sometimes you don't actually see the bear—you just hear him off in the woods somewhere crashing around or you sense his presence. Again, the important thing is not the bear itself, but how you feel about it.

A talented singer who had run aground in the commercial music industry retreated to the safety of giving music lessons. In her fantasy, she was dressed as a little girl, and when she saw the big bad bear coming, she scampered up a tree. Safe upon her high and remote perch, she watched as he went his way. Later, we returned to the meditation so that she could confront her fear. This time, she offered him a large jewel she had taken from her chest. He ate the jewel with relish and gave her a big bear hug!

Her talent—represented by the jewel from her chest—served to neutralize the bear. By eating it, he said he wanted to assimilate it into himself. The singer realized that withholding her talent from the world was harming her authentic Self—a performer who wanted to be onstage.

An actor, in a constant and unsuccessful struggle to get good parts, saw his bear as an adversary whose intention was to block his path. This bear made him very angry. He wanted to kill it, but he realized he was not strong enough, which left him feeling terribly frustrated. On a return trip, he took the bear a large pot of honey and made friends with it. The experience allowed the actor to accept that the world was not against him, that struggle is part of life. It is our attitude toward adversity that either creates or removes its sting.

EIGHT: THE HOUSE

The house represents your goals in life. You may be surprised at the difference between the image your inner mind presents to you and the conscious image you have of your aims in life. Remember, your sacred mind gives you the true picture.

One man, a powerful lawyer, stated that his life goal was to become politically powerful so that he would be able to help other people. He considered himself an altruist, interested only in the welfare of the people. However, the house image presented to him by his sacred mind told a different story. His house was an old stone hut, almost primitive, located in a remote place where there were no people at all. The surrounding territory was rugged and demanding, the ideal place for a loner who wanted to seclude himself away from all humanity. He had become a lawyer to please his liberal parents and had devoted himself to their code of altruism, under which cloak his authentic Self had been hidden.

Your house may have one or many rooms, be a cottage or a mansion, full of laughing people having a party or uninhabited. It may be cozily furnished with everything that makes you comfortable, sparsely furnished, or totally bare. What is important about this image is what you make of it, how you react to it.

One person found a houseful of partying guests—and was dismayed. She wanted to be left alone to paint, or so she thought. The fact was that she had retreated into her artwork to avoid the pain of shyness and the difficulty of making friends. However, her authentic Self loved being around people and longed for a house full of friends who were all having a good time. The image of her house distressed her so much she burst into tears. But they were healing tears, for the image allowed her to glimpse her authentic Self and its needs.

Whatever your house image, it is a vital component of who you are and where you are going on your spiritual journey. If your conscious goals conflict with the aims of your authentic Self, you are going to have difficulties reaching them, or if you do reach them, you will feel dissatisfied because they are not what your true Self desires. Finding out what blocks you on this level is fundamental to building your temple within.

NINE: THE VASE

The vase represents our perception of love. What we love and how we love is basic to all human life, and love, perhaps more than any other human characteristic, comes from the deepest, sacred level of our beings. We can no more rationally choose a love partner than we can choose what we dream tonight. We can marry for rational reasons: He's a good "catch" or his profession pleases your parents; she will be a good hostess and mother or her beauty will enhance his business aims. But love is another matter. Love springs from within, from that deepest level of the soul, which knows what is right for us. The image of the vase tells you about love and your perception of it.

Whatever your image of the vase, trust it to reveal your innermost secret feelings about what love means to you. If you fear or distrust love, or think it is difficult to find and keep, your vase may be cracked or broken, old and dirty, or hidden away in a closet. In a dramatic rejection of what she found, one woman said vehemently, "I don't *want* that vase! It's chipped and ugly, and I inherited it from my mother." We returned to the meditation and she smashed the old vase, which represented her mother's negative interpretation of love. She replaced it with a lovely new vase of her own choosing, for her authentic Self was a closet romantic who believed in love. Trying to love by her mother's standards was thwarting her fulfillment on both the personal and the spiritual levels.

Another woman found a beautiful crystal vase, but she was distressed because it was empty—in fact, it had never been used. She went out to the garden of her house and picked a bouquet of flowers to put in her vase. Upon contemplating both the image and her response to it, she discovered that her authentic Self was a very loving person who had not allowed herself to fulfill her affectionate nature.

TEN: THE FENCE

The fence represents our perception of death. Many people fear death or consider it to be an unfair intrusion into life. We all know rationally that death comes to everyone, that nobody lives forever, yet most of us consider death to be the enemy—something to be conquered, coerced into going away or, failing that, ignored. Yet death is as much a part of life as is birth. Whether there is life after death, in the sense of a continuance of *this* life, no one knows. I rather doubt it, but this does not mean that death is necessarily the end of everything. It marks the end of a chapter, not the end of the book. Or it is a sequel. Whatever you believe about death, it will come one day, and your perception of death, embedded as it is in your psyche, colors how you live. Fear of death is a great inhibitor to living your life fully. It prevents you from experiencing the sacred on a daily basis. The image of the fence reveals your issues about death. Facing it means looking at it from within your inner temple.

Having stared death in the face more than once, I believed that I was completely reconciled to my own demise. I did not think that I particularly cared whether or not there was an afterlife. However, my first view of the fence was of a high brick wall close behind my house, and I was furious that it cut off my view. This sent me in search of deeper levels of truth. Eventually my fence became a low stone wall, far off in the distance, with grasses and wildflowers growing through the cracks in the masonry. Beyond it, I could glimpse the sea gently rolling in upon the shore.

An old man I knew experienced a weathered picket fence, already lying flat on the ground. He saw himself stepping over it into a broad meadow filled with light and flowers. His life was almost over, and he was at peace with that.

Whatever your feelings about death, it remains a mystery for all of us. It's not death itself that's important—for it will come and others will come after us—but how we live that matters. Fear, anxiety, anger, and depression about death are only thoughts, and the sacred mind can choose what it wants to think. A positive relationship with the end of life makes the living of it more pleasurable and productive. Fear of death is a roadblock on the spiritual path. If you are angry or fearful about the fence, you can confront the feeling safely and make necessary changes.

One man, raised with visions of eternal hellfire, saw a frightening vision of flames leaping beyond a high concrete wall, like that of a prison. He returned to the meditation with a fire hose and, in drenching the hellish flames, realized he had nothing to fear. Hell is a construction of the mind, not a real place. He had believed that he no longer was influenced by his parents' old-fashioned religion, but the fear implanted in him as a child was still active. Armed with that knowledge, he was finally able to shed the rigid and crippling notions of his past and free his authentic Self. There are many images for the fence. Contemplate yours for the information it can give you.

Power of the Self-Image

Your self-image, the picture of who you think you are that you carry, consciously or subconsciously, around with you twenty-four hours a day has a powerful influence on your weight, your health, your prosperity, your self-esteem, your emotions, your spiritual life, your relationships, the very heart and pulse of your life.

Mary Orser and Richard A. Zarro, *Changing Your Destiny*

When you have studied the images you produced on your fantasy journey and have compared them to the symbolic interpretations, you can interpret your images your own way. It's your feelings that count.

Once you have completed this meditation, you can always retake the journey to change anything that didn't satisfy you. You have

A GODDESS EXERCISE

MAKING INNER IMAGE CHANGES

To make changes in any stage of your journey, simply follow the same procedure for getting "into" the journey, then go directly to the part you want to change—maybe you had a scary bear and want to make friends with it, or your cup wasn't representative of how you'd like to feel about yourself and you'd rather replace it with a more positive image. Remember that your images are not set in stone—they will change as you change, and you can change them at will by altering your own attitude toward anything about yourself that you don't like or wish to improve.

Be sure to record all the changes you make in your Goddess journal, along with the date you did the original journey and the date(s) you reentered it and made changes. Describe your experiences to yourself for future reference. You'll be amazed at how quickly you can improve all areas of your life by continuing contact with your Goddess center.

the ability to alter any of the images you have produced. This is the power of your Goddess within, who represents that part of you that recognizes the start of each day as an opportunity for a new start—a rebirth into your true Goddess Self.

You *always* stand at the beginning of a new cycle, at the edge of the unknown future. There is always something new for you to discover about yourself—and to love and admire about yourself!

However, before you decide to start making changes, take a moment to practice the following Acceptance Meditation. It's important to *first* accept yourself as you happen to be at this very minute. After you do that, feel free to get to work on any improvements you desire.

A GODDESS EXERCISE

ACCEPTANCE MEDITATION

To do this exercise, find a comfortable position and begin by taking several deep breaths to relax yourself completely. Close your eyes and imagine yourself standing before a magic mirror that has the power to show you your authentic Self—not just your physical reflection, but a reflection of your innermost reality, how you are when you are most yourself. Look carefully at this reflection and examine what you see without criticizing or making any judgments. Just look.

While looking at this reflection of your true Self, say softly and gently in your mind, *I accept you. I truly accept you for who you are and who you can be. I accept all of you. I know that by accepting you I empower myself to make any changes that I choose to make.*

Repeat this affirmation several times until you feel you are speaking the truth to yourself and that you are genuinely able to accept yourself with all your characteristics—even ones you might not like right now.

Remember that in Her image you are always becoming, budding, pregnant with possibility. You are full of potential to develop and grow. You have the ability to give birth to your Self through the Goddess within. Celebrate yourself!

RECORDING YOUR OWN INTERPRETATIONS OF THE SYMBOLIC JOURNEY

Now that you have read the symbolic interpretations for each step of the inner journey, record in your Goddess journal your own interpretations of your symbols. What they mean to you is what is important. Your interpretations may be different from the examples given. But they are yours and yours alone. For instance, a broken vase might mean the breakup of a relationship to one girl, but to another it might indicate that she is ambivalent about becoming sexually involved. Use your imagination and take whatever comes into your mind first when devising your own interpretations.

1. Your Special Place_____

2. Your Personal Path _____

3. Your Water _____

4. Your Key_____

5. Your Chest _____

6. Your Cup_____

7. Your Bear Encounter _____

8. Your House_____

9. Your Vase _____

10. Your Fence _____

Over time, you can take the entire goddess journey as many times as you like. Always wait at least a month between journeys to let your inner Self make its adjustments to this new process. As you work with your personal images, becoming more in tune with your symbol-making ability, you will find that your images change along with how you change, as you develop and grow into your true Goddess Girl Self.

Each time you take the goddess journey, keep a record of it, describing the changes that occur spontaneously and noting the date you journeyed. You can record your journeys in your Goddess journal or keep a separate notebook just for them. Over time, you will experience a progression of remarkable differences from journey to journey, and you will discover how to best use your own capacity for generating symbols that can help you understand and improve your life.

As you continue to explore the Goddess within, your life will become richer, more joyful, and more satisfying on every level. When you operate from your Goddess center you will feel connected—to your whole Self and to everything in the entire Universe. The following meditation is another good way to journey inside in search of the Goddess.

A Goddess Exercise

Finding Your Authentic Goddess Self

You will need half an hour of quiet time to do this meditation. It can take you very deeply into yourself, so be prepared for some surprises. Above all, do not be frightened or repulsed should you encounter anything you don't expect. We all have dark corners, and the only way to light them is to inhabit them. Or, you may be pleasantly surprised to discover your authentic Self is quite to your liking, only waiting for you to uncover it and be your friend.

Find a time when you can be alone and undisturbed. If possible, take a leisurely warm bath or shower using scented soap or salts. Dry yourself gently and dress in something soft, loose, and clean.

Now, breathe deeply several times and allow yourself to drift into a state of deep meditation. You are going to find a lovely spot somewhere outdoors—it could be in the woods, a park, a garden, on the beach, by a lakeshore, or anywhere else you fancy.

After you have envisioned this place, take a walk and look around. You are going to find a small, secret door someplace. It might be in the ground, under the water, in a tree, hidden under fallen leaves, under a hedge, or it might be the entrance to a secret garden.

When you find the secret door, open it carefully. It isn't locked, but it might have rusty hinges from lack of use. When you open the secret door, you find a passageway leading downward, a spiral staircase. Follow it down, counting from ten to one. As you move down this descending staircase clockwise in a spiral traverse, at ten, allow your body to relax further; at nine, your awareness sharpens and anticipates; at eight, you are enveloped in silence; at seven, you feel safe and comfortable; at six, five, four, as you descend the spiral way, you are in a state of complete relaxation and begin to sense there is magic here. At three, two, your senses tingle with expectation as you prepare to meet your true Self. At one, as you step from the last step of the spiral staircase, you have left the upper world behind and find yourself in a beautiful room that houses your authentic Self.

Look around at this room. You have seen it before. It was there the day you were born. Before you came to this earth, you knew who you were and you still know, but you have forgotten. This experience is like meeting someone that you knew as a child and loved very much but have lost touch with over the years. Now you meet yourself again and for the first time.

Take a comfortable seat in this lovely room, and ask your true Self to come forth. Imagine this Self standing in front of you and observe its form, figure, posture, and pose. Tell yourself you will recall this experience completely and that all the observations will remain as vivid memories, which you can call to mind at any time in the future. When you see an image of your authentic Self, observe details: clothing, facial expression, age, style. Allow this image to move and change and stay with it for a few moments.

Acknowledge this Self and take some time to get to know her. Ask your authentic Self if she has anything to say to you at this time. Express your love for your authentic Self and affirm your determination to live by and for her. If at first you feel uncomfortable, be patient until you become accustomed to this person, who is you at your best, the you that you truly are, the person you came to this earth to be.

Before beginning your ascent back to the ordinary world, make a symbolic gesture to your authentic Self. You can hug her and promise to return often. You might want to place a vase of fresh flowers on a table there as an indication you have visited. Do whatever comes to your mind at the time to express how you feel about the meeting.

After making your symbolic gesture, slowly ascend the spiral staircase, counting from one to ten, breathing evenly as you do, and return to the secret door, which is a sacred portal to the Goddess within. Follow your footsteps back to where you started and gradually bring yourself back to normal waking consciousness.

You can do this meditation as often as you like. As you become better acquainted with your authentic Goddess Self, you will learn more and more and develop a relationship. You can always go through the secret door and down the spiral staircase when you want to commune with your deepest, truest Self, which provides you with comfort and guidance.

In your journal or notebook write down what you experienced and, if you like, make a drawing of what you saw.

7

YOUR GODDESS BODY

In the ancient days when people lived the way of the Goddess, female bodies were considered sacred. This was because they were correctly seen as the primary source of all human life, while the Goddess was seen as the source of life altogether. Also, female bodies were mysterious (as they are even today in spite of scientific research into what makes the female body function or malfunction). One reason for this sense of mystery is that the female body is filled with unseen processes: The female reproductive organs are inside the body, whereas the male genitals are right out there in full sight. Girls and women ourselves cannot see our own genital areas without the aid of a mirror. So the mysterious aura continues into modern times.

These early women were not fundamentally different from us, but their attitudes toward themselves and their female bodies were as different from our attitudes as night and day. To the followers of the Goddess, women's bodies—along with their feminine characteristics—were important and necessary to the proper functioning of human life. The tragedy—and it can only be called by that strong word—that occurred when the Goddess was dethroned by the patriarchal gods is that women's bodies were devalued. Not only were they deemed inferior to men's bodies, they were considered to be sinful. Women's sexuality—celebrated as

sacred by the Goddess people—was turned into a snare, a trap, an evil power that women possessed against men.

As we have seen in the recounting of the Adam and Eve story, this enforced change in the way men regarded women's bodies was designed as a weapon against the Goddess. From then on, women were taught to be ashamed of their bodies and to feel guilty about their sexuality.

By contrast, in the time of the Goddess, female sexuality was celebrated in the sacred context of the temple. The temple women,

THE MYSTERY OF MENSTRUATION

Early people must have noticed that the transformation from life to death very often occurred with loss of blood. And it cannot have escaped their notice that women, the producers of new life, bled in synchrony with the Moon, month after month, until such time as the flow of blood was dammed, swelling the belly through the nine critical Moons that led to another birth.

It was probably not long after this realization that life and death, blood and birth, came to seem inseparable; this must have led to a belief in the power of blood to regenerate and revitalize. Women's seemingly miraculous ability to bleed monthly without dying and then to, equally miraculously, stop bleeding and produce a new life, led to menstruation being considered a sacred function.

Some early societies placed a taboo, or restriction, on menstruating girls and women, sequestering them away from the community at large. Sexual intercourse was often forbidden during menses, and today orthodox Jewish men are not allowed to even touch a menstruating woman. Of course, patriarchal systems considered menstruation unclean, but the original cultural taboos stemmed from the fear and awe in which natural female processes were held.

priestesses of the Goddess, were regarded as extremely holy. Their female bodies were considered to be, by way of sexual activity, the portal of initiation into the Goddess for men. When a temple woman bestowed her sexual gifts upon a man, she bestowed them as part of a sacred sexual rite. The man felt honored to be allowed to participate.

The patriarchal tribes of biblical times must have been ancient Puritans. They expressed horror at these sexual practices in the name of the Goddess, calling them prostitution. Unfortunately, the negative label stuck and later writers (all men) coined the phrase *temple prostitutes* to describe these holy women and their sexual activities in honor of their Goddess.

One Greek historian, Herodotus, a fervent supporter of the patriarchal system, was apparently deeply offended by the sexual activities of the holy women in the Goddess temples. We can only speculate on the psychosexual problems of Herodotus and his patriarchal fellows, but here's what he wrote:

> The worst Babylonian custom is the one that requires all women to go to the temple once in their lifetimes to have sexual relations with an unknown man. . . . The men walk past them and make their choices. The amount of money they offer makes no difference, the women will never refuse it, because that would be a grave sin. The money is rendered sacred by the sexual act. After this act, the woman is sanctified in the eyes of the goddess.

Commenting upon this passage, Jean Markale said in *The Great Goddess,* "Clearly he is describing the temple of Ishtar (Astarte), the Great Goddess of primitive Babylon, who . . . reappears [as] Cybele, Demeter, Artemis-Diana, Aphrodite-Venus, and Dana-Anna in the Celtic world."

These holy women were considered incarnations of the Goddess, and their sexual activity was "thus a liturgical act. . . . Such intimate contact was considered a true initiation, and thus, men could be united to the divinity, could somehow participate in the divine."

It was a clever trick of the patriarchal priests and writers to use the nasty word *prostitution* to refer to what was sacred and holy to the Goddess and Her people. Unfortunately, their ruse worked only too well. Today, *prostitute* is an ugly word, and the women to whom it is applied are looked upon as trash, or worse. But the clients of today's prostitutes are usually men. While calling the women who provide the services they desire by degrading names, they line up to buy those services.

I'm not suggesting that prostitution as it is practiced today is a good idea. It is a terrible abuse of girls and women all over the world. In many places, young girls are forced into being sex workers to satisfy rich male tourists who flock to countries where it has become informal national policy to offer such degrading tourist attractions. But I do think it is important for girls to understand the history behind why this sex industry flourishes, and just who is responsible for this outrageous use of the bodies of females.

HONORING YOUR SACRED BODY

Your body was made by the same force that created the Universe. This force has been making life-forms, including the human body, for aeons. It lives within you, and it contains millions of years of wisdom. As the vehicle of life, your body possesses its own inner wisdom, which is at work within you all the time—repairing and replacing cells, eliminating waste, nourishing tissues, fighting off germs, calming nerves, protecting from infection, balancing hormones, and, when necessary, healing contusions and wounds.

Each of your cells is a scientific genius, not only repairing itself, but having the capacity to renew and regenerate itself; in fact, every cell in your body replaces itself with a completely new cell every seven years. You literally produce a new body.

How is it then that girls and women tend to hate our bodies? Speaking of this self-hate, psychologist Edward C. Whitmont, MD, in his book *The Alchemy of Healing* said this: "Endemic in our own time is self-hate . . . a refusal of the ego to accept and work with what one happens to be."

It's long past time to change this, and you as a teen girl can begin the necessary return to the Goddess way by consciously learning to look at yourself differently. You must learn to see yourself as the remarkable creature you are. You must reject any former training you received that encouraged you to see yourself as ordinary or nothing special. You *are* special—a unique, irreplaceable female person with all of the qualities of the Goddess Herself. By learning to follow Her ways and Her guidance, you can learn to look at yourself—and your precious female body—more positively and with well-deserved appreciation. You only get one body in this lifetime. Learn to love it, treat it with the care and respect it deserves, and don't fall for the stupid media images of beauty and perfection that ignore the soul within your body.

I used to work in the business of fashion advertising. It takes at least seventeen highly paid experts and half a day or more of photography to produce one of those cover girls with that "natural" look. What a bunch of phony baloney!

Followers of the Hawaiian religious tradition called Huna believe that your body was created by your *unihipili*, which is your own personal elemental energy. This entity has created many bodies over time, for that is its work. Located in your solar plexus, your unihipili is the keeper of your personal archive, which is what the body is—the record of your life.

Like the Rosetta stone, for those who know how to read it, the body is a living record of life given, life taken, life hoped for, life healed. . . . To confine the beauty and value of the body to anything less than this magnificence is to force the body to live without its rightful spirit, its rightful form, its right to exultation. To be thought ugly or unacceptable because one's beauty is outside current fashion is deeply wounding to the natural joy that belongs to the wild nature.

Clarissa Pinkola Estes, *Women Who Run with the Wolves*

Your body ultimately knows itself far better than any other person can. In its cells have been stored every experience that has ever happened to you since before you were born. It knows more about you than your own mother, more about you even than your mind. Our bodies will teach us more than we can imagine, if only we will listen.

Mark Gerzon, *Listening to Midlife*

Here in this body are the sacred rivers; here are the sun and moon, as well as the pilgrimage places. I have not encountered another temple as blissful as my own body.

Saraha

THE SHAME GAME

Ours is a shame-based culture. And shame has long been used as a weapon against children, especially girls, and women. From earliest childhood, the idea of shame is associated with bodily functions and other people's opinions. All too often I hear girls say, "I could have just died of shame." Well, no one ever actually dies of shame, but it's a devastating feeling.

Shame is rarely attached to misdemeanors or masculine behaviors. Usually, it is reserved for females who are supposed to be ashamed of belonging to their tainted gender. So, shame gets hitched to the female body and its functions, especially reproductive ones—sex and menstruation. When I was in high school, having a menstrual period was terribly anxiety producing. I walked in fear of someone (especially a boy) noticing the bulge of my sanitary pad (we didn't have the thin pads then and I was an adult before I learned how to use a tampon). If a girl got blood on her skirt and it showed, she was subject to snide remarks and horrible embarrassment, as if she had committed a ghastly social error. Things are somewhat better today, but shame still rears its ugly head all too frequently in many of your lives and experiences.

Related to shame is embarrassment. Kids aren't particularly embarrassed to be caught with a joint (technically a crime), but if a negative incident occurs that is related to a girl's body or sexuality, she feels acute embarrassment and emotional pain.

Shame is among the most pernicious legacies of patriarchy, the one most in need of being stamped out forever. There is nothing to be ashamed of about your body, your gender, your sexuality, or your healthy human functions.

Repeat after me: "I refuse to accept the concept of shame as it relates to my body, my sexuality, my gender." Learn to be proud of being a girl. As you progress toward becoming a true Goddess Girl, this will become easier. You will be able to reject absolutely the sense of inferiority that comes with shame and its primary purpose of keeping females feeling inferior, which is what makes the patriarchy tick. The ability to humiliate and mortify females for being female gives the patriarchy power.

Another way the shame game works is through the concept of modesty. Girls are supposed to be modest (as are "proper ladies"). In working on this material, I decided to look up the word *modest* in the dictionary. Guess what? One meaning is the "absence of self-assertion!"

Another meaning for *modesty* is, "proper delicacy or purity of thought and manner." It's a no-brainer to see how that statement refers to sexuality. Purity of thought, indeed! Apparently, if something has to do with sex, it's not enough to say, "Just don't do it." The champions of modesty feel compelled to add. "Don't even *think* about it." Also found under *modesty* were, "Dishonor from loss of virginity. The private parts. Moral delinquency. Exposure of what modesty conceals." (Gee, what could *that* mean?)

Check out the following words I found under *modesty* in the thesaurus: *Humble. Meek. Lowly. Morally virtuous. Diffident. Coy. Decorous. Proper.*

Get the picture? This is a description of what girls (and adult women, too) are supposed to be like according to the dictates of the patriarchal society. I think it's time for girls to say in a very self-assertive way, "Hey, men, get over it! That was then, this is *now*." Do you agree?

ART AND THE BODY

Artists have always been fascinated by the human body. In the attempt to convey its inner qualities through the outer experience of seeing it, they have employed a wide variety of methods and techniques—from the lush curves of Rubens's nudes to the harsh geometries of Picasso's cubism. Flesh tones utilized by painters have covered a wide spectrum, from natural skin colors to bizarre shades never seen in the flesh. These attempts to plumb the magic and mystery of the body express the artist's conception of what the body reveals of the inner person. The body is the visible expression of the soul.

Buddhist meditation teacher Jack Kornfield makes this point in his essay, "Awakening a Sacred Presence," in *Nourishing the Soul.* When he realized he "used [his] body but didn't really inhabit it," he became aware that he had to "come into [his] body as a spiritual practice," because, "being aware of walking, eating, and moving is the ground of our awakening."

All of your experiences and memories are stored within your tissues. By becoming aware of your body and its needs and moods, you can connect with your inner truth, which is revealed by your instincts. Unfortunately, most of us have lost touch with the physical basis from which we derive. We ignore basic needs, override our natural drives with intellect or willpower, allow ourselves to become emotionally stressed from a variety of causes—some minor, some major. Having lost respect for our basic instincts, which are always right, we fail to listen to our bodies, fail to appreciate their sheer wonder.

Even though we hear that the body is the temple of the soul, we are taught conversely that the body is the repository of sin and the "sins of the flesh" are the most horrible. Not only are we often ashamed of or embarrassed by our sexuality and our sensuous nature, we hide our common bodily functions from view, as well, doing all we can to minimize their reality by subjecting ourselves to a multitude of artificial chemical agents, many of which are indeed a danger to both our physical and our spiritual health.

The human body is like a blank canvas upon which our imaginations create images. Too many of us suffer from a negative body image. Failing to appreciate that the body is the representative of the soul and thinking ourselves unacceptable as we are, we try to become something we are not to conform to some outside standard of fitness or beauty. And, when we do not conform because we cannot, we feel inferior, with our self-esteem damaged along with our soul. Though we may never resolve the debate about the precise time the soul enters the body, it is clear is that the soul inhabits the body and when either soul or body is neglected or denigrated, both suffer.

Ideas about the body vary with the times. Standards of beauty, health, and appropriateness concerning the body have fluctuated over the centuries, and even today different cultures have different bodily standards and views of the body, its nature and its use. But no matter what culture a person belongs to, to watch a human body at rest or in movement is to glimpse the soul of the person. We see our souls articulated in our gestures, movements, shapes, physiognomy, skin color, eye shine. We see disturbances to the soul expressed in bodily functions gone awry: skin eruptions, impaired movement, disease, malfunctioning organs are all symptoms of soul distress.

THE MAGIC OF LOVING TOUCH

An excellent way to get in touch with your body and begin to honor it as a sacred precinct, as the house of your Goddess within, is through touch. We can get in touch by touching ourselves. Unfortunately, most of us have been taught that touching ourselves is narcissistic or, worse, sinful. The result is that we touch ourselves only perfunctorily—as in the performance of personal hygiene—or furtively, in an erotic manner. Self-touch is one of the easiest and most effective means of getting to know your body, including your sexual feelings. Touching yourself in a loving way can be an

A Goddess Exercise

Self-Touch Meditation

To touch yourself positively, you must first let go of any feeling of embarrassment about putting your hands on your own body in a self-conscious manner. To begin, wash your hands and face thoroughly with a sweet-smelling soap and dry them on a soft, warm towel. You want to maximize the tactile experience in every way possible, and that means using your other senses in addition to your sense of touch. Next, put some lotion on your hands and rub them together until they are warm. Then, gently begin to stroke and caress your face, saying either silently or out loud, *I love you; you're beautiful* or other words of affection and praise. Spend ten minutes stroking your face and then look in the mirror at the lovely glow.

Another form of meditative self-touch can be done in the shower by consciously stroking any body part that is tense, in pain, or about which you feel negatively and speaking words of love and healing to it. Learning to cherish all parts of our bodies is a powerful way of realizing their sacredness every day. You can do this outside the shower as well—standing, sitting, or lying down. Before sleep is a good time to practice self-touch, especially if something hurts. Even if you can't reach the hurting part, such as your back, you can stroke the areas of your body that you can reach. You will find this a very soothing experience, and the more you use it, the more effective it will become.

Use this technique especially to reunite yourself with parts of your body that you have denied or despised. Because we are fed manufactured idealized images of beauty, girls learn to think our bodies are inadequate or inferior. Surveys show that even preteen girls already "hate" their hips, thighs, or breasts.

Until girls develop the good sense to reject these idealized media images, the poison they exude will continue to cause damage to girls' self-esteem.

However, right now you can take steps to heal the pain you have suffered because your body didn't fit the image-maker's ideal. Touch any part of you that you consider imperfect or a problem and give love to it. It's the only body you have, and it deserves your kind and loving care and attention. Practice the art of self-touch frequently, and you will get to know and love your body while learning about your sensuality and sexuality.

extremely positive experience, and because tactile experience is so fundamental, self-touch can be a meditative experience, whether it is sexually neutral or erotic.

Touching other people and animals brings us "in touch with" their soul energies. Many, however, are so blocked within that they are "touchy," or do not want to be touched. So negative has this simple, basic activity become, loaded as it is with taboos and connotations of incorrectness, that loving touch has become a rare experience in many lives.

Every mother uses the sacred power of touch whenever she kisses a child's small hurt "to make it better." And every loved child knows that mummy's kiss has tremendous power. Metaphorically speaking, you can kiss yourself.

TAKING CARE OF YOUR GODDESS BODY

Another way you can honor your body is simply by taking care of yourself. Learn about nutrition and eat properly. Don't make junk food a way of life. If you buy food at a supermarket yourself, read

I deliberately overeat to give my body the most voluptuous contours I can acquire. Growing fatter is one of the most intensely sensuous things that I have ever experienced.

Margaret Deidre O'Hartigan

Beauty comes in all shapes and sizes. Our goals should be health [and] stamina.

Emme Aronson

Women should try to increase their size rather than decrease it, because the bigger we are the more space we take up and the more we have to be reckoned with.

Roseanne Barr

Most of us think of transcendence as moving through spirit, taking us out of our bodies. Making space for the divine to enter through the vulnerability of our bodies is a very different experience. To open to our own humanness and our own humility—from *humus,* or the earth—is to accept our own deepest wounds. That is where the divine enters.

Marion Woodman,
"Sitting by the Well," in
Nourishing the Soul

No one can make you feel inferior without your consent.

Eleanor Roosevelt

the labels and avoid all kinds of additives. If you can't pronounce a word on the ingredients label, don't buy the product! "You are what you eat" isn't just a cute New Age saying.

And—you don't need me to tell you this—stay far, far away from illegal drugs. This is certainly not easy in our drug culture, with its intense pressures on girls to go along with the crowd. You have to make tough decisions every day and have the courage to stick with them. It's up to you to treat your body and mind with proper regard for the person you are and are in the process of becoming. Teens have a lot more freedom these days than in the past. That's good, but freedom means responsibility.

Alcohol, which is legal for adults, is all too easy for teens to obtain. Remember that your brain doesn't become fully developed until you are about twenty. Also remember that drunk girls are vulnerable to arrest and probation or even serious issues such as unprotected sex, disease, unwanted pregnancy—and rape.

GIVE YOURSELF THE GIFT OF REST

One of the primary and most often neglected forms of self-care is rest. Are you tired all the time? Teens today find yourselves under more and more pressure and have busier and busier schedules. Do you take on more than you can reasonably handle? Do parents or teachers or peers push you beyond your natural limits? If so, call a halt. If you don't get sufficient rest, your body will let you know by becoming sick. You don't want that to happen. So, learn to set limits.

Rest means giving yourself permission to be quiet, free of demands—your own and others. It is a place *within.* When you are truly resting, you have no place to go, nothing to do, nothing to accomplish. You are utterly at peace within yourself—at rest. It is a state of calm emptiness, like the still point at the hub of the turning wheel. Life goes on around us all the time, but we can withdraw into that center where all is still and unmoving to gain our deserved rest.

Rest isn't a given—it's a commodity in increasingly short supply in our busy lives. Those busy lives are usually something we are quite proud of—as if overfilled hours, days, weeks, months, years, earn extra credit in heaven. It's too bad that in our goal-driven society many people think the need for rest is a weakness, and that rest itself is nothing more than a lower-level activity that must be endured in order to get back to active pursuits. Though it does refresh you for what you must do, rest has a deeper and much more important internal purpose. When you rest, you activate your inner sacred realm, where you reconnect with your deep internal rhythms and with the inner wisdom that knows how to keep you in balance.

Rest is the glue that holds body, mind, and soul together. You know that when you are tired you tend to fall apart. Tired children are fretful, prone to accidents and tears. Tired people are grumpy, short-tempered, prone to argument and emotional upsets. They make mistakes, injure themselves and others, and become ill. You've heard the saying, "I'm just bone tired." That is what happens when we fail to get proper rest. We are tired right down to the marrow of our bones. Lack of genuine rest is a major factor in many teen problems and emotional upsets. When minds and bodies do not get the chance to recuperate fully from the daily wear and tear, like a stretched-out rubber band, they lose the ability to bounce back.

Many people confuse rest with laziness. Doing nothing is considered to be some kind of minor crime associated with having a bad character. The idea of doing "nothing" seems to be equated with the idea of *being* nothing, as if, instead of "I think therefore I am," the motto were, "I do, therefore I am." In our Puritan-based culture, doing nothing is a dangerous condition, a situation not to be tolerated. Too many of us had "idle hands are the devil's workshop" drummed into us when we were children.

Relax. See how it feels to be a human *being* instead of a human *doing* for a change.

However, that "nothing" is a valuable place, one you need to develop and protect. It is a refuge in times of stress, a sacred space within yourself, a source of strength, joy, and healing.

Rest is natural, as natural as breathing. But just as many people don't breathe deeply and fully (merely sipping the air instead of drinking it, thereby shorting themselves of the vital flow of oxygen) many of us have lost the ability to rest, have actually forfeited the knowledge of how rest is made. Rest means different things to different people. Only you can know what rests *you*. It does not necessarily imply lack of activity, but must include some cessation of it. Perhaps after the hike up the mountain you sit quietly and contemplate the vast emptiness of a cloudless blue sky. Remember, rest is a profound place within yourself. You must find it and identify it and experience it on your own. The very word *restful* has a soothing, calming sound to it. Think of a restful day and see what comes to mind.

CARING FOR YOUR ANIMAL SELF

The word *animal* has a bad connotation. We often use the word as a negative: "You're acting like an animal." We label some human behavior as animal when it is in fact something an animal would never do. Except in captivity or when they are stressed by shrinking habitats (both situations caused by humans), animals do not abuse themselves or their young. Animals do not litter their habitat. Animals do not rape, and they kill only for food.

In our patriarchal culture, we have been taught to denigrate our bodies as less valuable than our minds. With this upside-down view, we glorify the intellect, or rational intelligence, which we believe puts us in a class above all other creatures on Earth. Because we consider ourselves superior to animals, and therefore to our own animal natures, we deny, neglect, and repress our

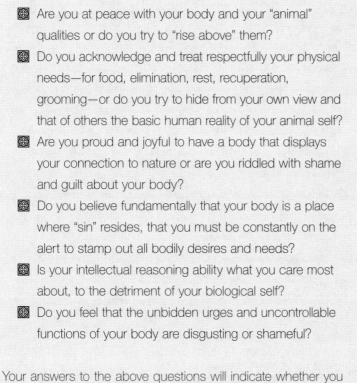

A GODDESS EXERCISE

TEST YOUR ANIMAL QUOTIENT

- Are you at peace with your body and your "animal" qualities or do you try to "rise above" them?
- Do you acknowledge and treat respectfully your physical needs—for food, elimination, rest, recuperation, grooming—or do you try to hide from your own view and that of others the basic human reality of your animal self?
- Are you proud and joyful to have a body that displays your connection to nature or are you riddled with shame and guilt about your body?
- Do you believe fundamentally that your body is a place where "sin" resides, that you must be constantly on the alert to stamp out all bodily desires and needs?
- Is your intellectual reasoning ability what you care most about, to the detriment of your biological self?
- Do you feel that the unbidden urges and uncontrollable functions of your body are disgusting or shameful?

Your answers to the above questions will indicate whether you see yourself as a totality or have a one-sided view of yourself.

Rejoice in Your Animal Self

Whenever we find ourselves denigrating our animal selves, we must stop and reflect that not only are our physical natures nothing to be ashamed of, they actually offer us much to be grateful for and to rejoice in. Minding the animal within is a vital part of the living of the Goddess way.

healthy animal instincts. This behavior has gotten us into a lot of trouble.

Our animal natures are not the problem—it is the *denial* of the animal in ourselves that has led to so much human conflict and unhappiness. When we relegate our animal natures to the bottom of the heap in terms of life's priorities, we end up with a culture in which people are fundamentally alienated from their own bodies. If we had

A GODDESS EXERCISE

HONORING YOUR ANIMAL SELF

Here are some things you can do to honor your animal self:

- Trust your instincts. Learn to listen to your body. It has wisdom through and through. Never forget that your body is a wondrous thing, full of marvels. If you deny its perfection and circumvent its instincts, you will be unhappy with your body and blame it for not feeling good or performing well. Learn that your body knows how to take care of itself if you will only allow it to guide you.

- Realize that your body is much more than its functions. It is not a machine but a living entity with intelligence and purpose. When you begin to relate to your body as having soul, you appreciate its unique beauty and expressiveness.

- Learn to think with your heart as well as with your head. The heart may be just a muscle to the surgeon doing a bypass, but to you it is the seat of love and courage. Astrologically, Leo rules the Sun, which represents both life purpose and the essence of human vitality. Leo the lion symbolizes the heart, the central pulse of one's being.

- Pay attention to symptoms. *Symptom* derives from the same root as *symbol*. Thus, symptoms are symbolic of a deeper process than mere physical discomfort. Ask yourself what it means when you become sick. Listen to the messages your body is sending you about what it needs.

- Don't accept the idea that your body or any of its natural functions, such as vaginal secretions or your menstrual periods, is in any way "disgusting." These functions are entirely natural and necessary. Unfortunately, we have been bludgeoned by the advertising industry to think that our necessary bodily activities, which keep us alive and healthy, are to be "corrected" by the use of this product or that. This conditioning produces toxic feelings of anxiety and shame.

▧ Refuse to accept anyone else's standards for how you should use your body. Instead, pay close attention to your body and learn to live in harmony with it. You are one single entity—not a body *and* a brain/mind *and* a soul/spirit. You are all of these, but they are not separate. Without a body, your mind wouldn't be able to think and you would have nothing with which to develop Goddess consciousness.

▧ Within the limits of possibility, learn to set your own pace for basic bodily needs like sleep, eating, exercising. Do what is right for you rather than following the advice of "experts" whose data often comes from experiments with laboratory rats. Eat when you are hungry. Sleep when you are tired. Exercise when you feel the need for movement. Don't believe you "should" follow somebody else's pre-scribed routine, unless, of course, you are under the care of an athletic coach or some other adult authority such as a dance instructor. We are inundated from all sides through the media with these shoulds, to the point that we are con-fused about what is best for us. The plain truth is that your body already knows what is best for you.

▧ Remember how you felt about your body as a child. Think of some of the things you did then that felt good. Make a list of things you would like to do that you once did. Think back to how you felt about your body as you entered puberty—what messages did you get about it? Were they negative or positive? Remember what you felt about getting your first period. Was it a good or bad feeling? If it was bad, do you still carry those negative feelings around today?

more regard for our animal natures, we would not be polluting ourselves and our environment at such a great rate. When we neglect or abuse our own bodies (or other people's) we miss out on many physical pleasures that are a vital part of the sacred experience.

LEARNING TO LOVE YOUR MANY-SPLENDORED BODY

Once you recognize that you are an integral whole—body and all its parts, mind and all its abilities, spirit/soul and all their potentials—you bring a new and revivifying force into your life. As you begin to experience genuine caring for your body, you discover that each part is in relationship to the total. Nothing operates independently. Discomfort or illness result when some part of the body withdraws from cooperative relationship with the rest because it does not feel recognized or loved. Recognize that each part of you is as important as every other part. For example, your colon may not seem as romantic or useful as your hands, but without its smooth and regular functioning you would become ill from toxic buildup. Try repeating the body affirmations in the following exercise to remind yourself how valuable each part of your body really is.

Becoming conscious of your body, its needs, and its relationships may seem a daunting task, but actually it is not difficult. You begin by regarding the whole, and then you become aware of any part that needs your conscious attention. By giving extra care to whatever is not working well, you foster the process of integration. Once you begin to truly care, and let your body know you are committed to a caring relationship with it, it will advise you of areas that need attention. Perhaps you need more rest, or less food. Maybe you need more comfortable shoes or a warmer coat. Massage or body therapy may be indicated.

A GODDESS EXERCISE

BODY AFFIRMATIONS

I now truly care about all of myself.
I acknowledge that my body is beautiful and good.
I accept and love all my parts.
I bless myself and all my parts. I care about their
    success, their happiness, and their good health.

Never mind if these statements seem hypocritical to you in the beginning. Pretend you are an actor getting into the part. Soon you will believe, for it is the truth. Say the above affirmations in different ways—with emphasis on one word or another. Repeat them softly, then loudly, then emphatically, then liltingly. Sing them if you like. After a while, you will realize that you actually do care about yourself, your whole self and all your parts. This will make you understand that you have always cared about yourself deeply, but that you were prevented from showing this care outwardly because of previous conditioning.

As an extension of this, ask yourself if you use your body as an excuse to prevent you from getting what you want out of life? If so, how? Or does your body help you to attain your goals? How? Set up a dialogue with your body and have a conversation with it every day. Imagine each of your organs separately and set up a dialogue with them. Ask your kidneys, your lungs, your heart, your spleen, your liver how they are and if they need anything. Thank them for the job they do so well. Pretend you are the boss giving out year-end bonuses for good performance. How would you rate each organ? Assign a color to each one and ask yourself what that color signifies.

As you begin to care, a tremendous burden falls from your shoulders, which may be tight from the tension of your not caring for a long time. Don't worry about being overwhelmed. Just do one thing at a time. Cultivate the habit of listening to your body without trying to drown out its communications with drugs or stimulants. As you progress, all your past social conditioning about your body and how imperfect or bad it is drop away like magic. You see that you are a unique, worthy, and *whole* person, fully deserving of all the care you can give yourself.

Today, after many centuries of considering the body as the repository of sin, many of us are reclaiming our bodies as the holy vessels they truly are. We are tuning in to the idea that the body is the original "church," or temple of the sacred. Traditional peoples have always used the body as part of sacred ritual, marking rites of passage by altering the body and undergoing physical trials. Some tribes use body paint made of the substance of the earth and of their own bodies (blood or semen), or they scar their bodies in prescribed ways.

A GODDESS EXERCISE

YOUR BODY SPEAKS

Pretend that your body is a character in a story. In your Goddess journal write a short essay in which your body expresses its feelings directly in dialogue.

We paint ourselves, too, but unlike indigenous peoples, we adorn our bodies for nonspiritual reasons: to attract the opposite sex, to impress others or, sadly, to disguise ourselves from who we really are. Teenagers pierce your bodies, get tattooed, spike and dye your hair bizarre colors, and dress in a manner guaranteed to displease your elders. My guess is that one reason for this is your feelings of being disregarded or invisible—but another explanation is that you are seeking new outlets for expression of your emerging spiritual awareness. And, lacking any formal or social rites of passage as guides, you are simply making up your own as you go along.

Misuse or abuse of the body results from misconceptions about the body and its importance in terms of the whole. Such acts indicate that you are not really in the body at all but are considering it as an object, separate from the Self. An essential truth is that the body cannot become the sacred vessel for your spiritual life until you are affirmatively and positively in it.

We must affirm ourselves for who we are, including the package we came in. Our bodies are not constructed by the life force to fulfill the fashion industry's current notion of beauty. Bodies come in all sizes and shapes and colors and abilities, each one beautiful and unique. There are many explanations given by metaphysics (for example, karma, past lives) for these differences, but no one truly knows why the range of human bodies is so great. What we do know is that it *is*. And the acceptance of what is, is a cornerstone of the structure of the Goddess way. What is important is that each human body houses a human soul and that each body takes that soul through its lifetime in one way or another, regardless of physical defects or anomalies.

You cannot revere the body as a temple at the same time you are criticizing it as "evil," "sinful," or "dirty." And you cannot polarize the body between extremes such as overeating and then going on a severe diet. Balance is necessary, even if difficult to achieve. Your body is the vehicle through which you experience spiritual ecstasy. Pleasure experienced in and through the body is a genuine aspect of the sacred. For example, in the writings of mystics, which appear in all religious traditions, the saints all describe physical conditions as part of their transformative spiritual experiences.

Negative Thoughts Can Make You Sick

Just as scientists have found that positive beliefs can engender wellness, they also have found that negative beliefs and influences can induce illness. . . . The brain sends messages throughout the body via neurotransmitters that signal the body to respond as if the thought were a real event.

Herbert Benson, MD,
Timeless Healing

A Goddess Exercise

Getting to Know Your Body

In the privacy of your own room at a comfortable temperature, undress and spend an hour communing with your naked self. Notice how you feel about being without clothing; register any feelings of discomfort, shame, or embarrassment. If you find yourself criticizing any of your body parts, stop and, instead of criticizing, send them love and appreciation. Thank your body for all it does for you.

Get some washable body paint and paint yourself. Pretend you are living free without any social constraints. What would you like to look like? Adorn your naked body with as much imagination and fantasy as you can and then dance around. Go a little wild and fanciful.

Write a short essay in your Goddess journal about how it felt to just hang out in your bare skin and how different it felt to dress in paint.

Imagine what you would think and how you would react if you had never before seen a human body. Observe all your moving parts and feel a sense of wonder at how the whole thing works together so marvelously. Consciously think of moving your finger or a toe, and be amazed at how your body responds to your commands. Draw a picture in your journal or notebook of your body as you imagine it looks to others. Draw a picture of your body as it looks to you. Compare the two.

Over the course of a week, keep a notebook about the running commentary you make to yourself about your body. Label one page Day 1, the next Day 2—all the way through Day 7. Pay attention to the circumstances in which you have negative thoughts about your body. Start to change the negative messages you send your body to positive ones. Write these down, converting the negative words you use into positive words. List all the positive things you can think of about your body and what it does for you.

My Goddess Body

Divide a page in your journal or notebook into three columns. Make three lists about your body. One about what you want to change. One about what you like as it is. And one about what you are grateful for.

- Things to Change
- Things to Leave Alone
- Things I'm Grateful For

THE GODDESS IN YOUR MOON

In chapter 5, I discussed the Moon as a primary symbol for the Great Goddess and gave suggestions about identifying with Her through the planetary placements in your astrological chart.

The Moon has a special affinity for things female. That's partly nature—women are chemically and physically different from men—and partly our culture's assigning nurturing and care-giving Moon roles to women. Still, the Moon is related to female physiology—breasts, ovaries, uterus, lactation, and the menstrual cycle. Female hormonal balance is quite different from the male, contributing to cyclical emotional fluctuations. The female average monthly cycle is approximately equal to the Moon's 28-day trip through the twelve signs of the zodiac.

Beginning at the time of puberty, your body awareness increases dramatically. Your body is going through rapid changes in growth and hormonal development. Unfortunately, at this time of bodily changes, many girls become terribly self-conscious about your bodies, which may begin to seem alien to you. It can be a confusing time for you. When you look at your reflection in the mirror, you might be pleased to see that your breasts are beginning to develop or your hips to round out—or you might be horrified. Is that really you in the mirror or is it someone else?

When we compare ourselves to the perfect bodies and faces we see on TV and in movies, we feel terrible because we think our bodies aren't "good enough." We agonize about whether others will find us attractive.

This kind of unfair comparison is a big mistake. When you become dissatisfied with your body, you cut yourself off from your Goddess Self. Your body is an important part of who you are—there's no other body on Earth exactly like yours—but your body isn't all of you. It is inextricably linked to your mind, heart, personality, character, abilities, aims, and goals. You inherited your physical body through the genes of your many ancestors, and you cannot change its fundamental form. You can, however, use it well and wisely, appreciating it for the marvelous instrument that it is, while recognizing that you possess a sacred authentic Self, of which your physical body is only a part.

If your Moon needs—the universal human requirements for physical and emotional nurturing—were fulfilled in childhood, your teen years will be a time of gradually and naturally becoming emotionally independent as you learn to care for yourself. But if your deepest inner needs were neglected or ignored, you may have major repair work to do. Children lacking fulfillment of their Moon needs often become immature teens who are always "needy" because they feel deeply deprived.

Close examination shows that we tend to nurture ourselves as we were nurtured—or not nurtured, as the case may be. If your mother took loving care of your physical and emotional needs—kept you clean and safe, fed and comfortable, and gave you lots of hugs and affection—chances are you have little trouble nurturing yourself. If, on the other hand, she was impatient with your small needs, was absent for some reason, or griped and complained about all she had to do for you, you quite probably have neglected your lunar self all your life.

My prescription for recovering from a lack of early nurturing is learning to love yourself unconditionally. The fact is that you cannot really love another until you first love yourself. If you didn't get the nurturing you needed when you needed it most, the solution is self-nurture.

Self-nurturance is an art because it requires the unlearning of unwanted, negative behaviors acquired in childhood. Usually people have adopted these behaviors as defenses or survival mechanisms. For example, as a youngest child, you might have learned to keep your thoughts and opinions to yourself to avoid ridicule from your older siblings. Or maybe special treats came few and far between at your house and you found that the best way to get your fair share was to grab it first—and your brother's too, if you could get away with it.

These strategies may have served their purpose when you devised them, but they hold you back as you grow older. The girl who never ventures an opinion may be assumed not to have any, or to be too "stuck up" to share them. The girl who muscles in at the front of the line or takes more than her fair share, without regard for others, certainly won't be winning any friends by doing so. Because these behaviors "worked" when you were a child, it's hard to believe you'll really be safe or get what you need if you give them up. The truth is that as you get older, negative behaviors prevent you from meeting your needs.

Each Moon sign has both positive and negative characteristics. The less you are in touch with your Moon self, the more likely you are to be expressing its negative characteristics. Don't worry if you are

Girls and Their Mothers

Girls have a very special tie to their mothers—we expect the female child to identify with the mother's female body, which is a connection quite different than mothers have with their sons. Girls' close and continuous experience of their mothers makes them models of what women are supposed to be like—even if the girl doesn't particularly like the model her mother represents. Nevertheless, it's extremely difficult for girls to free themselves from the mother's female model because of the symbiotic similarity between a mother and her daughter, who share the same female body characteristics.

Aries Moon Characteristics

Negative: Aggressive, foolhardy, pushy, hotheaded, impatient, rushing, overbusy, impetuous

Positive: Action-initiating, pioneering, energetic, enthusiastic, decisive, courageous, active

Taurus Moon Characteristics

Negative: Possessive, rigid, unyielding, stubborn, opinionated, materialistic, gluttonous

Positive: Stable, practical, productive, deliberate, affectionate, earthy, sensuous, artistic

Gemini Moon Characteristics

Negative: Superficial, scattered, distracted, restless, trite, babbling, fickle, fidgety

Positive: Thinking, communicating, reasoning, curious, quick-witted, versatile, flexible, agile

currently expressing negative ones. You can change that. Use the personal Goddess Girl self-renewal tips for your Moon Sign to learn how you can best nurture and renew yourself—both in body and in spirit. Because the Moon rules both your physical body and your emotions, your astrological Moon placement can give you valuable information about how to care for yourself in a deeply satisfying way. Remember that the Moon is a symbol of the Goddess.

GODDESS GIRL SELF-RENEWAL TIPS

Aries Moon: Your Goddess Girl self-renewal tip is to get plenty of physical activity. Whatever uses a lot of energy, such as sports or outdoor projects, helps you to work off excess emotional tension and curbs your restlessness. It's important for you to eat regularly and properly. Learn to stop doing things before you get overtired, especially when you are expecting your period. Slowing down is hard for you, but rest you must! Avoid rushing headlong into activities, and be sure to make frequent changes in routines to stave off boredom, which saps your energy.

Taurus Moon: Your Goddess Girl self-renewal tip is to surround yourself with nature and earth. You have a deep connection to earth and her rhythms. Being around growing plants and nurturing them, even if you're only taking care of a plant on your windowsill will nurture you. Pamper yourself with small luxuries, especially when you're feeling blue. Celebrate your monthly period with a ritual acknowledging your body's healthy functioning. Food is important to you, but if weight is a problem, eat light, tasty meals frequently to offset your tendency to overindulge. Then you can allow yourself the occasional gooey treat without feeling guilty.

Gemini Moon: Your Goddess Girl self-renewal tip is to talk your problems out with a friend you can trust. This is a must. You need to air troubles and grievances at length. Find good listeners, and give them equal time to talk, too. That way, you'll always have someone to talk to who won't feel that you are taking advantage. Don't let your periods make you feel alienated from your body. Avoid getting overtired, as your nervous system is high-strung. When in a state of unsatisfied restlessness, you tend to overdo in order to distract yourself. You need to learn how to be quiet and take sufficient downtime.

Cancer Moon: Your Goddess Girl self-renewal tip is proximity to water. Being near or in water, especially the sea, nourishes and reconnects you to the element your body needs most. If you can't get to the ocean, sit by a stream or soak in the tub. Sweet and starchy foods soothe your sensitive feelings, but avoid overindulgence. Learn to prepare healthy and tasty homemade meals. Mood swings can be problematic, especially during premenstrual times. Take frequent naps. Indulge in comfort foods. Make a nest of your bed in which to cuddle up and be cozy and pamper yourself.

Leo Moon: Your Goddess Girl self-renewal tip is to get positive feedback from others. Positive feedback is an absolute necessity for you. Ask for it! You need to look good to feel good, but don't let appearances rule your life. Sunshine will rejuvenate you. Your pride makes you insecure unless you are in the lead, but learn to share the spotlight. Working with younger kids lets you show your leadership abilities. If your periods make you grouchy, retreat to your den until you feel sunny again. Overdoing can bring on physical collapse or burnout, so keep activities at an even pace.

Virgo Moon: Your Goddess Girl self-renewal tip is to let up on perfectionism. While maintaining your need for fastidious cleanliness, don't self-criticize, especially during your periods when it's likely to be heightened. For you, self-nurture is not an indulgence,

Cancer Moon Characteristics

Negative: Oversensitive, insecure, clinging, illogical, acquisitive, self-indulgent, brooding, hoarding
Positive: Nurturing, feeling, caring, protecting, domestic, maternal, intuitive, devotional, sympathetic

Leo Moon Characteristics

Negative: Self-centered, self-glorifying, willful, grandiose, overbearing, attention-getting
Positive: Loving, creative, loyal, courageous, leading, playful, childlike, warm, honorable, generous

Virgo Moon Characteristics

Negative: Worrying, fault-finding, fussy, nit-picking, over-critical, nervous, introverted, self-effacing
Positive: Careful, orderly, discerning, discriminating, helpful, dutiful, meticulous, accurate, precise

Libra Moon Characteristics

Negative: Dependent on others' approval, inconsistent, indecisive, oppositional, judgmental, legalistic
Positive: Balancing, harmonious, diplomatic, appreciative, charming, graceful, considerate, socially aware

Scorpio Moon Characteristics

Negative: Relentless, secretive, coercive, vindictive, destructive, covetous, sarcastic, jealous
Positive: Transforming, regenerating, healing, intense, psychic, sexual, resourceful, determined

Sagittarius Moon Characteristics

Negative: Self-righteous, opinionated, exaggerating, blunt, hypocritical, judgmental, tactless, impractical
Positive: Understanding, far-seeing, expansive, optimistic, independent, athletic, travel-oriented, ethical

it's a necessity. Learn to relax more and just "hang out." The world won't stop turning if you take time off from your many projects and loaf for a day or two. Some of you fuss endlessly over health and others practice self-neglect. All of you need to get in touch with your sensuous nature and let go of control.

Libra Moon: Your Goddess Girl self-renewal tip is to have beauty in your environment, whether it is a vase of fresh flowers, a pretty quilt for your bed, or a beautifully arranged room. You rejuvenate best in a calm and refined atmosphere. The Libra Moon is relational—fill your life with music and beauty and with friends who will enjoy artistic activities with you. Cultivate a good friend with whom you can share intimate areas of your life that are hard to discuss, such as your periods. Avoid strife and gross behavior and people. Don't repress your anger—talk it out in a calm and rational manner.

Scorpio Moon: Your Goddess Girl self-renewal tip is to find solitude. Time to be alone regenerates you, especially in times of stress. Plan regular quiet time to delve into your private world and understand your feelings. Your emotional intensity, which is heightened just before and during your periods, can get out of balance. Learn to let go and try not to brood on past hurts. Practice the relaxation techniques in this book to dissolve bodily and sexual tensions. You need to be around water, even if it's only in the bathtub. Don't allow personal affairs to become obsessive, and avoid brooding over hurts.

Sagittarius Moon: Your Goddess Girl self-renewal tip is to travel. Travel restores and refreshes you; even short trips will help you feel your best. Spend time with travel books, magazines, TV programs, and websites. And get outdoors to go hiking or camping. But don't forget your body's needs, especially at the time of your periods. Relax and snuggle in for a couple of days before resuming normal activities. Use proper precautions to avoid injuries from sports or outdoor activities and take care when traveling in foreign lands to minimize mishaps or confusion.

Capricorn Moon: Your Goddess Girl self-renewal tip is to learn to live in the present. Security conscious, you are always thinking of the future rainy day. Learn to enjoy today's sunshine. Don't let work rule your life or you may get sick. Relaxing and enjoying what you already have is a good way to nurture yourself. Try to be more open with others and accept their sympathies. Don't let your natural pessimism get you down, especially during your periods. Remember that what you worry about rarely happens. Learn to release stress, have fun, and enjoy yourself more. Cultivate a hopeful outlook.

Aquarius Moon: Your Goddess Girl self-renewal tip is to seek out whatever is different and unusual. You thrive on the "far out"—the farther out the better. A natural rebel, you enjoy going against the grain of society, but don't overdo this. Emotions are hard for you to deal with, but ignoring them is dangerous. Let yourself feel your feelings, especially those that occur at the time of your periods. Find a way to use your thinking processes without becoming identified with them. The gyrations of abstract thought can cause eruptions of impatience and despondency.

Pisces Moon: Your Goddess Girl self-renewal tip is to allow the spiritual in your life. If you fail to recognize your deep need for a spiritual life and provide for it, you are in danger of becoming involved in drug abuse, alcoholism, or depression. Your periods may make you feel weepy, oversensitive, and self-pitying. Restore yourself through meditation, prayer, free-form dance, spontaneous art, and music. But learn the basics of self-care as well, such as good nutrition, hygiene, appropriate clothing for the weather, and

Capricorn Moon Characteristics

Negative: Competitive, worrier, overstructured, stiff, restrictive, authoritarian, austere, severe
Positive: Achieving, organized, serious, practical, focused, self-controlled, professional, wise, efficient

Aquarius Moon Characteristics

Negative: Know-it-all, rebellious, unreliable, perverse, tactless, disruptive, socially maladapted
Positive: Insightful, innovative, individualistic, free, independent, truth-seeking, reformist, intuitive

Pisces Moon Characteristics

Negative: Escapist, addictive, impractical, sentimentalist, illusory, self-sacrificing, self-pitying, guilty
Positive: Sensitive, imaginative, sympathetic, artistic, compassionate, aesthetic, subtle, idealistic

exercise, and practice them regularly. Balance your inner life with the material world.

WHAT ABOUT SEX?

To begin with, sex is a natural, normal, important part of life. It's also an extremely complex part. Sex isn't just about physical touching, kissing, fondling, or intercourse. Sex is about the whole person. You can not engage in sex—even casually or seemingly without emotional attachment to the other person—without involving your total self. With sex, *all* of you comes into play—your body *and* your feelings, thoughts, attitudes, emotions, and whatever notions about sex you have absorbed from your family, peers, and the general environment.

Sex affects the entire spectrum of human life. Of course it is how babies come into the world, and for that reason sex is a major factor in our communal life. But sexuality isn't just about having children, or about having fun. We all know that humans are sexual beings. But what most people—including adults—don't fully realize is that sexual energy is probably the most powerful energy humans possess. Sexuality literally pervades everything we think, feel, and do. It is so powerful that almost every society on Earth has tried to regulate it, for one purpose or another.

Many people fear sexuality—their own and that of others. Sexual feelings can be confusing, ambiguous, disturbing. Females, especially, have trouble coping with our sexual natures because of the distortion of female sexuality our patriarchal society has produced and continues to maintain.

The commercialization of female sexuality has put sex everywhere we look while at the same time depersonalizing what is humanity's most intimate form of communication. As a result, teen girls are faced with coping with their sexuality far too early, and

We tend to think of the erotic as an easy, tantalizing sexual arousal. I speak of the erotic as the deepest life force, a force which moves up towards living in a fundamental way.

Audre Lorde

under pressure. You can refuse to participate in this patriarchal scam. This doesn't mean you can't explore and enjoy your own sensuousness and sexual nature. What it means is that you have the power to take responsibility for the sexual choices you make.

Learning to understand your sexuality and its infinite complexity is a never-ending task. Life is always in a state of change, so sexuality will mean different things to different people at different times. Especially during adolescence—which by definition is a time of many changes happening rapid fire—you must constantly evolve and adjust to new situations. It's as though you were navigating a course through unknown waters without a map. Your relationships with family, friends, teachers, peers—and love interests—can pull you in all sorts of directions, and often one direction conflicts with another. This multiplicity creates a pretty complicated terrain through which you must make your way. That's why early sexual involvement, even if it does not include active sexual intercourse, is unwise.

Sexuality is a wonderful gift from the Goddess, but because our society does not provide its girls (or boys) with the kind of guidance and protection you need, exploring your sexuality can be a time of conflict and confusion. Right now, in your teen years, you are just at the beginning of a lifelong process that at times will be delightful, difficult, full of joy, marred by sorrow, extremely fulfilling, horribly painful. So how do you get started—or how do you continue what you have already started?

My answer—and it isn't necessarily the only one, nor is it a one-size-fits-all recommendation—is to first understand that your sexuality comes from the divine source of the Goddess. Goddess sexuality is sacred and should be treated accordingly.

Second, concentrate on learning as much as you can about yourself as a sexual being—by yourself. That can mean reading books; practicing self-touch, including masturbation (the only form of 100 percent safe sex!); and deep reflection.

There is so much to learn about your own unique sexual self and the best way is to go slowly. As a teen girl, you have a lifetime ahead of you to fully explore and experience your sexual nature. Don't let yourself be rushed into anything you aren't ready for. Don't allow yourself to be influenced by what "everybody's doing." Each girl begins sexual experimentation at a different age and from her own special point of view.

THE POWER OF SACRED SEXUALITY

Just as your body is unlike any other girl's body, so your sexual nature is yours alone. What is right or appropriate for someone else may do you harm. Keep in mind that as a Goddess Girl, you have the responsibility to honor your sexuality as the sacred and precious life force of the Goddess's divinity. When you firmly link yourself to the Goddess within, you learn the value of your sexuality as the wonderful gift the Goddess has bequeathed to you, Her daughter. It will become apparent to you, over time, that there is a vital connection between sex and spirit. And this understanding will be your Goddess guide to how you choose to express your sexuality, when, and with whom.

Because our patriarchal society does not condone, nor permit, the linking of sex and spirit, it is up to each person to forge that link. Eventually, with the help of every teen girl (and boys, too), those links will engender a new attitude that will gradually eliminate the negative effects from which female sexuality suffers today, such as physical and psychological abuse. And, the male-created rules and regulations—be they stated openly or imposed subtly—will come crashing down.

Your clear understanding of the positive aspects of your sexuality and its connection to your Goddess Self will eventually lead to fundamental changes for you personally (such as improved self-confidence, better body image, less dependency on having a boyfriend or girlfriend to feel good about yourself)—and reach outward to the whole of society, which is as yet only dimly aware of the need to integrate sexuality with spirituality.

A GODDESS GAME

A GODDESS SEXUALITY GAME

In your journal or notebook make a design by writing affirmations about your sexuality. Write up, down, sideways, around the margins, or whatever looks interesting. Use different colored pens and markers of different thicknesses to make an interesting design. Here are some sample sexuality affirmations:

- I love my sexuality.
- My sexuality is mine alone.
- Being sexual is my Goddess-given right.
- My sexuality is sacred.

Then create a symbol for your sexual self. You can draw symbolic images of the Goddess, make a picture of yourself as you see your sexual nature, or snip bits of colored paper or magazine pictures and paste them in your journal to make a collage representing your sexual nature.

8

KEEPING A GODDESS JOURNAL

Growing up can seem like a lonely trek through an unknown and unpopulated wilderness. Keeping a journal is a way of having the Goddess by your side all the time. I encourage you to keep a journal by your side as you read this book. Do the book's exercises there—and move beyond them to self-guided thought. Use any form you please—I find a bound notebook is best, as I tend to lose separate pieces of paper. A simple spiral notebook is inexpensive and widely available, or you may prefer something grander such as a clothbound book with blank pages. As you develop your contact with the Goddess, your journal will become a wonderful companion. All travelers are advised to keep a record of their journey. A spiritual journey is no exception. In fact, keeping a journal can, in and of itself, be a spiritual practice. On days when you are anxious or blue, having a conversation with your Goddess Self—your truest, most sacred, divine self—is a great help. Writing is magic—and the Goddess gave us that wonderful tool with which to express our deepest feelings and needs.

◈   Ask Her questions in your journal.

◈   Give thanks for Her blessings you received that day.

Spiritual Awareness

Developing spiritual awareness
involves the continual mixing of our
inner, private Self with the details of
our everyday, common-place life.

▩ Develop your relationship with Her wisdom.

▩ Write affirmations about what you want for yourself over and over—repetition sinks them into the
psyche and they become true.

▩ Let your writing be free and spontaneous. Don't
worry about spelling or grammar. Just let it flow
out of you.

▩ Give yourself permission to say anything.

▩ Record your Goddess Exercises.

When people learn that I write books, they say to me, "You
should write about *me*. My life would make a great book." And it
is true. Everyone's life is a book, and every girl could benefit
from writing the book of her own life. Writing in a journal is a
way of keeping track of your thoughts and feelings as you explore
your inner territory and develop a relationship with the Goddess
within. Your journal will be a friend who is always there to hear
your woes and celebrate your triumphs. You can think of it as
The Book of My Life. Rereading pages you have written in the past
can be an illuminating experience. You may wonder if the
person who wrote those lines a few weeks or a year ago was
really you.

Journal keeping was something that came to me late in life, but
now I produce several hundred pages a year, easily the length of
this book. And how I wish I had kept a copious journal during my
teen years! What a treasure-house that would be now!

A journal is a marvelous tool for just about any purpose you want
it to serve: companionship, a place to spill your thoughts and feelings, a friend who will keep your secrets, a factual record, the telling of your inner life. It can be used to communicate with the many

layers of yourself, to experiment with forms of expression, to mirror your many facets.

Keeping a journal is great way to explore your inner workings—writing about your life's experiences, both inward and outward, can bring fascinating insights and be full of delightful surprises. You'll find yourself connecting with your hidden, deeply private, side.

And a Goddess journal is the perfect place to express any negative feelings. Just the act of writing about what distresses you is a step toward finding the solution. By keeping your Goddess journal regularly, as you read this book and afterward, and telling Her what you are experiencing, you connect with the taproot of Goddess energy and receive guidance.

DIGGING FOR TREASURE AT THE CENTER OF YOURSELF

The charm of journal writing is that it is entirely private. You can think of this activity as the externalizing of your inner being, a way of manifesting into concrete reality all the thought forms and feelings that float around inside you.

By following the way of the Goddess, you are already on a spiritual quest. You may call it something else—a search for meaning, finding yourself, or getting in touch with what you really want to do in life. Labels are unimportant. The spiritual quest is life, and life is a spiritual quest.

To take a spiritual journey and keep a record of it, we needn't do anything dramatic, such as go off into a wilderness looking for visions or fast for days. That sort of spiritual vision quest can be a wonderfully illuminating experience and a thrilling adventure, but the real core of spirituality is tucked away in the corners of everyday life. Sunday, Monday, or Friday, rain or shine, cold or warm, all days are sacred in their happening and in their detail. Journal writing is a way of describing the territory you have traversed, of identifying and marking out the significant terrain—as such, it is also like mapmaking.

When fully experienced, journal writing has a liminal quality— it provokes a glow from within. I often imagine what it must have been like for archaeologist Howard Carter when, after years of searching and digging in the inhospitable Egyptian desert, he peered from amid the rubble into the gold-filled tomb of Tutankhamen and stood stunned before the wondrous sight of wall-to-wall gold and bejeweled riches beyond comparison. Symbolically speaking, this is the experience waiting for you as you proceed with what I call soul excavation, and begin to unearth your own inner treasures through the faithful keeping of your Goddess journal. By following your Goddess Self—what I call the "internal imperative"—you'll find the life path that will fulfill you and allow you to live out of your authentic Self.

Raising Consciousness

There is a well-known mythological symbol of two birds sitting in a tree—one is eating; the other is watching the one who eats. The symbol represents your two sides: the doer and the watcher. These might also be thought of as the actor and the recorder. The actor represents your outward existence, your struggles and achievements, your movements toward others, your participation. The recorder represents your inward life, your thoughts, feelings, attitudes, beliefs, hopes, and dreams. This part of yourself is the watcher, the one who reflects on what the actor is doing. It is contemplative. Carl Jung called these inner expressive powers archetypes, but we can think of them as vibrations to which we resonate at different levels.

Together, the actor and the recorder create consciousness. Just as thought without action produces no concrete results, action

Catch those Moments

A journal is somewhat like a butterfly net—we can use it to catch beautiful specimens, preserving them for future study and pleasure.

without thought is mere movement. Both are necessary to create a being conscious of itself and its actions. Do you remember your first conscious moment? There is a time when we first open our eyes to the world around us and see ourselves as both participating in that outer world and separate from it. Child specialists debate just when this happens in terms of age, but I see it as a continuous process.

Consciousness is our most precious possession. Without it, we are mere robots, only going through the motions of life, not really *living*. In the ability to think, reflect, and wonder, we possess treasures greater than any material riches on Earth.

We often feel confused about the difference between the words *conscience* and *consciousness*. Conscience is supposed to guide us in matters moral and ethical, but without awareness of the exact meaning of our actions, we cannot judge them. This is where consciousness comes in. When we become conscious of any negative effects associated with a behavior or thought pattern, we are in a position to change our behavior for the better. It is our ability to be aware that makes the difference. Consciousness makes awareness possible—it is our guiding inner companion who never goes away.

Without consciousness, we do not know who we are and cannot find out. This greatest of gifts should be guarded carefully and used wisely. The human mind can observe itself thinking—subject and object simultaneously. We can "see" ourselves doing what we do. The girl following the Goddess way is actually on a consciousness-raising mission. By seeking Her, you allow consciousness to emerge. It's as though you were peeling away the layers of an onion—with each layer removed you get closer to the center.

As you get closer, you begin to hear the whisperings of the Goddess's inner guidance. Subconscious information about the true implication of our actions may reach us first as a vague sensation, either mental or emotional. It can be a tension or a sense that something is about to happen. Consciousness may register no more than an ephemeral state of being, like the feeling that one has forgotten something important but cannot for the life of one remember what it is.

When we listen and pay attention to these sensations, to the still small voice, we hear the voice of the Goddess. The directions we need most often come from within, yet they can be mirrored by what is happening without. The question is: How can we sort through our multiplicity of feelings, sensations, intuitions, thoughts, and reactions to get to the core of the matter? The answer is through reflection. Consciousness thrives in the silence of reflection—and the Goddess Girl can use journal writing as valuable way to reflect.

Furniture of the Mind

The nineteenth-century American writer Willa Cather spoke of "the furniture of the mind," and said, "Miracles seem to rest . . . upon our perceptions being made finer so that for a moment our eyes can see and our ears can hear that which is about us always." We can furnish our minds with our conscious observations of everything both outside us and inside us.

YOUR OWN PERSONAL STORY MATTERS

Autobiography—which was once considered naive in academic writing classes—has become immensely popular among ordinary people. We're all interested in how others have lived, not only the famous or rich, but everyday folks just like us.

Teen self-help books based upon personal interviews with real teens are increasingly popular. True, a large segment of the population craves intimate details of the lives of international celebrities, but they wallow in this gossip and tabloid journalism to the detriment of their own personal life stories.

Maybe a pop rock singer or a Hollywood superstar seems to lead a more interesting life than yours, but you are the only person living your life.

Once you get to know yourself at your deeper levels, you will find you are a fascinating person. And you have the ultimate reward of actually experiencing your own life firsthand, not just living vicariously through TV and newspaper accounts of famous people, who, in person, might prove to be very dull indeed.

MY ITALIAN JOURNALING EXPERIENCE

Once, on a trip to Florence—alone and speaking little Italian—I felt totally cut off from my familiar life. One afternoon I bought some little notebooks to carry with me to jot down my impressions of the trip. An odd thing happened.

Sitting at an outdoor café for afternoon coffee, I took out one of the notebooks and began a stream-of-consciousness piece of writing that started out as a letter to a friend. I became so absorbed in writing that I forgot the time entirely and was startled when the waiter came to tell me the café was closing. I was amazed to discover that dusk was falling.

After that, I carried the notebooks everywhere, and they became my constant companions. I no longer felt awkward sitting alone in a café or restaurant. In fact, I eagerly looked forward to my time to write. My afternoon coffee break became a new and fulfilling pleasure.

I spent an entire afternoon observing a man in a piazza that was full of pigeons. They apparently knew him well, as he was covered from head to foot with the birds. They flew in and landed on his shoulders and his head and circled all about him as he scattered bread-crumbs. I was fascinated with this performance and enjoyed describing it for my friend. Now, I know that in this man's simple love for the pigeons and in their response to him, I was experiencing the Goddess at Her work.

By the time I left Florence, I had resolved some extremely important issues that were standing in the way of my making any further progress, creatively or spiritually. I had reached a rapport, not with another person but with myself.

GETTING STARTED AT JOURNAL WRITING

Many people are paralyzed when confronted with a blank page. They feel shy as if meeting a daunting stranger for the first time. Worries about "how to do it" rise up and inhibit the mind from transmitting to the hand the thoughts and feelings that seek written expression. But you needn't let yourself be stopped by self-doubt or worries about how anyone else would judge your writing. A journal is a private place and should be guarded from intrusion. You only need to start the flow and it will continue itself, creating a bridge between the inner and outer worlds, connecting action with reflection.

Writing is a sorting process. It is also a great teacher. A dialogue with yourself is never dull or uninteresting. So, please lay aside your fears that somehow you won't get it right. There's no right or wrong. It doesn't matter if you have terrible handwriting or are a master at calligraphy. You can make Ds in English or win prizes for composition. Your Goddess journal doesn't care about that. The Goddess just wants to hear what you think and feel regularly. If you do lack writing skills, what better way to improve them than by writing?

Write. That's all. And don't worry about the details. Just put them down as you see fit. You can also draw, doodle, paste in cutouts, or do anything else that pleases you. If you like structure, be neat and orderly. If you don't, scribble any old way (as long as you can read it later).

WHEN AND WHERE SHOULD I WRITE IN MY GODDESS JOURNAL?

There is no "right" time to write in your journal—occasionally you may give it more time; frequently, less time. Sometimes you write simply because you come to an activity in this book; sometimes

Just Write!

A famous author was once invited to conduct a college writing class as a visiting lecturer. This awesome man marched into the room full of eager wannabe writers who, with pencils poised, were waiting for pearls of wisdom to drop from the great man's mouth. Taking a firm stance behind the lectern, he barked out: "How many of you want to be writers?"

Seventy enthusiastically hopeful young arms shot up into the air simultaneously, waving like sea anemones. The master surveyed his class and then said softly, "Then get the hell home and *write*! Don't waste your time in writing classes."

With that, he turned on his heel and strode from the classroom leaving seventy young mouths gaping in his wake, for they realized they had heard Truth.

you inspire yourself to write. You are following your own rhythm—let the journal "speak" to you when it wants your attention. I do recommend writing as frequently as you can manage—daily if possible. The end of the day, in the quiet period just before bedtime, is a good time to write. This time of pre-sleep can influence your dreams. It's also good to combine journal writing with your relaxation and meditation periods. The time just after waking is excellent as well—I like to use this time to fit together the experiences of the previous day and the night's dreams. Whenever you write, for however long, you enhance your consciousness.

Like timing, writing locations will vary for each girl, depending on your personal conditions of space and privacy. To my mind, the ideal situation is to have a quiet, regular spot that is entirely private, at least for the time you are writing. As with doing relaxations and meditations (and journal keeping is a form of meditation), using the same place all the time is conducive to the activity. When the Goddess senses that you are in your writing spot and ready to make contact, you will shift into the right gear automatically. I sometimes sit at my computer and simply stare out the window at my garden for a few minutes until the flow begins.

However, I also know people who can placidly write in the middle of a traffic jam. One man I know carries his notebook in his glove compartment just for that purpose. He finds that when everyone around him is losing it, writing in his journal keeps him calm and collected. Others comfortably write while commuting on a train or bus. As with all the other exercises in this book, it's entirely up to you and your needs.

If you are already a journal keeper, keeping a Goddess journal will be no problem. If you are new to journal keeping, you may need some time to become acclimated to writing about yourself and your experiences on a regular basis. Writing is a form of self-healing, and having a dialogue with the Goddess should be enjoyable. Make it a habit to write self-created affirmations daily. Remind yourself that

Finding Patterns

Keeping a Goddess journal allows you to discover significant patterns—your life is not an accidental or random event; it has meaning and purpose. Your Goddess journal helps you to discover how the events of your life fit together into a meaningful whole. It gives you information about what you care about and what you find unimportant, what you enjoy and what you find unpleasant, what you're good at and what you struggle with. This information can help you live the life you were born to live in the best possible way for you.

you are a Goddess Girl with all the wonderful female qualities that She has given to you.

Time Well Spent

The amount of time you spend writing in your Goddess journal is entirely up to you and may vary depending on whatever else is going on in your life. During a six-month period when I was undergoing an intense healing after a plunge into the pit of depression, I wrote many pages every day. In fact, keeping my journal became, for that period of time, my life work.

Most people find themselves struggling with depression sometime in their lives, and teens often find themselves coping with it. Writing about those bad feelings can help to overcome them. If I hadn't recorded everything, I might have forgotten many of the lessons I learned, lost the details of my journey, or even had the whole experience fade away like last summer's flowers.

A GODDESS EXERCISE

THE MONITORING TECHNIQUE

As we go about our daily lives, we usually operate in a blur of automatic, preprogrammed thoughts and activities. Most of the time, our mental processes could be compared to a photograph that is slightly out of focus. Ordinarily, we focus sharply only in times of crisis. As a result, we are often bored and qualitatively "not there."

Many teens today live busy and highly programmed lives with an abundance of scheduled activities both in school and out of school. This makes everyday life such a blur of routine that it's easy to miss or neglect what is happening in your deepest Self. To combat this tendency toward lack of personal awareness, I have developed and teach a technique I call monitoring, which is a way of consciously focusing on the day's internal input, either as it is happening or during brief periods of reflection in the course of a day.

If the idea of learning to monitor your thoughts and feelings at first seems daunting, do not let that prevent you from attempting it. It's like learning to ride a bicycle. At first it seems clumsy and impossible and then—bingo—you are off and away with astonishing ease.

Begin by consciously storing in memory your thoughts, feelings, and reactions to the events of the day. It's especially important to monitor any events that might be contributors to a physical illness. If you're not feeling up to par, for example, if you feel a cold coming on, go over the events leading up to the sensation of having a congested head or a sore throat. When thoughts and feelings arise from the inner Self, do not ignore them or push them away; record them either mentally or physically so that they do not vanish into the well of forgetfulness. During the day, whenever you have a spot of unoccupied time—waiting for a bus, being driven in a car, standing in line—review what you have noted to fix it firmly in memory for later evaluation. If you have trouble remembering, train yourself to take brief notes during the day or following significant events, especially negative ones. Note the particulars of the situation along with your reactions. A few words will do—you will develop a kind of shorthand in time. Record your thoughts and feelings along with the physical circumstances in which they occurred. For example, if you get bad feelings about something that happens, notice what was going on physically at the time. The purpose is to give your memory a jog so that later when you look over your notes, you'll be able to recall the entire event with its "feeling tone."

At the end of the day, set aside a few minutes time to examine the entire day's input for insights about your inner workings, clues to your Goddess nature. The more you are aware of your inner and ongoing processes, the greater your ability to sort through your thoughts and feelings, especially difficult or painful ones.

If you use any meditations from this book or from other sources, use the same sort of notes to make a record of your experience. Doing a meditation is a good way to speed up the journey to your Goddess center. Notes of what you found there will be valuable reminders of how it felt to be connected to Her.

Rereading what you have written the next day or a year later can be an illuminating experience. For one thing, you may not be aware of how much progress you've made until you see where you were this time last year. Enjoy your journal—think of the Goddess as someone wonderful who loves you and wants only the best for you, who offers you loving guidance.

Your Goddess journal serves as a private record of your spiritual growth and is an excellent tool for coming to understand your individual pilgrimage on this Earth. In it, you will experience the adventure of your life—the discovery of your authentic Goddess Self.

If you find yourself responding to the idea of writing regularly in your journal with the excuse that you don't have the time, my answer is: We find the time for what we feel is important to us.

JOURNAL RX

James W. Pennebaker, PhD, a professor in the department of psychology at Southern Methodist University, developed a technique to help his patients cope with traumatic events in their lives. His method is to spend twenty minutes writing about the traumatic experience. You may want to try this. Write nonstop and don't be concerned about spelling or grammar.

Often, emotions will pour forth, even tears—but these are tears of release. This is an excellent method for gaining insights that can help with stress caused by trauma. Patients report that the writing exercise served to improve their emotional and physical well-being on a long-term basis.

When using this free-writing technique for dealing with trauma, it is important to continue it for at least four days in a row, or longer. The reason is that writing out feelings about deeply wounding experiences just once will reopen the wound but will not suffice to begin healing it. According to Pennebaker, the patients who wrote about their deepest feelings related to trauma experienced remarkable benefits in both physical and emotional health, compared to control groups who wrote only about trivial events. Their immune systems were strengthened, leading Pennebaker to conclude that "just putting upsetting experiences into words has profound psychological and physical benefits for our participants."

His reasoning is that repressing feelings is a physiological strain—blood pressure, heart rate, and muscle tension all increase when emotions are "stuffed," or blocked from expression. Pennebaker theorizes that when we express our long-buried emotions in words, we relieve the body as well as the mind of crippling stress. His studies have proved that the expression of thoughts and feelings can affect our overall health positively. He suggests the journal method be used to heal past traumas, as well as to relieve ongoing present-day stresses.

Important note: If you are seriously depressed or have any thoughts of suicide, get help from a responsible adult immediately. Writing about bad feelings can help, but you may need professional assistance from a doctor or therapist. Your journal is not a substitute for professional help or counseling.

Fun Tips for Journal Keeping

- Decide if you will write by hand or keyboard.
- If by hand, select loose-leaf paper or a bound book.
- Choose a book that opens flat.
- Do you prefer lined paper or unlined?
- The writing implement you use should be one that is permanent and does not smear. You may want to reserve a special pen or pencil just for journal writing.
- If using a keyboard, you can use three-hole-punched paper and keep your pages in a binder.
- Or, create a file folder, or a computer file.
- Browse in a stationery store for an assortment of pens, markers, or colored pencils and use them for a variety of moods and experiences. One client records all of her dreams in purple.

You have the time to watch TV, go to the movies, chat on the internet, hang out with friends, visit the mall, play sports, and lots of other activities. Your Goddess journal is meant to be another pleasure, not a chore. If at first it seems an unwelcome task or a burden, take heart and keep at it. This is a rewarding and important facet of your overall spiritual development.

Often I'm asked, "How much should I write?" Well, how long is a piece of string? This is a question that can only be answered by you and your personality. My only advice is to write what you want, where you want, for how long you want. If you feel you have nothing to say to yourself, don't write at all. You may write copiously or

A Goddess Exercise

Priming the Pump—Some Suggestions for Getting Started

Still not sure how to begin? Try some of the following short exercises to get flowing with journal keeping.

- Practice flow writing. To do this, simply write anything that comes to mind for fifteen minutes.
- Write an outline of the major turning points of your life for later elaboration.
- Ask yourself where you are now and write about it.
- Create a piece of artwork to represent your vision of the Goddess.
- Meditate upon a symbol that would express your personality and write about it or draw it.
- Find some pictures that express the Goddess to you and make a collage of them.
- Write a description of your solar self—the action side of your personality.
- Write a description of your lunar self—the side of yourself that takes time to reflect.
- Write a dialogue between your solar and lunar selves.
- Write a letter to yourself about why you are keeping this journal, what you intend to accomplish.
- Write a letter to the Goddess.

sparsely, and do either or both at different times in your life. There's no minimum and no maximum. Sometimes I jot down a few words; at other times, I write several pages. For those accustomed to taking notes, jotting a few lines in your own brand of shorthand suffices to jog your memories when you reread. Others find that starting to write in your journal sparks an outpouring of immense detail.

A Goddess Exercise

Make a Covenant with Your Goddess Journal

Think for a few minutes about why you are doing this and why you are willing to make a commitment to writing regularly in your journal. Then put this into words as your *purpose*. Here's a sample statement of purpose:

I'm keeping my Goddess journal for the purpose of getting in touch with Her within me, my intuition, and with the aim of generating more consciousness. My goal is to become more aware of messages from my sacred mind and to act on this information for my spiritual growth and development. I believe that keeping this journal will aid this process by providing me with a framework in which I can record and reflect upon my experiences and chart my progress.

Study what you have written for a few minutes and see if you are satisfied with your purpose. You may want to make changes.

When you are satisfied with your written statement of purpose, finish the following statement to sign a contract with yourself.

"Following my statement of purpose, I make a covenant with myself to pursue this effort on a regular basis. I promise to write in this journal _____."

Fill in the blank. You might decide on every day for fifteen minutes, or simply every day, or at least twice a week for half an hour, or for no less than one hour per week, or a total of X hours per month. You are making this agreement with yourself, and it's up to you to keep to the terms you make.

If at first you feel shy or have difficulty, don't worry. It's only stage fright and you will get over it. Remember, this is your personal Goddess journal and no one else ever need see it. If you feel uptight or restricted, go for a walk or do a relaxation exercise before writing. Remind yourself that you are doing this for *you*. It's not schoolwork, a book report, or a test. It's your artwork.

Consider your Goddess journal a gift you give yourself. You might think of it as a hobby. Rereading what you have written is a pleasant way to remind yourself of how much progress you have made. Like a photo album of a vacation trip, it will bring back the memories.

Think of your journal as a wise adviser and friend to whom you can turn whenever you need a boost or someone to talk with. Your journal is someone you can tell your day to without worrying about lack of interest. Enjoy it as you would enjoy spending time with any loved one who is genuinely interested in you, your problems, your daily life, your successes, your setbacks, your dreams, and your goals. In fact, you can consider the time you spend with your journal as time spent with the Goddess herself, the Source of All.

EXPLORE YOUR FEMALE FAMILY HISTORY

"Like mother, like daughter." Does that phrase give you the horrors or do feel proud to be like your mother? Whichever way you feel, as girls, we unconsciously model ourselves after our mothers and other important female relatives. Sometimes this is great, but sometimes we pick up beliefs or attitudes that hold us back us from becoming our authentic Selves. A good way to explore yourself, your beliefs, attitudes, talents, interests, sense of humor, strengths, and weaknesses is to learn more about your female ancestors. What were their hopes and dreams when they were girls like you? What did they end up doing with their lives? It pays to consciously explore your feminine history. Being aware of what has gone before will give you the jump on taking control of your own Goddess Girl life.

ONE WOMAN'S FEMALE FAMILY HISTORY

To give you an example of what a female family history might be like, I asked a friend to do hers and allow me to publish it in this book. When she sent me her story, she commented that "the female family history really touched a chord for me. I could see how a conscious exploration of the female family patterns of behavior, beliefs, response to the culture at large, roles assumed (as girl-friends, wives, and mothers) would be an incredibly illuminating—and freeing—exercise. It certainly was for me!" Her history follows.

Both of my grandmothers went to college, which was very unusual for women who were born in the late 1800s. My mother's mother entered college at the early age of sixteen. After graduation, she worked as a research librarian for ten years but stopped working when she married, as was expected of women of that era.

My father's mother went to college as an adult, when her children were grown and in college themselves. She graduated first in her class with a degree in accounting and was offered a job at the prestigious Chase Manhattan Bank in New York City. However, her husband—a prominent eye surgeon—refused to allow her to accept the job. He was afraid people would think he couldn't support his wife! So, she had no choice but to relegate her abilities to keeping his medical practice books and the household accounts.

My aunt, the same doctor's daughter, was a serious student of ballet when she was in high school. After

MOTHER LOSS

If you are a girl who has lost her mother—due to death, divorce, desertion, mental illness, or suicide—you are especially in need of knowing your female family history. Being motherless gives you special and unique problems. And very few social groups recognize the needs of girls without mothers. Most people take it for granted that a girl has a mother, or an adequate mother substitute. However, sadly, this is not always true. All too many girls are growing up without mothers. I myself was made motherless at the age of one when my mother died. And there wasn't any mother substitute figure in my life, so I understand what those of you without mothers have to face. And it's more than difficult.

For the very reason you were deprived of a mother, you need to access as much of your female family history as possible. Grandmothers, aunts, sisters, fathers, and brothers are valuable sources of information. Unfortunately, fathers rarely talk to their daughters about a missing mother. The younger you were when you lost your mother, the less likely you are to know about her and you may have to work hard to reconstruct her life. Asking questions is the only way you will learn what you need to know, so don't be held back by reticence or a sense of inappropriateness. You have a need to know, and the right to know whatever you can learn about your mother: who she was, how she lived, what she was like.

Storytelling creates a vital link between you and your lost mother. It will help you make sense of your past and cope with your present and future. For the motherless girl, taking her female family history is a way of fitting together the pieces of what is a puzzle, and to form a meaningful whole on which you can build your own life by healing the isolation you feel. Being without a mother can make you feel incomplete as a person, like missing a limb. And, indeed, you are missing a vital part of yourself. Of course, you have to compensate the best you can, and being on the Goddess path is a great benefit. Turning to the Goddess is extremely comforting, for She is the Great Mother and in Her image you were made.

That's why motherline stories help to ground a motherless girl in her gender, her family, and a feminine history. Without that history, a daughter is snipped from the female cord that connects the generations of women who preceded her—her ancestresses. Hearing from other female family members restores that separation to some extent and reconnects the motherless daughter to her long motherline. This is not only healing but it grants female authority to the girl who has no mother to confer it on her.

As you make the journey back to your own female roots—assuming this is possible, for sometimes, especially with adoptions or for those in foster care, the link is broken forever—you will meet ancestors who struggled with life in different historical times. This life-cycle perspective helps us understand that all things change. However, if you take the Goddess as your guide, you will find your connection to the archetypal Mother and the wisdom of the ancient Goddess way of life, which tells us that body and soul are inseparable.

seeing her dance in a recital, a scout from the New York City Ballet Theater School offered her a place in the famous company's academy. But my grandfather would not allow her to attend the school. His reason? "Nice girls don't pursue a career on the stage." Case closed.

Then, she decided that because she was also good at science, she wanted to become a doctor like her father. When she presented this idea to him, he informed her that he would not pay for her to go to medical school. Why? Because he didn't believe in women doctors. He did consent to send her to Smith College, at that time a training school for wives-to-be of well-to-do young men who were expected to succeed. After graduation, she married and became a homemaker.

At this point in taking my female family history I started feeling discouraged that these strong, intelligent, and talented women had been so held back by men telling them what they could and could not do. In fact, I was enraged. But I had more to learn that would dismay me.

My own mother graduated first in her high school class in Bennington, Vermont, and won a full scholarship to the college there. She worked at the college for several years after graduation but eventually moved to New York, where she met my father, a photographer and documentary filmmaker. After he'd asked her to marry him, he was offered a job on a filmmaking project in South America, so they combined their honeymoon with a working trip. While there, my mother took up photography herself, shooting black-and-white still photographs, while my father worked on the film project.

Here's the really sad part of my mother's story: When they returned to the States and settled down, she quit photography. As a child, I assumed that all those beautiful shots of South American scenes and people were my father's work—after all, *he* was the professional photographer. Many years later, I noticed my mother's name on the back of each print and understood that *she* had taken those glorious photographs. I was astounded and asked her why she had not continued taking pictures. She told me that she'd begun to realize that she might be a better photographer than her husband. She feared that her talent would show him up and "threaten the marriage."

I feel that my father would actually have been proud of my mother's talent and accomplishment, but women of her generation had been trained not to upstage their husbands, and that ingrained attitude affected her deeply. My mother didn't just sit at home; she started a library at the elementary school my sister and I attended and ran it for ten years. But—despite the fact that she held a master's degree in children's literature—it never occurred to her that she deserved to be paid for her work. She was just another married woman doing her part as a volunteer.

Needless to say, all of this affected my own life, but I wasn't aware to what degree until much later. Although I had heard these stories about my female relatives all my life, I didn't explore them consciously until I was in my forties. I had spent eighteen years in a difficult marriage, always putting the needs of my husband and my two children before my own (as I believed I was supposed to do according to unspoken patriarchal tradition). But after I separated from my husband and entered individual therapy, I began to explore my female family history more closely. It was then that I started to recognize the family pattern of extraordinary talent going to waste because of the unfair social restraints placed on girls and women.

Finally, I realized I could run my own life as I pleased. I heard that "still small voice" inside whispering to me, "You can do what you want. It's okay to succeed. Go ahead, follow your dreams."

A GODDESS EXERCISE

WRITE A FEMALE FAMILY HISTORY

Today, people are writing their histories, probing their families for personal recollections, and seeking connection to their ancestral past. Genealogical research is booming on the internet. By interviewing your mother, grandmother, aunts, and other female relatives, you can put together your own personal goddess history. Hearing the girlhood stories of your female relatives can be a great way to for you to connect to the Goddess. If you can, find photographs of them when they were teens and compare your body with the bodies of the women in your family. Looking at old photographs helps remind you that these women were once girls like you.

Times were different when your mother was growing up and especially when your grandmother was a girl. There were fewer opportunities for women than there are today. How did those limitations affect your female ancestors? Were they able to get around them? Did they have to fight to pursue careers that women take for granted today? Perhaps social expectations prevented some of your ancestors from following their dreams. Did they manage to make do with what was available and still find a way to live full and meaningful lives? Or were they disappointed with their lot in life? Learning about your ancestors' strengths in response to adversity can fill you with a sense of strength. If your ancestors were thwarted by unfair restrictions, your outrage at that injustice can give you the resolve to join the ongoing fight for equal rights.

Ask your female relatives about their lives. Then write down their stories. *Every* family has amazing stories to tell about its female members.

I realized that I'd been holding myself back because striking out on my own and making something of myself would feel like a betrayal of my own mother and my other female relatives, who had given up *their* dreams of career and success.

So I returned to school, taking writing classes and a graduate course designed to prepare students to work in the publishing industry, and became a writer and editor with a satisfying job that lets me utilize my talents and abilities to the utmost. It's not an easy life, but it's a rewarding one.

And as my daughter reached her teens, I made a point of sharing my female family history with her, letting her know she can be whatever she wants to be. A talented art student, she's working hard, honing her skills and practicing her craft. Nothing's going to keep this Goddess Girl from following her dreams.

9

GODDESS RITUALS

Rituals are an important part of the way of the Goddess. They help us reconnect ourselves to the cycles of Earth's living body and to the rhythms of the entire Universe. Through ritual, we open to the wonder and mystery of our roles as children of our Mother Earth.

Ritual is an art form whose aim is to connect us to the sacred meaning of our lives, to make our internal authentic Self visible to our external self and to others in the external world.

The external practice of ritual serves to makes us more receptive and aware of our thoughts, feelings, and actions. When we use ritual, we sanctify. And with sanctification we bring our lives closer to the sacred. It's said that you can light a candle because you need the light, or because it symbolizes the light you need.

Goddess ritual, insofar as it generates reverence for and celebrates that which is female . . . is fiercely empowering . . . [with] possibilities as limitless as the sunshine and the wind.

Sonia Johnson

RITUALS ANCIENT AND MODERN

In primordial times, life-sustaining fire was precious and therefore sacred. Live coals were transported with ceremony, protected in a vessel lined with moss, carried by a select elite, and welcomed with pomp and circumstance. The fire ritual gave people a heightened awareness of how valuable fire was to their lives. Being

allowed to blow on the embers to keep them glowing was considered a privilege.

Today, though we depend on it no less to sustain our existence than our ancient ancestors did, fire is commonplace. But—try to remember the last time you experienced a power outage and had to light candles against the sudden dark. You will discover that you unwittingly fell into the ritual of fire. Whatever you did, wherever you placed your candles, you did so with a renewed awareness of fire's light and warmth, and of the danger that lurks when it goes out.

The ancient Egyptians performed elaborate rituals to serve a variety of ends. These followed a precise order—any deviation would spoil the intended result. Magic, to which ritual is closely related, depends on each step in the proceeding being carried out exactly as prescribed.

Because Egyptian society was so closely bound to the land, with the food supply dependent on the annual flooding of the great Nile River, rituals often related to planting and harvesting, as well as to celestial events such as the phases of the moon and the appearances of the planets.

Egyptians perfomed special ceremonies of purification prior to performing the actual rituals. Priests bathed and removed their body hair before dressing in clean white linen robes kept for each separate ceremony. The pharaoh, as the representative of the Goddess as well as the ruler of the land, was the center of many annual or seasonal rituals. Because he was responsible for the spiritual health of his people, he was required to maintain the connection with the divine. Isis, the Egyptian Great Mother Goddess, upon whose lap the pharaoh sits, and from whose divinity he derives his power, both temporal and divine, was also the focus of regular rituals.

Whether elaborate and formal or simple and informal, ritual brings us into the presence of the sacred. Rituals have great power

A GODDESS EXERCISE

CONNECTING WITH RITUAL

Ask yourself these questions and answer them in your journal.

- What rituals do I use for ordinary everyday life? These may include how I prepare myself for bed, school, dates, visits to friends or relatives, meals, for playing sports or other recreation.

- What rituals do I observe as part of my spiritual practice? These may include churchgoing or any worshipful practice carried on through an outside or public forum, or purely private activity, such as doing yoga, meditating, or praying.

- Do I enjoy public ritual observations?

- Am I fully aware of my private rituals?

- How can I bring more awareness into my use of ritual?

- What do the rituals I use mean to me?

- What connections do I make through ritual?

- How can I include more ritual in my everyday activities?

- Does ritual serve to satisfy a need in me?

- Would I enjoy designing my own rituals?

Although the immanent Goddess of pre-history would not have been prayed to nor beseeched for favors, She was acknowledged, revered, honored, and participated in, Her many manifestations meditatively studied in order to enhance one's knowledge of one's extended Self. The Goddess religion was a shamanic practice in which Her wisdom was daily imparted through communication and identification with Her various shapes and forms through trance and . . . ritual.

Donna Wilshire,
Virgin, Mother, Crone

to influence the mind and emotions. Whether we are believers of a specific tradition or not, ritual seems to fill a basic need in the human psyche. Some cultures have formalized rituals that are an art form. The Japanese tea ceremony is one of these, as are flower arranging, calligraphy. You can make a ritual into artwork yourself simply by being superaware of your intent to do so. For example, you might make a ritual out of arranging the objects on your personal altar: Or you can create an art object to use for rituals.

Candle Magick

Many rituals use candles. According to the *Encyclopedia of Wicca and Witchcraft*, the practice of using candles for ritual purposes "evolved from the old lunar cults where torches were lit to invoke the Moon Goddess. The lit candle symbolizes the presence of the Moon Goddess, who is the Enchantress, Mistress of Magick. All acts of magick performed in the glow of her flame are empowered by the momentum of the Past."

A Goddess Exercise

Creating Rituals

Here are some suggestions for creating rituals that you can incorporate into your daily life:

- Create a welcoming ritual for any new possession, especially for an important one. In Japan, any new piece of equipment in a factory is formally blessed by a priest before it is used.

- Japanese Buddhists observe Needle Memorial Day, to honor all the needles that have been "killed in action," or worn out during the year. You can create a disposal ritual to "bury" the dead things you no longer use.

- Make a ritual to prepare yourself for each day's activity: Bless your clothing, schoolbooks, transportation, and whatever else you use daily. Thank them.

- Go on a pilgrimage to a place where you sense the presence of the Goddess—a natural setting like a park or wilderness site.

- Invite others to participate with you in creating a ritual to honor the Goddess in this setting. Make an earth ritual to celebrate the advent of each season. Perform this on the spring and fall equinoxes, on the summer and winter solstices.

- Ritually honor the moon at each new and full moon.

- Look up your own Moon sign and prepare a simple ritual to perform on the day the moon enters the sign it occupied when you were born. This is your lunar return.

- Make a ritual for the first day of school each year. Bless the past summer for its gifts. Give thanks for what you will learn in the new semester.

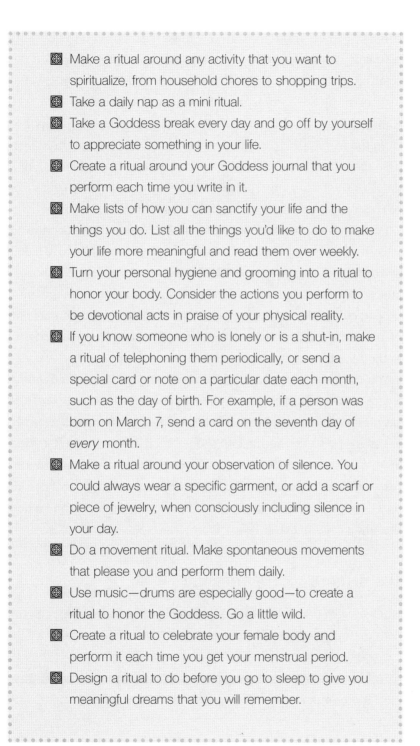

- Make a ritual around any activity that you want to spiritualize, from household chores to shopping trips.
- Take a daily nap as a mini ritual.
- Take a Goddess break every day and go off by yourself to appreciate something in your life.
- Create a ritual around your Goddess journal that you perform each time you write in it.
- Make lists of how you can sanctify your life and the things you do. List all the things you'd like to do to make your life more meaningful and read them over weekly.
- Turn your personal hygiene and grooming into a ritual to honor your body. Consider the actions you perform to be devotional acts in praise of your physical reality.
- If you know someone who is lonely or is a shut-in, make a ritual of telephoning them periodically, or send a special card or note on a particular date each month, such as the day of birth. For example, if a person was born on March 7, send a card on the seventh day of *every* month.
- Make a ritual around your observation of silence. You could always wear a specific garment, or add a scarf or piece of jewelry, when consciously including silence in your day.
- Do a movement ritual. Make spontaneous movements that please you and perform them daily.
- Use music—drums are especially good—to create a ritual to honor the Goddess. Go a little wild.
- Create a ritual to celebrate your female body and perform it each time you get your menstrual period.
- Design a ritual to do before you go to sleep to give you meaningful dreams that you will remember.

Candle Rituals

Designate a specific candle to burn during any activity you want to ritualize, from preparing for a test to dressing for a party. You can select a special candle for each day of the week and burn it for a few minutes in silence and solitude as a ritual meditation. You can make writing in your journal a ritual by lighting a candle and letting it burn while you write. Don't use designated candles for any other purpose than the one you have chosen. Put them away in a protected space (a drawer is good), wrapped in fresh tissue paper or a piece of clean cotton, between uses.

You must have a room or a certain hour of the day or so where you do not know what was in the morning paper, where you do not know who your friends are, you don't know what you owe anybody, or what they owe you—but a place where you can simply experience and bring forth who you are, and what you might be.

Joseph Campbell,
The Power of Myth

When I was a child, the Catholic mass was still said in Latin. Its complex pattern of sitting, standing, and kneeling, along with the rustling of the richly embroidered silken robes of the priest, the wafting of incense, the sprinkling of the congregation with holy water, and the tinkling of a little bell to signal a spoken response from the worshipers provoked in me an altered state of consciousness that often lasted all day. Conversely, the simple blessing of a meal, or the taking of a special drink in praise of the Goddess can be a significant ritual if done with sacred intent.

In today's busy world, we have all but lost our connection to meaningful ritual. For many, traditional religious rituals have faded in importance as people have become disconnected from the beliefs and values those rituals reinforced. They no longer serve any purpose in our modern lives. However, we can successfully create our own rituals to serve our own purposes. By doing so, we reconnect to the sacred in our everyday lives.

You may have already included ritual in your life without being aware of it—certain routines of our lives attain the importance of ritual, even becoming somewhat formalized, such as annual family gatherings that are marked by special food and drink and a fixed order in which events occur. Children naturally both create and respond to ritual—such as that of getting ready for bed—and can be upset if the precise sequence isn't followed: "No, no. I get in bed *first* and *then* you bring Teddy Bear."

THE RITUALS OF EVERYDAY LIFE

In *Care of the Soul,* Thomas Moore commented on the value of "ritualizing" everyday activities. He said:

> The ordinary arts we practice every day at home are of more importance to the soul than their simplicity might

suggest. For example, I can't explain it, but I enjoy doing dishes. I've had an automatic dishwasher in my home for over a year, and I have never used it. What appeals to me . . . is the reverie induced by going through the ritual of washing, rinsing, and drying.

Moore goes on to say that Marie-Louise von Franz, the Swiss psychologist observes that "weaving and knitting, too, are particularly good for the soul because they encourage reflection and reverie."

When I rented a house in the Catskills in New York, it came with a black rug on the living room floor. Of course, it picked up every piece of lint within miles and had to be vacuumed daily. In order to see all the tiny specks, I had to get down on my knees and crawl around on the floor. One day a friend surprised me at this task and asked: "What are you doing, a vacuum-cleaner ritual?" And I realized I had been doing just that! Thereafter, my daily vacuuming became a pleasurable ritual and the battleground of the black rug became holy ground.

Ritual connects us to mystery, and awareness of mystery is what opens the heart to the sacred dimension. Mystery can never be solved or explained—life is not a novel. Mystery shimmers and beckons. Like magic, mystery draws us to the center of our being—it takes us to the Goddess. Mystery, magic, and ritual—these give us a heightened awareness, they activate our subtle senses, taking us onward and upward into the etheric. Ritual shines a powerful beam of sacred light into our ordinary lives, brightens up the drab and the dull, polishes away the patina of the soul. It opens up to that sense of wonder—so that what we have lost is found in common moments. Ritual is the gateway through which we walk from the commonplace and into the rare, following the Goddess path.

SACRED SPACE

Handmaiden to ritual is sacred space. Throughout history, people have created sacred spaces where they performed their rituals, from elaborate temples to simple groves of trees. And these geographical locations have come to be considered as "power points"—Stonehenge in England, the Ganges River in India, the Western Wall in Jerusalem, Ayers Rock in Australia, the Temple of Delphi in Greece, St. Peter's Basilica in Rome, Mecca in Saudi Arabia, to mention the most famous of these sacred sites.

However, you do not have to travel anywhere to find sacred ground. The place where you are standing right now is holy ground. Or, as Black Elk said, when he was sitting on top of his mountain,

A GODDESS EXERCISE

PREPARING SACRED SPACE

To prepare a sacred space, first choose where you want it to be. If you have the luxury of a separate room, that is ideal, but any space you can spare will do. It could be an alcove, a niche, or just a corner of a room you use regularly. The important thing is your intention to keep this space sacred. Though most people want a space in their homes, your sacred space does not have to be indoors. For centuries people worshiped out in the open: in grottos or caves, in groves of trees that were sacred to the Goddess, or on mountaintops.

Once you have chosen the space, mark it out mentally (or walk around it). Some people define the area of their sacred space by using a small rug. When you have defined your space, proclaim its sacredness. With your arms outstretched, palms downward, say, "I now declare this space to be sacred."

If you like, your sacred space can contain an altar to the Goddess. An altar can be simple or elaborate. Depending on your available private space, you might set up a permanent altar—on your dresser or on a shelf or a small table in your room, on which you can put items of significance to you, such as pictures or photographs, one or more candles, crystals or other objects, a plant or fresh flowers.

If you don't have your own room and share space with a sibling, you can make a very simple arrangement of a few rocks or shells, a candle, a plant or a flower in some water. If space is really tight or others might not respect your sacred belongings, you can make your altar portable. Keep the things you like to use in your sacred space in a little pouch or box that's reserved especially for them. After you use them for meditation or for doing a ritual, you can pack them away until the next time.

When Native Americans perform rituals they cleanse the air by burning the herb sage. You can place a few leaves or a pinch of powdered sage in a shell or other flameproof dish and scent the air with its pleasant odor. Placing a container of water in your sacred space is another way to cleanse it. Water is thought to draw off negative spirits. It should be emptied after each use and set out fresh every time you use the space.

I now realize that the sacred space I created for myself, the room in which I do my writing, is really a reconstruction . . . of my boyhood space. When I go in there to write, I'm surrounded by books that have helped me to find my way. . . . When I sit down to do the writing, I pay close attention to little ritual details—where the notepads and pencils are placed, that sort of thing—so that everything is exactly as I remember it. . . . It's all a sort of 'set-up' that releases me.

Joseph Campbell
In *Reflections on the Art of Living*,
edited by Diane K. Osbon

"This is the center of the Earth. Where you are is the center of the Earth. The center of the Earth is everywhere."

You can create sacred space wherever you are: in your room, your backyard, or out in the woods. Anyplace on Earth can be read for spiritual significance. No matter what you believe about the origin of the species, whatever spiritual journey you choose must take place here on Earth. The starting point is wherever you happen to be at the moment.

No Churches

You don't need a special place to honor the Goddess and Her sacred ways. If you don't have a place in your home where you can set up your altar—*get out in the open spaces*, even a local park. Also, many natural features of Earth—ordinary or special, such as caves, mountains, trees, rock formations—are imbued with Her Sacred presence. Wherever you are, the Goddess is there.

In the long-gone days of Her ways, there was no need for temples, churches, and chapels within which worshipers believe in a God "out there" but not "in here."

The Goddess does not ask for *worship*—you don't need to fall on your face and declare yourself a sinner. You are already Her beloved child. In Her way, there is no getting away from what is Sacred, for All Is Sacred to Her.

A GODDESS EXERCISE

GETTING READY TO ENTER YOUR SACRED SPACE

After you have chosen and prepared your sacred space, create a meaningful ritual to follow in preparation for entering it. You might want to take a bath or shower, soothing yourself with scented oil afterward, and change into fresh, clean, loose-fitting clothes of natural fabrics (silk, linen, cotton, wool, rayon) that you reserve for ritual use. Then state your intent for your sacred space. Remember, where intention goes, energy flows. Allow profound silence to develop and . . . wait.

To create a ritual to use when entering your sacred space, or for any other purpose, you need only perform a few actions in a certain order. It could be something as simple as removing your shoes and outer clothing, washing your hands, lighting the candles, arranging a few fresh flowers in the vase you always use, having a ceremonial drink of tea, or water. Whatever actions you pick should represent what is meaningful to you.

These activities should have the effect of opening the way to your sacred space within in preparation for entering the sacred precinct without. In temples and shrines of old, there was an outer precinct through which one had to pass—often guarded by fierce-looking figures—in order to enter the holiest inner sanctum.

By performing ritual and putting yourself in the right inner space, you get ready for contact with the Goddess. Once you enter your sacred space, you should have a form to follow. Perhaps you sit on your cushion or chair and breathe quietly for a few moments and then begin meditating. I like to hold a large, smooth rose quartz crystal.

As you work with creating ritual, you will find what suits you best. Experiment until you feel that your sacred space resonates with your Goddess Self.

Joseph Campbell pointed out that in India a sacred place might consist of a red circle drawn around a stone, which creates a metaphor. He said, "When you look at that stone, you see it as a manifestation of Brahman, a manifestation of the mystery."

It's important to have a sense of reverence about your sacred space. Do not enter it unless you have properly prepared yourself. Do not permit others to enter it without your permission and the correct attitude. If you consistently treat your ritual space as sacred, it becomes imbued with a sense of the Goddess.

A GODDESS EXERCISE

THE GODDESS AS YOUR GUIDE

The Goddess is a wonderful guide. Her wisdom is limitless. You can use your Goddess journal to ask questions and receive answers. Here is a ritual to allow you to use the Goddess as your guide.

In this meditation, you are going to meet your Goddess and ask for guidance. To prepare yourself, do the following:

1. Articulate for yourself a question you would like to ask the Goddess. State the question as clearly and succinctly as you can. Vague questions beget vague answers. The more specific the question, the more specific the answer will be.

2. Do not ask a question that can be answered by a simple yes or no, such as, "Does so-and-so really love me?" Instead, ask, "What is the truth of my relationship to so-and-so at this time?" The purpose of this first effort to contact Her wisdom is for you to get to know the realms of your inner being.

3. Stick to your present situation and avoid broad generalities.

4. Do not ask a question requiring a prediction. Simply asking for guidance is always good. State the subject about which you wish guidance.

5. Be willing to trust the Goddess to take whatever form appears to you. Because all of life is energy, and the Goddess has the ability to take any form, there is no certain way of knowing how She will appear to you or in what manner She will communicate. Stay alert, for when we venture into the invisible world, we encounter mystery. There exist no neat categories of "this" and "that" that divide our rational world into recognizable events and objects. In the invisible world, all is shifting and changing, like a dream. So, when you open yourself up to the Goddess, do not be surprised at what may happen. If you draw a blank during the meditation, you can always try again later when you are more relaxed.

6. When the Goddess responds, pay attention to Her appearance. Ask Her for a name or a symbol by which you can address Her in the future.

After you have prepared yourself, find the time to be alone and undisturbed for half an hour. Using any of the breathing or relaxation methods already given, relax yourself completely and let go of the day's tensions and cares.

Mentally take yourself to a place somewhere in nature—a forest, the seaside, a flower-filled meadow, a lakeshore, a cove, a woods—whatever appeals to you. See in front of you a veiled object, full of mystery. A puff of wind blows away the covering, and the Goddess is revealed to you. Take whatever image comes and enter into a dialogue with Her. Introduce yourself, ask your question, and wait for an answer. If Her answer doesn't come at once, be patient. It may come in words, through intuition or telepathically, as an image, even as a snatch of song or an instruction to read a book or magazine article.

In these guided meditations, the specifics are not as important as making the contact. Whatever springs into your mind is the right answer, because you are using this process to contact your inner Goddess wisdom. The Goddess lives within the realm of the deepest part of your being, which is connected to all reality everywhere at all times and places.

After you have asked your question, notice the details of the place so that you can return here whenever you like. Fix it in your memory. When you get the answer to your question, thank the Goddess. Say you look forward to further dialogue with Her in the future.

If you do not get an answer, or if the answer seems to make no sense, accept that also and try again later. Remember, you are learning a new skill.

Before leaving, make an appointment to meet with Her again at a set time in the future and follow through on this with another meditation.

GODDESS GIRL ACTIVITIES

See if your friends would be interested in forming a group of Goddess Girls to learn more about the way of the Goddess and to study Her history. Make sure everyone is serious about learning the way of the Goddess. Select no fewer than three and no more than six girls to form your Goddess circle. Get together on a regular basis—it's best to pick a day and time that is convenient for everybody so that you always have the entire group assembled.

Use this book as a jumping off point. Then check your library and your local bookstores for other books about the Goddess. Read and discuss what you are learning and do any of the rituals already suggested or create a special ritual.

You could sing and dance in a circle, for example, to celebrate Her in all of you. Each girl could write a hymn to the Goddess for all to read or chant together. If possible, use musical instruments, especially percussion, in your rituals. Go on nature walks together, where you can be aware of Her presence.

And always celebrate yourselves as Goddess Girls! The real Sacred is everywhere—it is the power and the joy, the source of meaning. And it includes the sacred you. For as a Goddess Girl, you embody in your femaleness the Sacred.

PLANETARY TABLES

HOW TO FIND THE SUN SIGN

The following table shows which dates the sun occupies each of the twelve signs of the zodiac.

Aries	March 21-22—April 19-20
Taurus	April 20-21—May 20-21
Gemini	May 21-22—June 21-22
Cancer	June 22-23—July 22-23
Leo	July 23-24—August 23-24
Virgo	August 23-24—September 22-23
Libra	September 23-24—October 23-24
Scorpio	October 24-25—November 21-22
Sagittarius	November 22-23—December 21-22
Capricorn	December 22-23—January 19-20
Aquarius	January 20-21—February 18-19
Pisces	February 19-20—March 20-21

HOW TO FIND THE MOON SIGN

Find the year of your birth in the tables provided. Then find the birth month at the top of the appropriate table. Find the date of birth in the column below. If it is not listed, then the sign given for the listed date that is closest to and preceding the birth date is the moon sign. For instance, if you were born on February 2, 2000, you see that for February 1, Capricorn is the sign, meaning your moon sign is Capricorn.

If your birth occurred on a day that starts a new sign (February 4 in this example), your moon may be in the preceding sign. The only way to be absolutely sure is to have a chart done professionally or by a computer service. In lieu of this, read the text for both signs, and see which seems more like you.

1990

JAN	FEB	MAR	APR	MAY	JUN	JUL	AUG	SEP	OCT	NOV	DEC
1 PIS	1 TAU	2 GEM	1 CAN	3 VIR	1 LIB	1 SCO	2 CAP	1 AQU	1 PIS	2 TAU	1 GEM
3 ARI	3 GEM	5 CAN	3 LEO	5 LIB	4 SCO	4 SAG	5 AQU	3 PIS	3 ARI	4 GEM	3 CAN
5 TAU	5 CAN	7 LEO	5 VIR	8 SCO	6 SAG	6 CAP	7 PIS	6 ARI	5 TAU	6 CAN	5 LEO
7 GEM	8 LEO	9 VIR	8 LIB	10 SAG	9 CAP	9 AQU	9 ARI	8 TAU	7 GEM	8 LEO	7 VIR
9 CAN	10 VIR	12 LIB	10 SCO	13 CAP	11 AQU	11 PIS	12 TAU	10 GEM	9 CAN	10 VIR	9 LIB
11 LEO	12 LIB	14 SCO	13 SAG	15 AQU	14 PIS	13 ARI	14 GEM	12 CAN	11 LEO	12 LIB	12 SCO
13 VIR	15 SCO	16 SAG	15 CAP	17 PIS	16 ARI	15 TAU	16 CAN	14 LEO	14 VIR	15 SCO	14 SAG
16 LIB	17 SAG	19 CAP	18 AQU	20 ARI	18 TAU	17 GEM	18 LEO	16 VIR	16 LIB	17 SAG	17 CAP
18 SCO	20 CAP	21 AQU	20 PIS	22 TAU	20 GEM	19 CAN	20 VIR	19 LIB	18 SCO	20 CAP	19 AQU
21 SAG	22 AQU	24 PIS	22 ARI	24 GEM	22 CAN	21 LEO	22 LIB	21 SCO	21 SAG	22 AQU	22 PIS
23 CAP	24 PIS	26 ARI	24 TAU	26 CAN	24 LEO	24 VIR	25 SCO	24 SAG	23 CAP	25 PIS	24 ARI
26 AQU	26 ARI	28 TAU	26 GEM	28 LEO	26 VIR	26 LIB	27 SAG	26 CAP	26 AQU	27 ARI	26 TAU
28 PIS	28 TAU	30 GEM	28 CAN	30 VIR	29 LIB	28 SCO	30 CAP	29 AQU	28 PIS	29 TAU	28 GEM
30 ARI			30 LEO			31 SAG			30 ARI		30 CAN

1991

JAN	FEB	MAR	APR	MAY	JUN	JUL	AUG	SEP	OCT	NOV	DEC
1 LEO	2 LIB	2 LIB	3 SAG	2 CAP	1 AQU	1 PIS	2 TAU	3 CAN	2 LEO	2 LIB	2 SCO
4 VIR	4 SCO	4 SCO	5 CAP	5 AQU	4 PIS	3 ARI	4 GEM	5 LEO	4 VIR	5 SCO	4 SAG
6 LIB	7 SAG	6 SAG	8 AQU	7 PIS	6 ARI	6 TAU	6 CAN	7 VIR	6 LIB	7 SAG	7 CAP
8 SCO	9 CAP	9 CAP	10 PIS	10 ARI	8 TAU	8 GEM	8 LEO	9 LIB	8 SCO	10 CAP	9 AQU
11 SAG	11 AQU	11 AQU	12 ARI	12 TAU	10 GEM	10 CAN	11 VIR	11 SCO	11 SAG	12 AQU	12 PIS
13 CAP	14 PIS	14 PIS	15 TAU	14 GEM	12 CAN	12 LEO	13 LIB	13 SAG	13 CAP	15 PIS	14 ARI
16 AQU	17 ARI	16 ARI	17 GEM	16 CAN	14 LEO	14 VIR	15 SCO	15 CAP	16 AQU	17 ARI	17 TAU
18 PIS	19 TAU	18 TAU	19 CAN	18 LEO	16 VIR	16 LIB	17 SAG	18 AQU	18 PIS	19 TAU	19 GEM
20 ARI	21 GEM	20 GEM	21 LEO	20 VIR	19 LIB	18 SCO	20 CAP	21 PIS	21 ARI	21 GEM	21 CAN
23 TAU	23 CAN	22 CAN	23 VIR	22 LIB	21 SCO	21 SAG	22 AQU	23 ARI	23 TAU	23 CAN	23 LEO
25 GEM	25 LEO	25 LEO	25 LIB	25 SCO	23 SAG	23 CAP	25 PIS	25 TAU	25 GEM	25 LEO	25 VIR
27 CAN	27 VIR	27 VIR	28 SCO	27 SAG	26 CAP	26 AQU	27 ARI	28 GEM	27 CAN	28 VIR	27 LIB
29 LEO		29 LIB	30 SAG	30 CAP	29 AQU	28 PIS	29 TAU	30 CAN	29 LEO	30 LIB	29 SCO
31 VIR		31 SCO				31 ARI	31 GEM		31 VIR		

1992

JAN	FEB	MAR	APR	MAY	JUN	JUL	AUG	SEP	OCT	NOV	DEC
1 SAG	2 AQU	3 PIS	1 ARI	1 TAU	2 CAN	1 LEO	2 LIB	2 SAG	2 CAP	1 AQU	1 PIS
3 CAP	4 PIS	5 ARI	4 TAU	3 GEM	4 LEO	3 VIR	4 SCO	5 CAP	5 AQU	3 PIS	3 ARI
6 AQU	7 ARI	8 TAU	6 GEM	5 CAN	6 VIR	5 LIB	6 SAG	7 AQU	7 PIS	6 ARI	6 TAU
8 PIS	9 TAU	10 GEM	8 CAN	8 LEO	8 LIB	7 SCO	8 CAP	10 PIS	10 ARI	8 TAU	8 GEM
11 ARI	12 GEM	12 CAN	10 LEO	10 VIR	10 SCO	10 SAG	11 AQU	12 ARI	12 TAU	11 GEM	10 CAN
13 TAU	14 CAN	14 LEO	12 VIR	12 LIB	12 SAG	12 CAP	13 PIS	15 TAU	14 GEM	13 CAN	12 LEO
15 GEM	16 LEO	16 VIR	15 LIB	14 SCO	15 CAP	15 AQU	16 ARI	17 GEM	17 CAN	15 LEO	14 VIR
17 CAN	18 VIR	18 LIB	17 SCO	16 SAG	17 AQU	17 PIS	18 TAU	19 CAN	19 LEO	17 VIR	16 LIB
19 LEO	20 LIB	20 SCO	19 SAG	19 CAP	20 PIS	20 ARI	21 GEM	21 LEO	21 VIR	19 LIB	19 SCO
21 VIR	22 SCO	23 SAG	21 CAP	21 AQU	22 ARI	22 TAU	23 CAN	24 VIR	23 LIB	21 SCO	21 SAG
23 LIB	24 SAG	25 CAP	24 AQU	24 PIS	25 TAU	24 GEM	25 LEO	26 LIB	25 SCO	24 SAG	23 CAP
25 SCO	27 CAP	27 AQU	26 PIS	26 ARI	27 GEM	27 CAN	27 VIR	28 SCO	27 SAG	26 CAP	26 AQU
28 SAG	29 AQU	30 PIS	29 ARI	28 TAU	29 CAN	29 LEO	29 LIB	30 SAG	29 CAP	28 AQU	28 PIS
30 CAP				31 GEM		31 VIR	31 SCO				31 ARI

1993

JAN	FEB	MAR	APR	MAY	JUN	JUL	AUG	SEP	OCT	NOV	DEC
2 TAU	1 GEM	2 CAN	1 LEO	2 LIB	1 SCO	2 CAP	1 AQU	2 ARI	2 TAU	1 GEM	3 LEO
4 GEM	3 CAN	5 LEO	3 VIR	4 SCO	3 SAG	4 AQU	3 PIS	5 TAU	4 GEM	3 CAN	5 VIR
7 CAN	5 LEO	7 VIR	5 LIB	6 SAG	5 CAP	7 PIS	6 ARI	7 GEM	7 CAN	5 LEO	7 LIB
9 LEO	7 VIR	9 LIB	7 SCO	9 CAP	7 AQU	10 ARI	8 TAU	10 CAN	9 LEO	8 VIR	9 SCO
11 VIR	9 LIB	11 SCO	9 SAG	11 AQU	10 PIS	12 TAU	11 GEM	12 LEO	11 VIR	10 LIB	11 SAG
13 LIB	11 SCO	13 SAG	11 CAP	13 PIS	12 ARI	15 GEM	13 CAN	14 VIR	13 LIB	12 SCO	13 CAP
15 SCO	13 SAG	15 CAP	14 AQU	16 ARI	15 TAU	17 CAN	15 LEO	16 LIB	15 SCO	14 SAG	15 AQU
17 SAG	16 CAP	17 AQU	16 PIS	18 TAU	17 GEM	18 LEO	17 VIR	18 SCO	17 SAG	16 CAP	18 PIS
19 CAP	18 AQU	20 PIS	19 ARI	21 GEM	19 CAN	21 VIR	19 LIB	20 SAG	19 CAP	18 AQU	20 ARI
22 AQU	21 PIS	22 ARI	21 TAU	23 CAN	22 LEO	23 LIB	21 SCO	22 CAP	22 AQU	21 PIS	23 TAU
24 PIS	23 ARI	25 TAU	24 GEM	25 LEO	24 VIR	25 SCO	24 SAG	24 AQU	24 PIS	23 ARI	25 GEM
27 ARI	26 TAU	27 GEM	26 CAN	28 VIR	26 LIB	27 SAG	26 CAP	27 PIS	27 ARI	26 TAU	28 CAN
29 TAU	28 GEM	30 CAN	28 LEO	30 LIB	28 SCO	30 CAP	28 AQU	29 ARI	29 TAU	28 GEM	30 LEO
			30 VIR		30 SAG		31 PIS			30 CAN	

1994

JAN	FEB	MAR	APR	MAY	JUN	JUL	AUG	SEP	OCT	NOV	DEC
1 VIR	2 SCO	1 SCO	1 CAP	1 AQU	2 ARI	2 TAU	1 GEM	2 LEO	2 VIR	2 SCO	2 SAG
3 LIB	4 SAG	3 SAG	4 AQU	3 PIS	5 TAU	4 GEM	3 CAN	4 VIR	4 LIB	4 SAG	4 CAP
5 SCO	6 CAP	5 CAP	6 PIS	6 ARI	7 GEM	7 CAN	6 LEO	6 LIB	6 SCO	6 CAP	6 AQU
8 SAG	8 AQU	7 AQU	9 ARI	8 TAU	10 CAN	9 LEO	8 VIR	8 SCO	8 SAG	8 AQU	8 PIS
10 CAP	11 PIS	10 PIS	11 TAU	11 GEM	12 LEO	11 VIR	10 LIB	10 SAG	10 CAP	11 PIS	10 ARI
12 AQU	13 ARI	12 ARI	14 GEM	13 CAN	14 VIR	14 LIB	12 SCO	13 CAP	12 AQU	13 ARI	13 TAU
14 PIS	16 TAU	15 TAU	16 CAN	16 LEO	16 LIB	16 SCO	14 SAG	15 AQU	14 PIS	15 TAU	15 GEM
17 ARI	18 GEM	17 GEM	18 LEO	18 VIR	18 SCO	18 SAG	16 CAP	17 PIS	17 ARI	18 GEM	18 CAN
19 TAU	20 CAN	20 CAN	21 VIR	20 LIB	20 SAG	20 CAP	18 AQU	19 ARI	19 TAU	20 CAN	20 LEO
22 GEM	23 LEO	22 LEO	23 LIB	22 SCO	23 CAP	22 AQU	21 PIS	22 TAU	22 GEM	23 LEO	23 VIR
24 CAN	25 VIR	24 VIR	25 SCO	24 SAG	25 AQU	25 PIS	23 ARI	24 GEM	24 CAN	25 VIR	25 LIB
26 LEO	27 LIB	26 LIB	27 SAG	26 CAP	27 PIS	27 ARI	26 TAU	27 CAN	27 LEO	28 LIB	27 SCO
28 VIR		28 SCO	29 CAP	28 AQU	29 ARI	29 TAU	28 GEM	29 LEO	29 VIR	30 SCO	29 SAG
31 LIB		30 SAG		31 PIS			31 CAN		31 LIB		31 CAP

1995

JAN	FEB	MAR	APR	MAY	JUN	JUL	AUG	SEP	OCT	NOV	DEC
2 AQU	1 PIS	2 ARI	1 TAU	1 GEM	2 LEO	2 VIR	3 SCO	1 SAG	2 AQU	1 PIS	3 TAU
4 PIS	3 ARI	5 TAU	3 GEM	3 CAN	4 VIR	4 LIB	5 SAG	3 CAP	5 PIS	3 ARI	5 GEM
7 ARI	5 TAU	7 GEM	6 CAN	6 LEO	7 LIB	6 SCO	7 CAP	5 AQU	7 ARI	5 TAU	8 CAN
9 TAU	8 GEM	10 CAN	9 LEO	8 VIR	9 SCO	8 SAG	9 AQU	7 PIS	9 TAU	8 GEM	10 LEO
12 GEM	10 CAN	12 LEO	11 VIR	10 LIB	11 SAG	10 CAP	11 PIS	9 ARI	12 GEM	10 CAN	13 VIR
14 CAN	13 LEO	14 VIR	13 LIB	13 SCO	13 CAP	12 AQU	13 ARI	12 TAU	14 CAN	13 LEO	15 LIB
16 LEO	15 VIR	17 LIB	15 SCO	15 SAG	15 AQU	14 PIS	15 TAU	14 GEM	17 LEO	15 VIR	17 SCO
19 VIR	17 LIB	19 SCO	17 SAG	17 CAP	17 PIS	17 ARI	18 GEM	17 CAN	19 VIR	18 LIB	19 SAG
21 LIB	19 SCO	21 SAG	19 CAP	19 AQU	19 ARI	19 TAU	20 CAN	19 LEO	21 LIB	20 SCO	21 CAP
23 SCO	22 SAG	23 CAP	21 AQU	21 PIS	22 TAU	22 GEM	23 LEO	22 VIR	23 SCO	22 SAG	23 AQU
25 SAG	24 CAP	25 AQU	24 PIS	24 ARI	24 GEM	24 CAN	25 VIR	24 LIB	26 SAG	24 CAP	25 PIS
27 CAP	26 AQU	27 PIS	26 ARI	26 TAU	27 CAN	27 LEO	28 LIB	26 SCO	28 CAP	26 AQU	28 ARI
30 AQU	28 PIS	30 ARI	28 TAU	28 GEM	29 LEO	29 VIR	30 SCO	28 SAG	30 AQU	28 PIS	30 TAU
				31 CAN		31 LIB		30 CAP		30 ARI	

1996

JAN	FEB	MAR	APR	MAY	JUN	JUL	AUG	SEP	OCT	NOV	DEC
1 GEM	3 LEO	1 LEO	2 LIB	2 SCO	2 AQU	2 PIS	2 ARI	1 TAU	3 CAN	2 LEO	2 VIR
4 CAN	5 VIR	3 VIR	4 SCO	4 SAG	4 PIS	4 ARI	4 TAU	3 GEM	5 LEO	4 VIR	4 LIB
6 LEO	8 LIB	6 LIB	7 SAG	6 CAP	6 ARI	6 TAU	7 GEM	6 CAN	8 VIR	6 LIB	6 SCO
9 VIR	10 SCO	8 SCO	9 CAP	8 AQU	9 TAU	9 GEM	9 CAN	8 LEO	10 LIB	9 SCO	9 SAG
11 LIB	12 SAG	10 SAG	11 AQU	10 PIS	11 GEM	11 CAN	12 LEO	11 VIR	13 SCO	11 SAG	11 CAP
14 SCO	14 CAP	13 CAP	13 PIS	12 ARI	13 CAN	13 LEO	14 VIR	13 LIB	15 SAG	13 CAP	13 AQU
16 SAG	16 AQU	15 AQU	15 ARI	15 TAU	16 LEO	16 VIR	17 LIB	15 SCO	17 CAP	16 AQU	15 PIS
18 CAP	18 PIS	17 PIS	17 TAU	17 GEM	18 VIR	18 LIB	19 SCO	18 SAG	19 AQU	18 PIS	17 ARI
20 AQU	20 ARI	19 ARI	20 GEM	19 CAN	21 LIB	21 SCO	21 SAG	20 CAP	21 PIS	20 ARI	19 TAU
22 PIS	23 TAU	21 TAU	22 CAN	22 LEO	23 SCO	23 SAG	24 CAP	22 AQU	23 ARI	22 TAU	22 GEM
24 ARI	25 GEM	23 GEM	25 LEO	25 VIR	26 SAG	25 CAP	26 AQU	24 PIS	26 TAU	24 GEM	24 CAN
26 TAU	27 CAN	26 CAN	27 VIR	28 LIB	28 CAP	29 AQU	28 PIS	26 ARI	28 GEM	27 CAN	26 LEO
29 GEM		28 LEO	30 LIB	31 SCO	30 AQU	31 PIS	30 ARI	28 TAU	30 CAN	29 LEO	29 VIR
31 CAN		31 VIR						30 GEM			31 LIB

1997

JAN	FEB	MAR	APR	MAY	JUN	JUL	AUG	SEP	OCT	NOV	DEC
3 SCO	1 SAG	1 SAG	1 AQU	1 PIS	1 TAU	1 GEM	2 LEO	3 LIB	3 SCO	1 SAG	1 CAP
5 SAG	4 CAP	3 CAP	4 PIS	4 ARI	4 GEM	3 CAN	4 VIR	5 SCO	5 SAG	4 CAP	3 AQU
7 CAP	6 AQU	5 AQU	6 ARI	5 TAU	6 CAN	5 LEO	7 LIB	8 SAG	8 CAP	6 AQU	5 PIS
9 AQU	8 PIS	7 PIS	8 TAU	8 GEM	9 LEO	8 VIR	9 SCO	10 CAP	10 AQU	8 PIS	8 ARI
11 PIS	10 ARI	9 ARI	10 GEM	9 CAN	11 VIR	10 LIB	12 SAG	12 AQU	12 PIS	10 ARI	10 TAU
13 ARI	12 TAU	11 TAU	12 CAN	11 LEO	13 LIB	13 SCO	14 CAP	15 PIS	14 ARI	12 TAU	12 GEM
15 TAU	14 GEM	13 GEM	14 LEO	14 VIR	16 SCO	15 SAG	16 AQU	17 ARI	16 TAU	14 GEM	14 CAN
18 GEM	16 CAN	16 CAN	17 VIR	17 LIB	18 SAG	18 CAP	18 PIS	19 TAU	18 GEM	17 CAN	16 LEO
20 CAN	19 LEO	18 LEO	19 LIB	19 SCO	20 CAP	20 AQU	20 ARI	21 GEM	20 CAN	19 LEO	19 VIR
23 LEO	21 VIR	21 VIR	22 SCO	22 SAG	22 AQU	22 PIS	22 TAU	23 CAN	23 LEO	21 VIR	21 LIB
25 VIR	24 LIB	23 LIB	24 SAG	24 CAP	24 PIS	24 ARI	24 GEM	25 LEO	25 VIR	24 LIB	24 SCO
28 LIB	26 SCO	26 SCO	27 CAP	26 AQU	26 ARI	26 TAU	27 CAN	28 VIR	28 LIB	26 SCO	26 SAG
30 SCO		28 SAG	29 AQU	28 PIS	29 TAU	28 GEM	29 LEO	30 LIB	30 SCO	29 SAG	28 CAP
		30 CAP		30 ARI		30 CAN	31 VIR				31 AQU

1998

JAN	FEB	MAR	APR	MAY	JUN	JUL	AUG	SEP	OCT	NOV	DEC
2 PIS	2 TAU	2 TAU	2 CAN	2 LEO	3 LIB	3 SCO	2 SAG	3 AQU	2 PIS	1 ARI	2 GEM
4 ARI	4 GEM	4 GEM	4 LEO	5 VIR	5 SCO	5 SAG	4 CAP	5 PIS	4 ARI	3 TAU	4 CAN
6 TAU	7 CAN	6 CAN	7 VIR	7 LIB	8 SAG	8 CAP	6 AQU	7 ARI	6 TAU	5 GEM	6 LEO
8 GEM	9 LEO	8 LEO	9 LIB	10 SCO	10 CAP	10 AQU	8 PIS	9 TAU	8 GEM	7 CAN	9 VIR
10 CAN	11 VIR	11 VIR	12 SCO	12 SAG	13 AQU	12 PIS	11 ARI	11 GEM	10 CAN	9 LEO	11 LIB
13 LEO	13 LIB	13 LIB	14 SAG	15 CAP	15 PIS	14 ARI	13 TAU	13 CAN	13 LEO	11 VIR	14 SCO
15 VIR	16 SCO	16 SCO	17 CAP	16 AQU	17 ARI	16 TAU	15 GEM	15 LEO	15 VIR	14 LIB	16 SAG
18 LIB	19 SAG	18 SAG	19 AQU	19 PIS	19 TAU	18 GEM	17 CAN	17 VIR	17 LIB	16 SCO	19 CAP
20 SCO	21 CAP	21 CAP	21 PIS	21 ARI	21 GEM	21 CAN	19 LEO	19 LIB	20 SCO	19 SAG	21 AQU
23 SAG	23 AQU	23 AQU	23 ARI	23 TAU	23 CAN	23 LEO	21 VIR	22 SCO	23 SAG	21 CAP	23 PIS
25 CAP	25 PIS	25 PIS	25 TAU	25 GEM	25 LEO	25 VIR	24 LIB	25 SAG	25 CAP	24 AQU	25 ARI
27 AQU	27 ARI	27 ARI	27 GEM	28 CAN	28 VIR	28 LIB	26 SCO	27 CAP	27 AQU	26 PIS	28 TAU
29 PIS		29 TAU	29 CAN	31 LEO	30 LIB	30 SCO	29 SAG	29 AQU	30 PIS	28 ARI	30 GEM
31 ARI		31 GEM					31 CAP			30 TAU	

1999

JAN	FEB	MAR	APR	MAY	JUN	JUL	AUG	SEP	OCT	NOV	DEC
1 CAN	1 VIR	1 VIR	2 SCO	2 SAG	3 AQU	2 PIS	1 ARI	2 GEM	1 CAN	1 VIR	1 LIB
3 LEO	4 LIB	3 LIB	4 SAG	4 CAP	5 PIS	5 ARI	3 TAU	4 CAN	3 LEO	4 LIB	3 SCO
5 VIR	6 SCO	6 SCO	7 CAP	7 AQU	8 ARI	7 TAU	6 GEM	6 LEO	5 VIR	6 SCO	6 SAG
7 LIB	9 SAG	8 SAG	9 AQU	9 PIS	10 TAU	9 GEM	7 CAN	8 VIR	8 LIB	9 SAG	8 CAP
10 SCO	11 CAP	11 CAP	12 PIS	11 ARI	12 GEM	11 CAN	10 LEO	10 LIB	10 SCO	11 CAP	11 AQU
12 SAG	14 AQU	13 AQU	14 ARI	13 TAU	14 CAN	13 LEO	12 VIR	12 SCO	12 SAG	14 AQU	13 PIS
15 CAP	16 PIS	15 PIS	16 TAU	16 GEM	16 LEO	15 VIR	14 LIB	15 SAG	15 CAP	16 PIS	16 ARI
17 AQU	18 ARI	17 ARI	18 GEM	17 CAN	18 VIR	17 LIB	16 SCO	17 CAP	17 AQU	18 ARI	18 TAU
19 PIS	20 TAU	19 TAU	20 CAN	19 LEO	20 LIB	20 SCO	19 SAG	20 AQU	20 PIS	21 TAU	20 GEM
22 ARI	22 GEM	21 GEM	22 LEO	21 VIR	23 SCO	22 SAG	21 CAP	22 PIS	22 ARI	23 GEM	22 CAN
24 TAU	24 CAN	23 CAN	24 VIR	23 LIB	25 SAG	24 CAP	24 AQU	24 ARI	24 TAU	25 CAN	24 LEO
26 GEM	26 LEO	26 LEO	27 LIB	26 SCO	28 CAP	27 AQU	26 PIS	27 TAU	26 GEM	27 LEO	26 VIR
28 CAN		28 VIR	29 SCO	28 SAG	30 AQU	30 PIS	28 ARI	29 GEM	28 CAN	29 VIR	28 LIB
30 LEO		30 LIB		31 CAP			30 TAU		30 LEO		31 SCO

2000

JAN	FEB	MAR	APR	MAY	JUN	JUL	AUG	SEP	OCT	NOV	DEC
3 SAG	1 CAP	2 AQU	1 PIS	3 TAU	1 GEM	2 LEO	1 VIR	2 SCO	1 SAG	3 AQU	2 PIS
5 CAP	4 AQU	4 PIS	3 ARI	5 GEM	3 CAN	4 VIR	3 LIB	4 SAG	4 CAP	5 PIS	5 ARI
7 AQU	6 PIS	7 ARI	5 TAU	7 CAN	5 LEO	7 LIB	5 SCO	6 CAP	6 AQU	8 ARI	7 TAU
10 PIS	8 ARI	9 TAU	7 GEM	9 LEO	7 VIR	9 SCO	8 SAG	9 AQU	9 PIS	10 TAU	9 GEM
12 ARI	11 TAU	11 GEM	9 CAN	11 VIR	9 LIB	11 SAG	10 CAP	11 PIS	11 ARI	12 GEM	11 CAN
14 TAU	13 GEM	13 CAN	11 LEO	13 LIB	12 SCO	14 CAP	13 AQU	14 ARI	13 TAU	14 CAN	13 LEO
16 GEM	15 CAN	15 LEO	14 VIR	15 SCO	14 SAG	16 AQU	15 PIS	16 TAU	16 GEM	16 LEO	15 VIR
18 CAN	17 LEO	17 VIR	16 LIB	18 SAG	17 CAP	19 PIS	18 ARI	18 GEM	18 CAN	18 VIR	18 LIB
20 LEO	19 VIR	20 LIB	18 SCO	20 CAP	19 AQU	21 ARI	20 TAU	20 CAN	20 LEO	20 LIB	20 SCO
23 VIR	21 LIB	22 SCO	21 SAG	23 AQU	22 PIS	24 TAU	22 GEM	23 LEO	22 VIR	23 SCO	22 SAG
25 LIB	23 SCO	24 SAG	23 CAP	25 PIS	24 ARI	26 GEM	24 CAN	24 VIR	24 LIB	25 SAG	25 CAP
27 SCO	26 SAG	27 CAP	26 AQU	28 ARI	26 TAU	28 CAN	26 LEO	26 LIB	26 SCO	27 CAP	27 AQU
29 SAG	28 CAP	29 AQU	28 PIS	30 TAU	28 GEM	30 LEO	28 VIR	29 SCO	29 SAG	30 AQU	30 PIS
			30 ARI		30 CAN		30 LIB		31 CAP		

2001

JAN	FEB	MAR	APR	MAY	JUN	JUL	AUG	SEP	OCT	NOV	DEC
1 ARI	2 GEM	1 GEM	2 LEO	1 VIR	2 SCO	1 SAG	3 AQU	1 PIS	1 ARI	2 GEM	2 CAN
4 TAU	4 CAN	4 CAN	4 VIR	3 LIB	4 SAG	4 CAP	5 PIS	4 ARI	4 TAU	4 CAN	4 LEO
6 GEM	6 LEO	6 LEO	6 LIB	6 SCO	7 CAP	6 AQU	8 ARI	6 TAU	6 GEM	7 LEO	6 VIR
8 CAN	8 VIR	8 VIR	8 SCO	8 SAG	9 AQU	9 PIS	10 TAU	9 GEM	8 CAN	9 VIR	8 LIB
10 LEO	10 LIB	10 LIB	10 SAG	10 CAP	11 PIS	11 ARI	12 GEM	11 CAN	10 LEO	11 LIB	10 SCO
12 VIR	12 SCO	12 SCO	13 CAP	13 AQU	14 ARI	14 TAU	15 CAN	13 LEO	13 VIR	13 SCO	12 SAG
14 LIB	15 SAG	14 SAG	15 AQU	15 PIS	16 TAU	16 GEM	17 LEO	15 VIR	15 LIB	15 SAG	15 CAP
16 SCO	17 CAP	16 CAP	18 PIS	18 ARI	19 GEM	18 CAN	19 VIR	17 LIB	17 SCO	17 CAP	17 AQU
18 SAG	20 AQU	19 AQU	20 ARI	20 TAU	21 CAN	20 LEO	21 LIB	19 SCO	19 SAG	20 AQU	20 PIS
21 CAP	22 PIS	22 PIS	23 TAU	22 GEM	23 LEO	22 VIR	23 SCO	21 SAG	22 CAP	22 PIS	22 ARI
23 AQU	25 ARI	24 ARI	25 GEM	24 CAN	25 VIR	24 LIB	25 SAG	24 CAP	23 AQU	25 ARI	25 TAU
26 PIS	27 TAU	26 TAU	27 CAN	27 LEO	27 LIB	26 SCO	27 CAP	26 AQU	26 PIS	27 TAU	27 GEM
28 ARI		29 GEM	29 LEO	29 VIR	29 SCO	29 SAG	30 AQU	29 PIS	28 ARI	30 GEM	29 CAN
31 TAU		31 CAN		31 LIB		31 CAP			31 TAU		31 LEO

2002

JAN	FEB	MAR	APR	MAY	JUN	JUL	AUG	SEP	OCT	NOV	DEC
2 VIR	1 LIB	2 SCO	1 SAG	2 AQU	1 PIS	1 ARI	2 GEM	1 CAN	1 LEO	1 LIB	1 SCO
4 LIB	3 SCO	4 SAG	3 CAP	5 PIS	4 ARI	4 TAU	5 CAN	3 LEO	3 VIR	3 SCO	3 SAG
6 SCO	5 SAG	6 CAP	5 AQU	7 ARI	6 TAU	6 GEM	7 LEO	5 VIR	5 LIB	5 SAG	5 CAP
9 SAG	7 CAP	9 AQU	8 PIS	10 TAU	9 GEM	8 CAN	9 VIR	7 LIB	7 SCO	7 CAP	7 AQU
11 CAP	10 AQU	11 PIS	10 ARI	12 GEM	11 CAN	11 LEO	11 LIB	9 SCO	9 SAG	10 AQU	9 PIS
13 AQU	12 PIS	14 ARI	13 TAU	15 CAN	13 LEO	13 VIR	13 SCO	12 SAG	11 CAP	12 PIS	12 ARI
16 PIS	15 ARI	16 TAU	15 GEM	17 LEO	15 VIR	15 LIB	15 SAG	14 CAP	13 AQU	15 ARI	14 TAU
18 ARI	17 TAU	19 GEM	18 CAN	19 VIR	18 LIB	17 SCO	18 CAP	16 AQU	16 PIS	17 TAU	17 GEM
21 TAU	20 GEM	21 CAN	20 LEO	21 LIB	20 SCO	19 SAG	20 AQU	19 PIS	18 ARI	20 GEM	19 CAN
23 GEM	22 CAN	24 LEO	22 VIR	23 SCO	22 SAG	21 CAP	22 PIS	21 ARI	21 TAU	22 CAN	22 LEO
26 CAN	24 LEO	26 VIR	24 LIB	25 SAG	24 CAP	24 AQU	25 ARI	24 TAU	23 GEM	24 LEO	24 VIR
28 LEO	26 VIR	28 LIB	26 SCO	28 CAP	26 AQU	26 PIS	27 TAU	26 GEM	26 CAN	27 VIR	26 LIB
30 VIR	28 LIB	30 SCO	28 SAG	30 AQU	29 PIS	28 ARI	30 GEM	29 CAN	28 LEO	29 LIB	28 SCO
			30 CAP			31 TAU			30 VIR		30 SAG

2003

JAN	FEB	MAR	APR	MAY	JUN	JUL	AUG	SEP	OCT	NOV	DEC
1 CAP	2 PIS	1 PIS	3 TAU	2 GEM	1 CAN	1 LEO	2 LIB	2 SAG	1 CAP	2 PIS	2 ARI
3 AQU	5 ARI	4 ARI	5 GEM	5 CAN	4 LEO	3 VIR	4 SCO	4 CAP	4 AQU	5 ARI	4 TAU
6 PIS	7 TAU	6 TAU	8 CAN	7 LEO	6 VIR	5 LIB	6 SAG	6 AQU	6 PIS	7 TAU	6 GEM
8 ARI	10 GEM	9 GEM	10 LEO	10 VIR	8 LIB	7 SCO	8 CAP	8 PIS	8 ARI	10 GEM	9 CAN
11 TAU	12 CAN	11 CAN	12 VIR	12 LIB	10 SCO	10 SAG	10 AQU	11 ARI	11 TAU	12 CAN	12 LEO
13 GYM	14 LEO	14 LEO	14 LIB	14 SCO	12 SAG	12 CAP	12 PIS	13 TAU	13 GEM	15 LEO	14 VIR
16 CAN	16 VIR	16 VIR	16 SCO	16 SAG	14 CAP	14 AQU	15 ARI	16 GEM	16 CAN	17 VIR	16 LIB
18 LEO	18 LIB	18 LIB	18 SAG	18 CAP	16 AQU	16 PIS	17 TAU	18 CAN	18 LEO	19 LIB	19 SCO
20 VIR	21 SCO	20 SCO	20 CAP	20 AQU	19 PIS	18 ARI	20 GEM	21 LEO	21 VIR	21 SCO	21 SAG
22 LIB	23 SAG	22 SAG	23 AQU	22 PIS	21 ARI	21 TAU	22 CAN	22 VIR	23 LIB	23 SAG	23 CAP
24 SCO	25 CAP	24 CAP	25 PIS	25 ARI	23 TAU	23 GEM	24 LEO	25 LIB	25 SCO	25 CAP	25 AQU
26 SAG	27 AQU	26 AQU	27 ARI	27 TAU	26 GEM	26 CAN	27 VIR	27 SCO	27 SAG	27 AQU	27 PIS
29 CAP		29 PIS	30 TAU	30 GEM	28 CAN	28 LEO	29 LIB	29 SAG	29 CAP	29 PIS	29 ARI
31 AQU		31 ARI				30 VIR	31 SCO		31 AQU		

2004

JAN	FEB	MAR	APR	MAY	JUN	JUL	AUG	SEP	OCT	NOV	DEC
1 TAU	2 CAN	3 LEO	1 VIR	1 LIB	2 SAG	1 CAP	1 PIS	2 TAU	2 GEM	1 CAN	1 LEO
3 CEM	4 LEO	5 VIR	4 LIB	3 SCO	4 CAP	3 AQU	4 ARI	5 GEM	5 CAN	3 LEO	3 VIR
6 CAN	7 VIR	7 LIB	6 SCO	5 SAG	6 AQU	5 PIS	6 TAU	7 CAN	7 LEO	6 VIR	6 LIB
8 LEO	9 LIB	9 SCO	9 SAG	7 CAP	8 PIS	7 ARI	8 GEM	10 LEO	10 VIR	8 LIB	8 SCO
10 VIR	11 SCO	12 SAG	10 CAP	9 AQU	10 ARI	10 TAU	11 CAN	12 VIR	12 LIB	10 SCO	10 SAG
13 LIB	13 SAG	14 CAP	12 AQU	11 PIS	12 TAU	12 GEM	13 LEO	14 LIB	14 SCO	13 SAG	12 CAP
15 SCO	15 CAP	16 AQU	14 PIS	14 ARI	15 GEM	15 CAN	16 VIR	16 SCO	16 SAG	15 CAP	14 AQU
17 SAG	17 AQU	18 PIS	16 ARI	16 TAU	17 CAN	17 LEO	18 LIB	19 SAG	18 CAP	17 AQU	16 PIS
19 CAP	20 PIS	20 ARI	19 TAU	19 GEM	20 LEO	20 VIR	20 SCO	21 CAP	20 AQU	19 PIS	19 ARI
21 AQU	22 ARI	23 TAU	21 GEM	21 CAN	22 VIR	22 LIB	23 SAG	23 AQU	23 PIS	21 ARI	21 TAU
23 PIS	24 TAU	25 GEM	24 CAN	24 LEO	25 LIB	24 SCO	25 CAP	25 PIS	25 ARI	23 TAU	23 GEM
25 ARI	27 GEM	28 CAN	26 LEO	26 VIR	27 SCO	26 SAG	27 AQU	27 ARI	27 TAU	26 GEM	25 CAN
28 TAU	29 CAN	30 LEO	29 VIR	28 LIB	29 SAG	28 CAP	29 PIS	30 TAU	29 GEM	28 CAN	28 LEO
30 GEM				31 SCO		30 AQU	31 ARI				31 VIR

2005

JAN	FEB	MAR	APR	MAY	JUN	JUL	AUG	SEP	OCT	NOV	DEC
2 LIB	1 SCO	2 SAG	3 AQU	2 PIS	3 TAU	2 GEM	1 CAN	2 VIR	2 LIB	1 SCO	2 CAP
4 SCO	3 SAG	4 CAP	5 PIS	5 ARI	5 GEM	5 CAN	3 LEO	5 LIB	4 SCO	3 SAG	4 AQU
6 SAG	5 CAP	6 AQU	7 ARI	7 TAU	7 CAN	7 LEO	6 VIR	7 SCO	7 SAG	5 CAP	7 PIS
8 CAP	7 AQU	8 PIS	9 TAU	9 GEM	10 LEO	10 VIR	8 LIB	9 SAG	9 CAP	7 AQU	9 ARI
10 AQU	9 PIS	10 ARI	11 GEM	11 CAN	12 VIR	12 LIB	11 SCO	11 CAP	11 AQU	9 PIS	11 TAU
12 PIS	11 ARI	13 TAU	14 CAN	14 LEO	15 LIB	15 SCO	13 SAG	14 AQU	13 PIS	11 ARI	13 GEM
15 ARI	13 TAU	15 GEM	16 LEO	16 VIR	17 SCO	17 SAG	15 CAP	16 PIS	15 ARI	14 TAU	15 CAN
17 TAU	15 GEM	17 CAN	19 VIR	18 LIB	19 SAG	19 CAP	17 AQU	18 ARI	17 TAU	16 GEM	18 LEO
19 GEM	18 CAN	20 LEO	21 LIB	21 SCO	21 CAP	21 AQU	19 PIS	20 TAU	19 GEM	18 CAN	20 VIR
22 CAN	21 LEO	22 VIR	23 SCO	23 SAG	23 AQU	23 PIS	21 ARI	22 GEM	22 CAN	21 LEO	23 LIB
24 LEO	23 VIR	25 LIB	25 SAG	25 CAP	25 PIS	25 ARI	24 TAU	24 CAN	24 LEO	23 VIR	25 SCO
27 VIR	25 LIB	27 SCO	28 CAP	27 AQU	28 ARI	27 TAU	26 GEM	27 LEO	27 VIR	26 LIB	28 SAG
29 LIB	28 SCO	29 SAG	30 AQU	29 PIS	30 TAU	29 GEM	28 CAN	29 VIR	29 LIB	28 SCO	30 CAP
		31 CAP		31 ARI			31 LEO			30 SAG	

2006

JAN	FEB	MAR	APR	MAY	JUN	JUL	AUG	SEP	OCT	NOV	DEC
1 AQU	1 ARI	1 ARI	1 GEM	1 CAN	2 VIR	2 LIB	1 SCO	2 CAP	1 AQU	2 ARI	1 TAU
3 PIS	3 TAU	3 TAU	3 CAN	3 LEO	5 LIB	5 SCO	3 SAG	4 AQU	4 PIS	4 TAU	3 GEM
5 ARI	6 GEM	5 GEM	6 LEO	6 VIR	7 SCO	7 SAG	6 CAP	6 PIS	6 ARI	6 GEM	6 CAN
7 TAU	8 CAN	7 CAN	8 VIR	8 LIB	9 SAG	9 CAP	8 AQU	8 ARI	8 TAU	8 CAN	8 LEO
9 GEM	10 LEO	10 LEO	11 LIB	11 SCO	12 CAP	11 AQU	10 PIS	10 TAU	10 GEM	10 LEO	10 VIR
12 CAN	13 VIR	12 VIR	14 SCO	13 SAG	14 AQU	13 PIS	12 ARI	12 GEM	12 CAN	13 VIR	13 LIB
14 LEO	16 LIB	15 LIB	16 SAG	15 CAP	16 PIS	15 ARI	14 TAU	14 CAN	14 LEO	15 LIB	15 SCO
17 VIR	18 SCO	17 SCO	18 CAP	18 AQU	18 ARI	17 TAU	16 GEM	17 LEO	17 VIR	18 SCO	18 SAG
19 LIB	20 SAG	20 SAG	20 AQU	20 PIS	20 TAU	20 GEM	18 CAN	19 VIR	19 LIB	20 SAG	20 CAP
22 SCO	23 CAP	22 CAP	23 PIS	22 ARI	22 GEM	22 CAN	21 LEO	22 LIB	22 SCO	23 CAP	22 AQU
24 SAG	25 AQU	24 AQU	25 ARI	24 TAU	25 CAN	24 LEO	23 VIR	24 SCO	24 SAG	25 AQU	24 PIS
26 CAP	27 PIS	26 PIS	27 TAU	26 GEM	27 LEO	27 VIR	26 LIB	27 SAG	26 CAP	27 PIS	27 ARI
28 AQU		28 ARI	29 GEM	28 CAN	29 VIR	29 LIB	28 SCO	29 CAP	29 AQU	29 ARI	29 TAU
30 PIS		30 TAU		31 LEO			31 SAG		31 PIS		31 GEM

2007

JAN	FEB	MAR	APR	MAY	JUN	JUL	AUG	SEP	OCT	NOV	DEC
2 CAN	1 LEO	2 VIR	1 LIB	1 SCO	2 CAP	2 AQU	2 ARI	1 TAU	2 CAN	3 VIR	3 LIB
4 LEO	3 VIR	5 LIB	3 SCO	3 SAG	4 AQU	4 PIS	4 TAU	3 GEM	4 LEO	5 LIB	5 SCO
7 VIR	5 LIB	7 SCO	6 SAG	6 CAP	7 PIS	6 ARI	6 GEM	5 CAN	7 VIR	8 SCO	8 SAG
9 LIB	8 SCO	10 SAG	8 CAP	8 AQU	9 ARI	8 TAU	9 CAN	7 LEO	9 LIB	10 SAG	10 CAP
12 SCO	10 SAG	12 CAP	11 AQU	10 PIS	11 TAU	10 GEM	11 LEO	9 VIR	12 SCO	13 CAP	13 AQU
14 SAG	13 CAP	14 AQU	13 PIS	12 ARI	13 GEM	12 CAN	13 VIR	12 LIB	14 SAG	15 AQU	15 PIS
16 CAP	15 AQU	17 PIS	15 ARI	14 TAU	14 CAN	14 LEO	15 LIB	14 SCO	17 CAP	18 PIS	17 ARI
19 AQU	17 PIS	19 ARI	17 TAU	16 GEM	17 LEO	17 VIR	18 SCO	17 SAG	19 AQU	20 ARI	19 TAU
21 PIS	19 ARI	21 TAU	19 GEM	18 CAN	19 VIR	19 LIB	20 SAG	19 CAP	21 PIS	22 TAU	21 GEM
23 ARI	21 TAU	23 GEM	21 CAN	21 LEO	22 LIB	22 SCO	23 CAP	21 AQU	23 ARI	24 GEM	23 CAN
25 TAU	23 GEM	25 CAN	23 LEO	23 VIR	24 SCO	24 SAG	25 AQU	24 PIS	25 TAU	26 CAN	25 LEO
27 GEM	25 CAN	27 LEO	26 VIR	25 LIB	27 SAG	27 CAP	27 PIS	26 ARI	27 GEM	28 LEO	27 VIR
29 CAN	28 LEO	29 VIR	28 LIB	28 SCO	29 CAP	29 AQU	29 ARI	28 TAU	29 CAN	30 VIR	30 LIB
				31 SAG		31 PIS		30 GEM	31 LEO		

2008

JAN	FEB	MAR	APR	MAY	JUN	JUL	AUG	SEP	OCT	NOV	DEC
1 SCO	3 CAP	1 CAP	2 PIS	2 ARI	2 GEM	2 CAN	2 VIR	1 LIB	3 SAG	2 CAP	2 AQU
4 SAG	5 AQU	3 AQU	4 ARI	4 TAU	4 CAN	4 LEO	5 LIB	3 SCO	5 CAP	5 AQU	4 PIS
6 CAP	7 PIS	6 PIS	6 TAU	6 GEM	6 LEO	6 VIR	7 SCO	6 SAG	8 AQU	7 PIS	6 ARI
9 AQU	10 ARI	8 ARI	8 GEM	8 CAN	8 VIR	8 LIB	9 SAG	8 CAP	10 PIS	9 ARI	9 TAU
11 PIS	12 TAU	10 TAU	10 CAN	10 LEO	11 LIB	10 SCO	12 CAP	11 AQU	13 ARI	11 TAU	11 GEM
13 ARI	14 GEM	12 GEM	12 LEO	12 VIR	13 SCO	13 SAG	14 AQU	13 PIS	15 TAU	13 GEM	13 CAN
15 TAU	16 CAN	14 CAN	15 VIR	14 LIB	15 SAG	15 CAP	17 PIS	15 ARI	17 GEM	15 CAN	15 LEO
18 GEM	18 LEO	16 LEO	17 LIB	17 SCO	18 CAP	18 AQU	19 ARI	17 TAU	19 CAN	17 LEO	17 VIR
20 CAN	20 VIR	18 VIR	20 SCO	19 SAG	21 AQU	20 PIS	21 TAU	19 GEM	21 LEO	19 VIR	19 LIB
22 LEO	23 LIB	21 LIB	22 SAG	22 CAP	23 PIS	23 ARI	23 GEM	22 CAN	23 VIR	22 LIB	21 SCO
24 VIR	25 SCO	23 SCO	25 CAP	25 AQU	25 ARI	25 TAU	25 CAN	24 LEO	25 LIB	24 SCO	24 SAG
26 LIB	28 SAG	26 SAG	27 AQU	27 PIS	28 TAU	27 GEM	27 LEO	26 VIR	28 SCO	27 SAG	26 CAP
29 SCO		28 CAP	30 PIS	29 ARI	30 GEM	29 CAN	30 VIR	28 LIB	30 SAG	29 CAP	29 AQU
31 SAG		31 AQU		31 TAU		31 LEO		30 SCO			31 PIS

2009

JAN	FEB	MAR	APR	MAY	JUN	JUL	AUG	SEP	OCT	NOV	DEC
3 ARI	1 TAU	3 GEM	1 CAN	2 VIR	1 LIB	3 SAG	2 CAP	3 PIS	3 ARI	1 TAU	1 GEM
5 TAU	3 GEM	5 CAN	3 LEO	5 LIB	3 SCO	5 CAP	4 AQU	5 ARI	5 TAU	4 GEM	3 CAN
7 GEM	5 CAN	7 LEO	5 VIR	7 SCO	6 SAG	7 AQU	7 PIS	8 TAU	7 GEM	6 CAN	5 LEO
9 CAN	7 LEO	9 VIR	7 LIB	9 SAG	8 CAP	10 PIS	9 ARI	10 GEM	9 CAN	8 LEO	7 VIR
11 LEO	10 VIR	11 LIB	10 SCO	12 CAP	10 AQU	13 ARI	11 TAU	12 CAN	11 LEO	10 VIR	9 LIB
13 VIR	12 LIB	13 SCO	12 SAG	14 AQU	13 PIS	15 TAU	14 GEM	14 LEO	14 VIR	12 LIB	11 SCO
15 LIB	14 SCO	16 SAG	15 CAP	17 PIS	16 ARI	17 GEM	16 CAN	16 VIR	16 LIB	14 SCO	14 SAG
18 SCO	16 SAG	18 CAP	17 AQU	19 ARI	18 TAU	18 CAN	18 LEO	18 LIB	18 SCO	17 SAG	16 CAP
20 SAG	19 CAP	21 AQU	20 PIS	21 TAU	20 GEM	21 LEO	20 VIR	20 SCO	20 SAG	19 CAP	19 AQU
23 CAP	21 AQU	23 PIS	23 ARI	23 GEM	22 CAN	22 VIR	22 LIB	23 SAG	23 CAP	22 AQU	21 PIS
25 AQU	24 PIS	26 ARI	24 TAU	25 CAN	24 LEO	24 LIB	24 SCO	25 CAP	25 AQU	24 PIS	24 ARI
28 PIS	26 ARI	28 TAU	26 GEM	28 LEO	26 VIR	26 SCO	26 SAG	28 AQU	28 PIS	26 ARI	26 TAU
30 ARI	28 TAU	30 GEM	28 CAN	30 VIR	28 LIB	30 SAG	29 CAP	30 PIS	30 ARI	29 TAU	28 GEM
			30 LEO		30 SCO		31 AQU				30 CAN

2010

JAN	FEB	MAR	APR	MAY	JUN	JUL	AUG	SEP	OCT	NOV	DEC
2 LEO	2 LIB	2 LIB	2 SAG	2 CAP	1 AQU	1 PIS	2 TAU	1 GEM	2 LEO	1 VIR	2 SCO
4 VIR	4 SCO	4 SCO	5 CAP	4 AQU	3 PIS	3 ARI	4 GEM	3 CAN	4 VIR	3 LIB	4 SAG
6 LIB	7 SAG	6 SAG	7 AQU	7 PIS	6 ARI	6 TAU	6 CAN	5 LEO	6 LIB	5 SCO	6 CAP
8 SCO	9 CAP	8 CAP	10 PIS	9 ARI	8 TAU	8 GEM	8 LEO	7 VIR	8 SCO	7 SAG	9 AQU
10 SAG	11 AQU	11 AQU	12 ARI	12 TAU	10 GEM	10 CAN	10 VIR	9 LIB	10 SAG	9 CAP	11 PIS
13 CAP	14 PIS	13 PIS	14 TAU	14 GEM	13 CAN	12 LEO	12 LIB	11 SCO	13 CAP	11 AQU	14 ARI
15 AQU	16 ARI	16 ARI	17 GEM	16 CAN	15 LEO	14 VIR	14 SCO	13 SAG	15 AQU	14 PIS	16 TAU
18 PIS	19 TAU	18 TAU	19 CAN	18 LEO	17 VIR	16 LIB	16 SAG	15 CAP	18 PIS	16 ARI	19 GEM
20 ARI	21 GEM	21 GEM	21 LEO	20 VIR	19 LIB	18 SCO	19 CAP	17 AQU	20 ARI	19 TAU	21 CAN
23 TAU	23 CAN	23 CAN	23 VIR	23 LIB	21 SCO	20 SAG	22 AQU	20 PIS	23 TAU	21 GEM	23 LEO
25 GEM	26 LEO	25 LEO	25 LIB	25 SCO	23 SAG	23 CAP	24 PIS	23 ARI	25 GEM	24 CAN	25 VIR
27 CAN	28 VIR	27 VIR	27 SCO	27 SAG	26 CAP	25 AQU	27 ARI	25 TAU	27 CAN	26 LEO	27 LIB
29 LEO		29 LIB	30 SAG	29 CAP	28 AQU	28 PIS	29 TAU	28 GEM	30 LEO	28 VIR	29 SCO
31 VIR		31 SCO				30 ARI		30 CAN		30 LIB	

2011

JAN	FEB	MAR	APR	MAY	JUN	JUL	AUG	SEP	OCT	NOV	DEC
1 SAG	1 AQU	1 AQU	2 ARI	2 TAU	3 CAN	2 LEO	1 VIR	1 SCO	1 SAG	1 AQU	1 PIS
3 CAP	4 PIS	3 PIS	4 TAU	4 GEM	5 LEO	5 VIR	3 LIB	3 SAG	3 CAP	4 PIS	4 ARI
5 AQU	6 ARI	6 ARI	7 GEM	7 CAN	7 VIR	7 LIB	5 SCO	6 CAP	5 AQU	6 ARI	6 TAU
8 PIS	9 TAU	8 TAU	9 CAN	9 LEO	9 LIB	9 SCO	8 SAG	8 AQU	8 PIS	9 TAU	9 GEM
10 ARI	11 GEM	11 GEM	12 LEO	11 VIR	12 SCO	11 SAG	9 CAP	10 PIS	10 ARI	11 GEM	11 CAN
13 TAU	14 CAN	13 CAN	14 VIR	13 LIB	14 SAG	13 CAP	12 AQU	13 ARI	13 TAU	14 CAN	13 LEO
15 GEM	16 LEO	15 LEO	16 LIB	15 SCO	16 CAP	15 AQU	14 PIS	15 TAU	15 GEM	16 LEO	16 VIR
17 CAN	18 VIR	17 VIR	18 SCO	17 SAG	18 AQU	18 PIS	17 ARI	18 GEM	18 CAN	18 VIR	18 LIB
19 LEO	20 LIB	19 LIB	20 SAG	19 CAP	20 PIS	20 ARI	19 TAU	20 CAN	20 LEO	20 LIB	20 SCO
21 VIR	22 SCO	21 SCO	22 CAP	22 AQU	23 ARI	23 TAU	22 GEM	23 LEO	22 VIR	23 SCO	22 SAG
23 LIB	24 SAG	23 SAG	24 AQU	24 PIS	25 TAU	25 GEM	24 CAN	25 VIR	24 LIB	25 SAG	24 CAP
26 SCO	26 CAP	26 CAP	27 PIS	27 ARI	28 GEM	28 CAN	26 LEO	27 LIB	26 SCO	27 CAP	26 AQU
28 SAG		28 AQU	29 ARI	29 TAU	30 CAN	30 LEO	28 VIR	29 SCO	28 SAG	29 AQU	28 PIS
30 CAP		30 PIS		31 GEM			30 LIB		30 CAP		31 ARI

2012

JAN	FEB	MAR	APR	MAY	JUN	JUL	AUG	SEP	OCT	NOV	DEC
2 TAU	1 GEM	2 CAN	1 LEO	3 LIB	1 SCO	2 CAP	1 AQU	2 ARI	1 TAU	3 CAN	3 LEO
5 GEM	4 CAN	4 LEO	3 VIR	5 SCO	3 SAG	4 AQU	3 PIS	4 TAU	4 GEM	5 LEO	5 VIR
7 CAN	6 LEO	7 VIR	5 LIB	7 SAG	5 CAP	7 PIS	5 ARI	7 GEM	7 CAN	8 VIR	7 LIB
10 LEO	8 VIR	9 LIB	7 SCO	9 CAP	7 AQU	9 ARI	08 TAU	9 CAN	9 LEO	10 LIB	9 SCO
12 VIR	10 LIB	11 SCO	9 SAG	11 AQU	9 PIS	11 TAU	10 GEM	12 LEO	11 VIR	12 SCO	11 SAG
14 LIB	12 SCO	13 SAG	11 CAP	13 PIS	12 ARI	14 GEM	13 CAN	14 VIR	13 LIB	14 SAG	13 CAP
16 SCO	15 SAG	15 CAP	13 AQU	15 ARI	14 TAU	17 CAN	15 LEO	16 LIB	16 SCO	16 CAP	15 AQU
18 SAG	17 CAP	17 AQU	16 PIS	18 TAU	17 GEM	19 LEO	18 VIR	18 SCO	18 SAG	18 AQU	18 PIS
20 CAP	19 AQU	20 PIS	18 ARI	20 GEM	19 CAN	21 VIR	20 LIB	20 SAG	20 CAP	20 PIS	20 ARI
23 AQU	21 PIS	22 ARI	21 TAU	23 CAN	22 LEO	23 LIB	22 SCO	22 CAP	22 AQU	23 ARI	22 TAU
25 PIS	24 ARI	24 TAU	23 GEM	25 LEO	24 VIR	26 SCO	24 SAG	24 AQU	24 PIS	25 TAU	25 GEM
27 ARI	26 TAU	27 GEM	26 CAN	28 VIR	26 LIB	28 SAG	26 CAP	27 PIS	26 ARI	28 GEM	27 CAN
30 TAU	29 GEM	29 CAN	28 LEO	30 LIB	28 SCO	30 CAP	28 AQU	29 ARI	29 TAU	30 CAN	30 LEO
			30 VIR		30 SAG		30 PIS		31 GEM		

HOW TO FIND THE VENUS SIGN

Under the year of your birth, find the birth date. If your birth was on the first or last day of a particular time period, it's possible that Venus might be posted in a preceding or following sign. For example, if the time period is from August 6 to September 10, and your birth occurred on September 10, then Venus might be in the next sign. The only way to be absolutely sure is to have a chart done professionally or by a computer service. If you are unsure, read the adjacent sign to decide which is more applicable.

1990

Jan 1 – Jan 16	AQU
Jan 17 – Mar 3	CAP
Mar 4 – Apr 5	AQU
Apr 6 – May 3	PIS
May 4 – May 29	ARI
May 30 – Jun 24	TAU
Jun 25 – Jul 19	GEM
Jul 20 – Aug 13	CAN
Aug 14 – Sep 6	LEO
Sep 7 – Sep 30	VIR
Oct 1 – Oct 24	LIB
Oct 25 – Nov 17	SCO
Nov 18 – Dec 11	SAG
Dec 12 – Dec 31	CAP

1991

Jan 1 – Jan 4	CAP
Jan 5 – Jan 28	AQU
Jan 29 – Feb 21	PIS
Feb 22 – Mar 18	ARI
Mar 19 – Apr 12	TAU
Apr 13 – May 8	GEM
May 9 – Jun 5	CAN
Jun 6 – Jul 10	LEO
Jul 11 – Aug 21	VIR
Aug 22 – Oct 6	LEO
Oct 7 – Nov 8	VIR
Nov 9 – Dec 5	LIB
Dec 6 – Dec 31	SCO

1992

Jan 1 – Jan 24	SAG
Jan 25 – Feb 18	CAP
Feb 19 – Mar 13	AQU
Mar 14 – Apr 6	PIS
Apr 7 – May 1	ARI
May 2 – May 25	TAU
May 26 – Jun 18	GEM
Jun 19 – Jul 13	CAN
Jul 14 – Aug 6	LEO
Aug 7 – Aug 31	VIR
Sep 1 – Sep 24	LIB
Sep 25 – Oct 19	SCO
Oct 20 – Nov 13	SAG
Nov 14 – Dec 8	CAP
Dec 9 – Dec 31	AQU

1993

Jan 1 – Jan 3	AQU
Jan 4 – Feb 2	PIS
Feb 3 – Jun 5	ARI
Jun 6 – Jul 5	TAU
Jul 6 – Aug 1	GEM
Aug 2 – Aug 27	CAN
Aug 28 – Sep 21	LEO
Sep 22 – Oct 15	VIR
Oct 16 – Nov 8	LIB
Nov 9 – Dec 2	SCO
Dec 3 – Dec 26	SAG
Dec 27 – Dec 31	CAP

1994

Jan 1 – Jan 19	CAP
Jan 20 – Feb 12	AQU
Feb 13 – Mar 8	PIS
Mar 9 – Apr 1	ARI
Apr 2 – Apr 25	TAU
Apr 26 – May 20	GEM
May 21 – Jun 14	CAN
Jun 15 – Jul 10	LEO
Jul 11 – Aug 7	VIR
Aug 8 – Sep 7	LIB
Sep 8 – Dec 31	SCO

1995

Jan 1 – Jan 7	SCO
Jan 8 – Feb 4	SAG
Feb 5 – Mar 2	CAP
Mar 3 – Mar 27	AQU
Mar 28 – Apr 21	PIS
Apr 22 – May 16	ARI
May 17 – Jun 10	TAU
Jun 11 – Jul 4	GEM
Jul 5 – Jul 29	CAN
Jul 30 – Aug 22	LEO
Aug 23 – Sep 15	VIR
Sep 16 – Oct 9	LIB
Oct 10 – Nov 2	SCO
Nov 3 – Nov 27	SAG
Nov 28 – Dec 21	CAP
Dec 22 – Dec 31	AQU

1996

Jan 1 – Jan 14	AQU
Jan 15 – Feb 8	PIS
Feb 9 – Mar 5	ARI
Mar 6 – Apr 3	TAU
Apr 4 – Aug 6	GEM
Aug 7 – Sep 6	CAN
Sep 7 – Oct 3	LEO
Oct 4 – Oct 28	VIR
Oct 29 – Nov 22	LIB
Nov 23 – Dec 16	SCO
Dec 17 – Dec 31	SAG

1997

Jan 1 – Jan 9	SAG
Jan 10 – Feb 2	CAP
Feb 3 – Feb 26	AQU
Feb 27 – Mar 22	PIS
Mar 23 – Apr 15	ARI
Apr 16 – May 10	TAU
May 11 – Jun 3	GEM
Jun 4 – Jun 28	CAN
Jun 29 – Jul 23	LEO
Jul 24 – Aug 17	VIR
Aug 18 – Sep 11	LIB
Sep 12 – Oct 7	SCO
Oct 8 – Nov 4	SAG
Nov 5 – Dec 11	CAP
Dec 12 – Dec 31	AQU

1998

Jan 1 – Jan 9	AQU
Jan 10 – Mar 4	CAP
Mar 5 – Apr 5	AQU
Apr 6 – May 3	PIS
May 4 – May 29	ARI
May 30 – Jun 24	TAU
Jun 25 – Jul 19	GEM
Jul 20 – Aug 12	CAN
Aug 13 – Sep 6	LEO
Sep 7 – Sep 30	VIR
Oct 1 – Oct 24	LIB
Oct 25 – Nov 17	SCO
Nov 18 – Dec 11	SAG
Dec 12 – Dec 31	CAP

1999

Jan 1 – Jan 4	CAP
Jan 5 – Jan 28	AQU
Jan 29 – Feb 21	PIS
Feb 22 – Mar 17	ARI
Mar 18 – Apr 12	TAU
Apr 13 – May 8	GEM
May 9 – Jun 5	CAN
Jun 6 – Jul 12	LEO
Jul 13 – Aug 15	VIR
Aug 16 – Oct 7	LEO
Oct 8 – Nov 8	VIR
Nov 9 – Dec 5	LIB
Dec 6 – Dec 30	SCO
Dec 31 – Dec 31	SAG

2000

Jan 1 – Jan 24	SAG
Jan 25 – Feb 17	CAP
Feb 18 – Mar 12	AQU
Mar 13 – Apr 6	PIS
Apr 7 – Apr 30	ARI
May 1 – May 25	TAU
May 26 – Jun 18	GEM
Jun 19 – Jul 12	CAN
Jul 13 – Aug 6	LEO
Aug 7 – Aug 30	VIR
Aug 31 – Sep 24	LIB
Sep 25 – Oct 18	SCO
Oct 19 – Nov 12	SAG
Nov 13 – Dec 7	CAP
Dec 8 – Dec 31	AQU

2001

Jan 1 – Jan 2	AQU
Jan 3 – Feb 1	PIS
Feb 2 – Jun 5	ARI
Jun 6 – Jul 4	TAU
Jul 5 – Jul 31	GEM
Aug 1 – Aug 25	CAN
Aug 26 – Sep 19	LEO
Sep 20 – Oct 14	VIR
Oct 15 – Nov 7	LIB
Nov 8 – Dec 1	SCO
Dec 2 – Dec 25	SAG
Dec 26 – Dec 31	CAP

2002

Jan 1 – Jan 17	CAP
Jan 18 – Feb 10	AQU
Feb 11 – Mar 6	PIS
Mar 7 – Mar 31	ARI
Apr 1 – Apr 24	TAU
Apr 25 – May 19	GEM
May 20 – Jun 13	CAN
Jun 14 – Jul 9	LEO
Jul 10 – Aug 6	VIR
Aug 7 – Sep 6	LIB
Sep 7 – Dec 31	SCO

2003

Jan 1 – Jan 6	SCO
Jan 7 – Feb 3	SAG
Feb 4 – Mar 1	CAP
Mar 2 – Mar 26	AQU
Mar 27 – Apr 20	PIS
Apr 21 – May 15	ARI
May 16 – Jun 8	TAU
Jun 9 – Jul 13	GEM
Jul 14 – Jul 27	CAN
Jul 28 – Aug 21	LEO
Aug 22 – Sep 14	VIR
Sep 15 – Oct 8	LIB
Oct 9 – Nov 1	SCO
Nov 2 – Nov 25	SAG
Nov 26 – Dec 20	CAP
Dec 21 – Dec 31	AQU

2004

Jan 1 – Jan 13	AQU
Jan 14 – Feb 7	PIS
Feb 8 – Mar 4	ARI
Mar 5 – Apr 2	TAU
Apr 3 – Aug 6	GEM
Aug 7 – Sep 5	CAN
Sep 6 – Oct 2	LEO
Oct 3 – Oct 27	VIR
Oct 28 – Nov 21	LIB
Nov 22 – Dec 15	SCO
Dec 16 – Dec 31	SAG

2005

Jan 1 – Jan 8	SAG
Jan 9 – Feb 1	CAP
Feb 2 – Feb 25	AQU
Feb 26 – Mar 21	PIS
Mar 22 – Apr 14	ARI
Apr 15 – May 8	TAU
May 9 – Jun 2	GEM
Jun 3 – Jun 27	CAN
Jun 28 – Jul 21	LEO
Jul 22 – Aug 15	VIR
Aug 16 – Sep 10	LIB
Sep 11 – Oct 6	SCO
Oct 7 – Nov 4	SAG
Nov 5 – Dec 14	CAP
Dec 15 – Dec 31	AQU

2006

Jan 1 – Mar 4	CAP
Mar 5 – Apr 4	AQU
Apr 5 – May 2	PIS
May 3 – May 28	ARI
May 29 – Jun 22	TAU
Jun 23 – Jul 17	GEM
Jul 18 – Aug 11	CAN
Aug 12 – Sep 5	LEO
Aug 6 – Sep 29	VIR
Sep 30 – Oct 23	LIB
Oct 24 – Nov 16	SCO
Nov 17 – Dec 10	SAG
Dec 11 – Dec 31	CAP

2007

Jan 1 – Jan 2	CAP
Jan 3 – Jan 26	AQU
Jan 27 – Feb 20	PIS
Feb 21 – Mar 16	ARI
Mar 17 – Apr 10	TAU
Apr 11 – May 7	GEM
May 8 – Jun 4	CAN
Jun 5 – Jul 13	LEO
Jul 14 – Aug 7	VIR
Aug 8 – Oct 7	LEO
Oct 8 – Nov 7	VIR
Nov 8 – Dec 4	LIB
Dec 5 – Dec 29	SCO
Dec 30 – Dec 31	SAG

2008

Jan 1 – Jan 23	SAG
Jan 24 – Feb 16	CAP
Feb 17 – Mar 11	AQU
Mar 12 – Apr 5	PIS
Apr 6 – Apr 29	ARI
Apr 30 – May 23	TAU
May 24 – Jun 17	GEM
Jun 18 – Jul 11	CAN
Jul 12 – Aug 4	LEO
Aug 5 – Aug 29	VIR
Aug 30 – Sep 22	LIB
Sep 23 – Oct 17	SCO
Oct 18 – Nov 11	SAG
Nov 12 – Dec 6	CAP
Dec 7 – Dec 31	AQU

2009

Jan 1 – Jan 2	AQU
Jan 3 – Feb 1	PIS
Feb 2 – Apr 10	ARI
Apr 11 – Apr 23	PIS
Apr 24 – Jun 5	ARI
Jun 6 – Jul 4	TAU
Jul 5 – Jul 30	GEM
Jul 31 – Aug 25	CAN
Aug 26 – Sep 19	LEO
Sep 20 – Oct 13	VIR
Oct 14 – Nov 6	LIB
Nov 7 – Nov 30	SCO
Dec 1 – Dec 24	SAG
Dec 25 – Dec 31	CAP

2010

Jan 1 – Jan 17	CAP
Jan 18 – Feb 10	AQU
Feb 11 – Mar 6	PIS
Mar 7 – Mar 30	ARI
Mar 31 – Apr 23	TAU
Apr 24 – May 18	GEM
May 19 – Jun 13	CAN
Jun 14 – Jul 9	LEO
Jul 10 – Aug 5	VIR
Aug 6 – Sep 7	LIB
Sep 8 – Nov 6	SCO
Nov 7 – Nov 28	LIB
Nov 29 – Dec 31	SCO

2011

Jan 1 – Jan 6	SCO
Jan 7 – Feb 3	SAG
Feb 4 – Mar 1	CAP
Mar 2 – Mar 26	AQU
Mar 27 – Apr 20	PIS
Apr 21 – May 14	ARI
May 15 – Jun 8	TAU
Jun 9 – Jul 3	GEM
Jul 4 – Jul 27	CAN
Jul 28 – Aug 20	LEO
Aug 21 – Sep 14	VIR
Sep 15 – Oct 9	LIB
Oct 09 – Nov 1	SCO
Nov 02 – Nov 25	SAG
Nov 26 – Dec 19	CAP
Dec 20 – Dec 31	AQU

2012

Jan 1 – Jan 13	AQU
Jan 14 – Feb 7	PIS
Feb 8 – Mar 4	ARI
Mar 5 – Apr 2	TAU
Apr 3 – Aug 6	GEM
Aug 7 – Sep 5	CAN
Sep 6 – Oct 2	LEO
Oct 3 – Oct 27	VIR
Oct 28 – Nov 21	LIB
Nov 22 – Dec 15	SCO
Dec 16 – Dec 32	SAG

HOW TO FIND THE MARS SIGN

Under the year of your birth, find the birth date. If your birth was on the first or last day of a particular period, it's possible that Mars might be placed in the preceding or following sign. The only way to be absolutely sure is to have a chart done by a computer service or by a professional astrologer. In lieu of this, read the text for both signs, to decide which seems more applicable.

1990

Jan 1 – Jan 29	SAG
Jan 30 – Mar 11	CAP
Mar 12 – Apr 20	AQU
Apr 21 – May 30	PIS
May 31 – Jul 12	ARI
Jul 13 – Aug 30	TAU
Aug 31 – Dec 13	GEM
Dec 14 – Dec 31	TAU

1991

Jan 1 – Jan 20	TAU
Jan 21 – Apr 2	GEM
Apr 3 – May 26	CAN
May 27 – Jul 15	LEO
Jul 16 – Aug 31	VIR
Sep 1 – Oct 16	LIB
Oct 17 – Nov 28	SCO
Nov 29 – Dec 31	SAG

1992

Jan 1 – Jan 8	SAG
Jan 9 – Feb 17	CAP
Feb 18 – Mar 27	AQU
Mar 28 – May 5	PIS
May 6 – Jun 14	ARI
Jun 15 – Jul 26	TAU
Jul 27 – Sep 11	GEM
Sep 12 – Dec 31	CAN

1993

Jan 1 – Apr 27	CAN
Apr 28 – Jun 22	LEO
Jun 23 – Aug 11	VIR
Aug 12 – Sep 26	LIB
Sep 27 – Nov 8	SCO
Nov 9 – Dec 19	SAG
Dec 20 – Dec 31	CAP

1994

Jan 1 – Jan 27	CAP
Jan 28 – Mar 6	AQU
Mar 7 – Apr 14	PIS
Apr 15 – May 23	ARI
May 24 – Jul 3	TAU
Jul 4 – Aug 16	GEM
Aug 17 – Oct 4	CAN
Oct 5 – Dec 11	LEO
Dec 12 – Dec 31	VIR

1995

Jan 1 – Jan 22	VIR
Jan 23 – Mar 25	LEO
Mar 26 – Jul 20	VIR
Jul 21 – Sep 6	LIB
Sep 7 – Oct 20	SCO
Oct 21 – Nov 30	SAG
Dec 1 – Dec 31	CAP

1996

Jan 1 – Jan 7	CAP
Jan 8 – Feb 14	AQU
Feb 15 – Mar 24	PIS
Mar 25 – May 2	ARI
May 3 – Jun 12	TAU
Jun 13 – Jul 25	GEM
Jul 26 – Sep 9	CAN
Sep 10 – Oct 29	LEO
Oct 30 – Dec 31	VIR

1997

Jan 1 – Jan 2	VIR
Jan 3 – Mar 8	LIB
Mar 9 – Jun 18	VIR
Jun 19 – Aug 13	LIB
Aug 14 – Sep 28	SCO
Sep 29 – Nov 8	SAG
Nov 9 – Dec 17	CAP
Dec 18 – Dec 31	AQU

1998

Jan 1 – Jan 24	AQU
Jan 25 – Mar 4	PIS
Mar 5 – Apr 12	ARI
Apr 13 – May 23	TAU
May 24 – Jul 5	GEM
Jul 6 – Aug 20	CAN
Aug 21 – Oct 7	LEO
Oct 8 – Nov 26	VIR
Nov 27 – Dec 31	LIB

1999

Jan 1 – Jan 25	LIB
Jan 26 – May 5	SCO
May 6 – Jul 4	LIB
Jul 5 – Sep 2	SCO
Sep 3 – Oct 16	SAG
Oct 17 – Nov 25	CAP
Nov 26 – Dec 31	AQU

2000

Jan 1 – Jan 3	AQU
Jan 4 – Feb 11	PIS
Feb 12 – Mar 22	ARI
Mar 23 – May 3	TAU
May 4 – Jun 16	GEM
Jun 17 – Jul 31	CAN
Aug 1 – Sep 16	LEO
Sep 17 – Nov 3	VIR
Nov 4 – Dec 23	LIB
Dec 24 – Dec 31	SCO

2001

Jan 1 – Feb 13	SCO
Feb 14 – Sep 7	SAG
Sep 8 – Oct 26	CAP
Oct 27 – Dec 7	AQU
Dec 8 – Dec 31	PIS

2002

Jan 1 – Jan 17	PIS
Jan 18 – Feb 28	ARI
Mar 1 – Apr 12	TAU
Apr 13 – May 27	GEM
May 28 – Jul 12	CAN
Jul 13 – Aug 28	LEO
Aug 29 – Oct 14	VIR
Oct 15 – Nov 30	LIB
Dec 1 – Dec 31	SCO

2003

Jan 1 – Jan 15	SCO
Jan 16 – Mar 3	SAG
Mar 4 – Apr 20	CAP
Apr 21 – Jun 15	AQU
Jun 16 – Dec 15	PIS
Dec 16 – Dec 31	ARI

2004

Jan 1 – Feb 2	ARI
Feb 3 – Mar 20	TAU
Mar 21 – May 6	GEM
May 7 – Jun 22	CAN
Jun 23 – Aug 9	LEO
Aug 10 – Sep 25	VIR
Sep 26 – Nov 9	LIB
Nov 10 – Dec 24	SCO
Dec 25 – Dec 31	SAG

2005

Jan 1 – Feb 5	SAG
Feb 6 – Mar 19	CAP
Mar 20 – Apr 29	AQU
Apr 30 – Jun 10	PIS
Jun 11 – Jul 26	ARI
Jul 27 – Dec 31	TAU

2006

Jan 1 – Feb 16	TAU
Feb 17 – Apr 13	GEM
Apr 14 – Jun 2	CAN
Jun 3 – Jul 21	LEO
Jul 22 – Sep 7	VIR
Sep 8 – Oct 22	LIB
Oct 23 – Dec 5	SCO
Dec 6 – Dec 31	SAG

2007

Jan 1 – Jan 15	SAG
Jan 16 – Feb 25	CAP
Feb 26 – Apr 5	AQU
Apr 6 – May 14	PIS
May 15 – Jun 23	ARI
Jun 24 – Aug 6	TAU
Aug 7 – Sep 27	GEM
Sep 28 – Dec 30	CAN
Dec 31	GEM

2008

Jan 1 – Mar3	GEM
Mar 4 – May 8	CAN
May 9 – Jun 30	LEO
Jul 1 – Aug 18	VIR
Aug 19 – Oct 3	LIB
Oct 4 – Nov 15	SCO
Nov 16 – Dec 26	SAG
Dec 27 – Dec 31	CAP

2009

Jan 1 – Feb 3	CAP
Feb 4 – Mar 14	AQU
Mar 15 – Apr 21	PIS
Apr 22 – May 30	ARI
May 31 – Jul 11	TAU
Jul 12 – Aug 24	GEM
Aug 25 – Oct 15	CAN
Oct 16 – Dec 31	LEO

2010

Jan 1 – Jun 6	LEO
Jun 7 – Jul 28	VIR
Jul 29 – Sep 13	LIB
Sep 14 – Oct 27	SCO
Oct 28 – Dec 6	SAG
Dec 7 – Dec 31	CAP

2011

Jan 1 – Jan 14	CAP
Jan 15 – Feb 22	AQU
Feb 23 – Apr 1	PIS
Apr 2 – May 10	ARI
May 11 – Jun 20	TAU
Jun 21 – Aug 2	GEM
Aug 3 – Sep 18	CAN
Sep 19 – Nov 10	LEO
Nov 11 – Dec 14	VIR

2012

Jan 1 – Jul 2	VIR
Jul 3 – Aug 22	LIB
Aug 23 – Oct 6	SCO
Oct 7 – Nov 16	SAG
Nov 17 – Dec 25	CAP
Dec 26 – Dec 31	AQU

FURTHER READING

My hope is that this book encourages you to go to your library and read other books on the Goddess and topics related to her. There are now dozens of these books available, many written by women. There are a couple of websites included in this list—follow your parents' rules for internet use.

Abadie, M. J. *Teen Astrology: The Ultimate Guide to Making Your Life Your Own*. Rochester, VT: Bindu Books, 2001.

Bell, Ruth. *Changing Bodies, Changing Lives*. 3rd ed. New York: Three Rivers Press, 1998.

Campbell, Joseph. *Occidental Mythology*. New York: Viking Penguin, 1991.

Columbia University's Health Education Program. *The "Go Ask Alice" Book of Answers*. New York: Holt Paperbacks, 1998.

Edelman, Hope. *Motherless Daughters: The Legacy of Loss*. 2nd ed. Da Capo Press, 2006.

Eisler, Riane. *The Chalice and the Blade: Our History, Our Future*. San Francisco: HarperOne, 1988.

Gadon, Elinor W. *The Once and Future Goddess: A Sweeping Visual Chronicle of the Sacred Female and Her Reemergence in the Cult*. New York: HarperCollins Publishers, 1989.

Hopman, Ellen Evert, and Lawrence Bond. *People of the Earth: The New Pagans Speak Out*. Rochester, VT: Inner Traditions, 1995.

Johnson, Buffie. *Lady of the Beasts: The Goddess and Her Sacred Animals*. 2nd ed. Rochester, VT: Inner Traditions, 1994.

Keller, Catherine. *From a Broken Web: Separation, Sexism, and Self*. Boston: Beacon Press, 1988.

Markale, Jean. *The Great Goddess: Reverence of the Divine Feminine from the Paleolithic to the Present*. Rochester, VT: Inner Traditions, 1999.

Monaghan, Patricia. *The New Book of Goddesses & Heroines*. 3rd ed. Woodbury, MN: Llewellyn Publications, 1997.

Pagels, Elaine. *Adam, Eve, and the Serpent*. New York: Random House, 1988.

Sex, Etc. sexetc.org. Teen-to-Teen Sexuality Education Project by Answer.

Sjoo, Monica, and Barbara Mor. *The Great Cosmic Mother: Rediscovering the Religion of the Earth*. New York: Harper & Row, 1987.

Spretnak, Charlene, ed. *The Politics of Women's Spirituality: Essays by Founding Mothers of the Movement*. New York: Anchor Books, 1981.

Stone, Merlin. *When God Was a Woman*. New York: Harvest/ Harcourt Brace & Company, 1976.

Whitmont, Edward C. *The Return of the Goddess*. New York: Continuum International Publishing Group, 1997.

Wilshire, Donna. *Virgin, Mother, Crone: Myths and Mysteries of the Triple Goddess*. Rochester, VT: Inner Traditions, 1993.